NEW SCIENCE LIBRARY

presents traditional topics from a modern perspective, particularly those associated with the hard sciences—physics, biology, and medicine—and those of the human sciences—psychology, sociology, and philosophy.

The aim of this series is the enrichment of both the scientific and spiritual view of the world through their mutual dialogue and exchange.

New Science Library is an imprint of Shambhala Publications.

General editor Ken Wilber

Jeremy Hayward, Consulting Editor
Francisco Varela, Consulting Editor

ALSO BY FRANCES VAUGHAN
Awakening Intuition
Beyond Ego: Transpersonal Dimensions in Psychology (with Roger Walsh)
Accept this Gift (with Roger Walsh)

The Inward Arc

Healing and Wholeness in Psychotherapy and Spirituality

Frances Vaughan

NEW SCIENCE LIBRARY
Shambhala
Boston & London
1986

NEW SCIENCE LIBRARY
An imprint of Shambhala Publications, Inc.
314 Dartmouth Street
Boston, Massachusetts 02116

Printed in the United States of America
Distributed in the United States by Random House
and in Canada by Random House of Canada Ltd.

Library of Congress Cataloging in Publication Data
Vaughan, Frances E.
  The inward arc.
  Includes index.
  1. Psychotherapy. 2. Spirituality. 3. Mental health. I. Title.
RC480.5.V35 1985   616.89'14   85-2504
ISBN 0-87773-324-4 (pbk.)
ISBN 0-394-74201-X (Random House : pbk.)

For all companions on the way

Contents

Acknowledgments

I especially want to express my appreciation to Ken Wilber for the depth and breadth of his vision, and to thank him for his encouragement and assistance in bringing this book into existence. I am grateful to Roger Walsh for his companionship, love, and editorial comments, and I also want to thank Angeles Arrien, Arthur Hastings, John Levy, Duane Elgin, Ann Niehaus, Nancy Berry, and Emily Hilburn Sell for their valuable assistance.

Preface

In my work as a psychotherapist I have observed people growing and changing over many years. I have been struck, over and over again, by the fact that people get better when they learn to see themselves and their world differently. In particular, to perceive or envision wholeness can have a powerful effect on the healing process, yet we have few models of psychological health and wholeness in our culture.

Writing this book has been an exercise in bringing the intellect into alignment with experience for the purpose of communication. In it I have shared processes and ways of thinking that have been useful to me and others along the way. I have found great joy and satisfaction in studying consciousness, learning from experience that although words are no substitute for experience, they certainly can be helpful. In the art of psychotherapy the skillful use of words is part of the healing process. Words are also used in spiritual guidance to point the way to spiritual awakening. States of consciousness, health, and well-being are difficult to describe verbally, but can often be recognized and sometimes transmitted. It is not enough to understand or even to taste them. If our experience is to benefit others, it is necessary to communicate what we have learned.

I have devoted much of my professional life to healing emotional, mental, and existential dis-ease. Personally, I have been on a continually unfolding spiritual path ever since I can remember. In this book I have attempted to offer a new vision of healing and wholeness for the purpose of enhancing well-being at any level on the spectrum of consciousness and pointing the way to liberation.

The Inward Arc

The desire and pursuit of the whole is called love.— *Plato*

Introduction

> A human being is a part of the whole, called by us "Universe"—a part limited in time and space. He experiences himself, his thoughts and feelings as something separated from the rest—a kind of optical delusion of consciousness.
> —*Albert Einstein*[1]

In recent years health has become a popular topic, but attention has been predominantly focused on physical wellness rather than on the states of consciousness that underlie healthy functioning. We know that physical, emotional, and mental well-being are intimately connected, but the longing for genuine emotional, mental, and spiritual healing remains unsatisfied by advances in medical technology. Today individuals everywhere are searching for ways to cope with despair in the midst of unprecedented threats to human survival that are all human caused. Everything has changed except our way of thinking, and changing our minds has thus become a psychological challenge of utmost importance. A new vision of healing and wholeness must be planetary as well as personal.

Spiritual teachings tell us that in our ignorance we tend to perpetuate conditions causing fear and suffering. Yet even as we seem to be drifting toward catastrophe, we choose to continue living, affirming the value of existence as we know it, perhaps trusting that as we grow in understanding we may experience the universal love, peace, and joy that sages and mystics of all ages have proclaimed are available to those who recognize wholeness. Our ability to correct what Einstein called the "optical delusion of consciousness" that imprisons us in a state of alienation and seeming isolation depends on a new vision of relational exchange at all levels on the spectrum of consciousness.

According to the perennial philosophy,[2] human beings are part of a wholeness that constitutes the fabric of the universe, the ground of being. This integral wholeness does not exist as a separate entity, yet everything exists within it. This wholeness is called by different names in different languages and different religious traditions. In this context I will use the term *the Absolute* to refer to this ultimate wholeness. I will not attempt to prove, justify, or explain this concept, but I will ask the reader to bear in mind that it does not refer to a personal Deity, but to the underlying unity or basic nature of existence, the universe of matter and energy, and everything within it.[3]

The intrinsic wholeness of a person cannot be considered apart from the totality of which it is only a tiny part. Yet within each one the totality is enfolded. Physicist David Bohm has called this enfolded totality the implicate order. He says,

In the implicate order the totality of existence is enfolded within each region of space (and time). So, whatever part, element, or aspect we may abstract in thought, this still enfolds the whole and is therefore intrinsically related to the totality from which it has been abstracted.[4]

Within this whole, each human being may experience him or herself as an independent separate self in search of wholeness. In healthy psychological development a person grows toward intrinsic wholeness and a recognition of the relationship of the individual to the larger whole within which each one exists.

In human development the conscious journey to wholeness begins with self-consciousness and evolves through superconsciousness to self-transcendence. The full cycle of development is envisioned by Ken Wilber as a circle (see Figure 1).[5] According to this view the outward arc of personal egoic development precedes the inward arc of transpersonal spiritual awakening. As self-consciousness emerges in healthy human development the self evolves through stages of identification with various self-concepts that tend to become increasingly expanded and inclusive as the journey unfolds. The goal of the journey is awakening or, in some traditions, enlightenment. This process can be viewed as self-healing that comes to completion in wholeness. Intrinsic wholeness for the individual is conceived to be an integration of physical, emotional, mental, existential, and spiritual aspects of well-being. According to Wilber, the psyche, like the cosmos, is many layered, composed of successively higher-ordered wholes and integrations.[6]

As the individual psyche evolves through various stages of self-awareness, a series of basic structures or levels of consciousness emerges. Basic structures emerge in time as consciousness awakens, and they remain as a foundation for further development.[7] By analogy, these *levels* or basic structures of consciousness can be viewed as the rungs of a ladder of human evolution which remain in place regardless of where an individual may be on the ladder. The self, which seems to climb the ladder, goes through a series of *stages* in the process of climbing, perceiving itself and reality in different ways as it progresses. At each stage a broader, more encompassing self-concept replaces the previous one in a higher-order integration. Basic structures are not replaced, but included in a larger unity. Thus, for example, when one transcends exclusive identification with body-as-self, the body is not replaced, but subsumed as one aspect of a more inclusive mind/body unity.

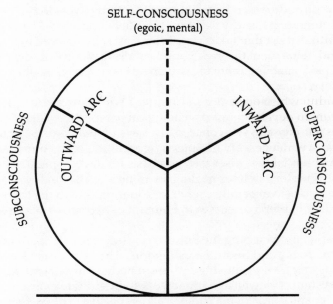

Figure 1. The General Life Cycle

If health is defined as a condition of optimum integrated functioning and relational exchange at all levels of consciousness, healing must take all aspects of well-being into account. Furthermore, the health of society depends on the health of its members. Healing ourselves therefore is essential to healing societal conflicts and ensuring planetary survival.[8]

The idea of healing the whole person is not new, but accessing inner healing for the psyche is an art in which few practitioners are truly skilled. Today, as consciousness studies become increasingly widespread, some psychologists are beginning to appreciate the importance of taking spiritual issues into account in the process of psychological healing. Recently the California State Psychological Association set up a task force on spirituality to investigate the state of the art.[9] Traditionally trained clinicians were found to be completely unprepared to deal with spiritual concerns, although they are frequently called upon to do so. Although the words inscribed over the entrance to the hospital at Columbia Presbyterian Medical Center in New York say "Healing Comes From The Most High," few health professionals seem to be aware of it.

This book is an attempt to provide a conceptual framework for understanding healthy functioning at stages of development beyond those usually addressed by traditional Western psychology. It offers a way of integrating healthy psychological development with the perennial spiritual quest that takes people beyond self-centered egoic concerns and helps them through periods of disillusionment, depression, and despair, enabling them to participate creatively in healing and wholeness.

Our investigation begins in Chapter 1 with a discussion of health for the whole person from a psychological perspective. Chapter 2 explores identity and self-concept as a basis for deepening our understanding of wholeness. In Chapter 3, recognition of the transpersonal Self as a potentiality is discussed as a basis for developing healing abilities. Chapter 4 defines healing awareness as the quality of attention one brings to experience when one identifies with the transpersonal Self. Chapter 5 discusses the pursuit of happiness as a precursor of the spiritual quest.

Chapter 6, "Mapping the Spiritual Path," views the path through Christian, yogic, and Buddhist metaphors. The heroic journey and Dante's *Divine Comedy* illustrate Western paths. The ancient yogic chakra system is viewed as a framework for identifying various levels of consciousness from a psychological perspective. The ox-herding pictures present stages of enlightenment as portrayed in Zen Buddhism. Chapter 7 examines questions pertaining to personal power and spiritual mastery and points out possible pitfalls on any path.

Chapter 8 explores creativity and dreaming as expressions of insight and inspiration for healing at all levels. Chapter 9 focuses on healing relationships as an essential aspect of emerging awareness of wholeness and optimal relational exchange at any stage of development. Chapter 10 discusses transpersonal vision as a faculty that can be trained to transcend fragmented perceptions of reality in a new vision of wholeness.

Traditionally, psychological growth and the spiritual quest have been perceived as separate and fundamentally antagonistic pursuits. Most Western psychology has tended to dismiss spiritual searching as escapist, delusional, or, at best, a psychological crutch. Spiritual disciplines, on the other hand, have tended to regard psychology as an irrelevant distraction on the path of spiritual awakening. Here these two apparently divergent approaches to the relief of human suffering are viewed as complementary and interdependent aspects of healing and the journey to wholeness.

Many psychologically sophisticated people are disenchanted with both traditional and contemporary approaches to spiritual growth that perpetuate or exacerbate psychological problems. Yet the desire for authentic transcendence and a deeper understanding of the psyche cannot be satisfied by psychological growth strategies alone. After many years of work in both psychotherapy and spiritual practice, I see both as necessary for healing and wholeness. Our discussion here, therefore, explores the interface of psychological and spiritual work. I hope this book may contribute to clarifying some misunderstandings and enable us to apply what we know about healing more effectively for the benefit of all.

1 Healing the Whole Person: A Psychological Perspective

To heal is to make whole.
And what is whole can have no missing parts
that have been kept outside.   —*A Course in Miracles*[1]

The inward arc of human development calls for a wider vision of healing and wholeness and a redefinition of the purpose of psychotherapy. If optimum health for the whole person depends on healthy integrated functioning at all levels of consciousness, efforts to maintain it must consider all aspects of well-being. Genuine healing cannot be limited to treatment of physical disorders. Attention to emotional and mental aspects of well-being must be included. From a psychological perspective, coming to terms with existential questions of identity, meaning, and purpose in life is widely recognized as crucial to mental health.[2] Transpersonal psychotherapy, extending the domain of psychological inquiry to include spiritual experiences,[3] now suggests that on the inward arc of human development healing remains incomplete unless the human aspiration for transcendence is taken into account.

In this chapter we will briefly review some of the assumptions that are commonly accepted among growth-oriented psychotherapists regarding physical, emotional, and mental health, and examine some of the beliefs underlying existential and spiritual approaches to well-being. In addition to addressing these five levels of health, healing the whole person is viewed in the context of global human concerns. Just as treating symptoms of disease brings some relief but does not heal the whole person, treating individuals without taking their world into account is limited in its effectiveness. Since a healthy person does not exist in isolation, but in an intricate network of relationships, intrinsic wholeness for the person cannot be separated from the larger whole of which each one is a part.

Optimum psychological health is inextricably interwoven with all other aspects of well-being. Wholeness therefore depends on a balanced integration of physical, emotional, mental, existential, and spiritual levels of consciousness. Health is not a static condition that is achieved once and for all, but a dynamic ongoing process of optimum functioning, satisfaction, and relational exchange on all levels.

Characteristics of health for each level of human development—physical, emotional, mental, existential, and spiritual—are reviewed here with the understanding that they each describe only a portion of the whole spectrum of consciousness or what the perennial philosophy calls the Great Chain of Being. Ken Wilber describes the hierarchical arrangement of these levels as follows:

Notice that each level in the Great Chain *transcends but includes* its predecessor(s). That is, each higher level contains functions, capacities, or structures not found on, or explainable solely in terms of, a lower level. The higher level does not violate the principles of the lower, it simply is not exclusively bound to or explainable by them. The higher transcends but includes the lower, and *not vice versa,* just as a three-dimensional sphere includes or contains two-dimensional circles, but not vice-versa. . . .

Thus, life transcends but includes matter; mind transcends but includes life; soul transcends but includes mind; and spirit transcends but includes soul. . . . Spirit is that which transcends everything *and* includes everything. Or, in traditional terms, spirit is both completely transcendent to the world and completely immanent in the world.[4]

Physical Health

Physical health is what we tend to think of first when we speak of health in general, and healing is commonly believed to pertain to relief of physical symptoms. In the absence of physical pain a great deal of emotional and mental suffering may be endured in the belief that seeking help is acceptable only when there is some physical condition that requires treatment. Contemporary society values adequate medical care for physical health, but the importance of emotional and mental well-being for general health is less appreciated.

In recent years holistic approaches to health care have called attention to the role of the patient in the healing process, and primary responsibility for health maintenance has shifted from the medical establishment to the person. Preventive health care at the physical level emphasizes the importance of nutrition, exercise, and relaxation. Popular concern with physical health has become somewhat of a national obsession in recent years and does not need further elaboration here, except to point out that these factors also affect emotional and mental health.

Inadequate attention to diet, exercise, and relaxation contributes to stress-related illnesses as well as to psychological states of anxiety and depression. One may learn from experience that anxiety symptoms are alleviated when caffeine is eliminated from the diet. Likewise, a person who is depressed can easily learn that he or she feels much better when exercising regularly. Unfortunately, even when one knows how to treat symptoms on a physical level, one often does not do it. Failure to maintain optimum physical health is not just ignorance. People who know what would be good for their physical health nevertheless ignore it. In affluent societies many people suffer more from overindulgence than from ignorance or deprivation.

Maintenance of optimum physical health must therefore take into account psychological factors as well as biological information about what is good for the body. Optimum well-being assumes physical fitness, but mental health is not necessarily contingent on physical health, nor is physical health necessarily contingent on mental health. Some people who appear to be mentally and emotionally healthy may experience physical illness, and vice versa. However, although physical health does not guarantee mental health, it can be a powerful contributing factor.

All human beings share basic biological experiences such as birth, growth, sex, and death. Regardless of culture or creed, the necessities of physical survival must be met. Once basic survival needs are satisfied, however, people seek health and wholeness in many different ways. From a psychological perspective, health for the whole person implies a state of well-being in which freedom from pain is combined with an enhanced capacity for pleasure and satisfaction in work and relationships. When adequate conditions for physical well-being are established, our attention may turn to the next, more subtle level of well-being, and hence we become concerned with emotional health.

Emotional Health

The relationship between physical and emotional well-being is not clearly defined, but we know that these two aspects of health interact with and affect each other. Most physical illnesses are at least partly psychosomatic. This does not mean that they are imaginary, but that they are caused in part by mental or emotional factors. In psychotherapy, when healing is focused on emotional and mental disorders, physical symptoms often clear up, although symptom relief is the most superficial aspect of psychological work. Symptom relief is certainly a worthy goal, but unless underlying causes are uprooted, symptoms may recur in another form.

Prescriptions for maintaining emotional health are less well known than prescriptions for physical health, but they are no secret. A basic principle for maintaining emotional health is to acknowledge feelings. We ignore feelings at our own risk. Repression, suppression, or denial of feelings creates emotional stress and may exact a heavy price in somatic symptoms. One cannot expect to feel well if one is not in touch with feelings.

The necessity of getting in touch with feelings in order to experience oneself as healthy and whole is widely recognized in most forms of psychotherapy. Emotional health means identifying feelings, taking them into account in determining behavior, and expressing them appropriately. Communicating feelings is essential for maintaining satisfying personal relationships. Open, free feeling-exchange enhances and enriches relationships, and intimacy depends on one's capacity for sharing deep personal feelings. To the extent that feelings are suppressed or withheld, one feels constricted, cut off, alienated, and alone.

Everyone has the capacity for a broad spectrum of emotions. We all experience some fear and love, joy and sadness, frustration, anger, gratitude, and satisfaction in life. How one handles these emotions depends partly on cultural conditioning and partly on the willingness to value them and accept responsibility for them. Unfortunately, when one tries to suppress negative emotions and express only positive ones, one may discover that one cannot suppress only some feelings and not others. Emotional health depends on the willingness to experience all feelings. This does not mean wallowing in them or indulging in inappropriate behavior or loss of control. It does mean acknowledging emotions and taking them into account in making choices and decisions.

Emotional health does not mean that one experiences only positive emotions. It does mean that one is not afraid to experience a full range of emotions and that one is capable of acting on them appropriately without feeling overwhelmed. It also implies a capacity for deep emotional intimacy and satisfying personal relationships.

Taking responsibility for emotional health means being willing to feel deeply even when one is afraid to do so. It may be easier to acknowledge feelings when one feels loved and safe with another person. A therapeutic relationship can provide a safe, healing environment in which a person experiencing emotional difficulties can re-experience painful feelings that were repressed in the past and learn to express real feelings in the present. When a natural capacity for free feeling-exchange is rediscovered, emotional health can be re-established.

Just as physical health implies freedom from bodily pain, emotional health implies freedom from the emotional pain inherent in inappropriate fear, guilt, and anger. Sometimes emotional health is mistakenly equated with the capacity to express anger. While learning to express anger can have a therapeutic effect for those people who tend to deny or suppress it, indiscriminate expressions of anger do not contribute to emotional health. Although it is important to *be able* to express or communicate anger when it arises, just being angry can contribute more to illness than to health. Chronic anger not only contributes to mental and physical stress, it also blocks creativity and alienates others.

The problem of dealing with anger is commonly encountered as soon as one pays attention to emotional health. When anger is acknowledged and one is free to express and release it without fear, it can be used as feedback to call attention to change that is needed. Sometimes it indicates that we are doing violence to ourselves or others in some way. Anger is always reactive, and is often associated with fear. We tend to get angry when we feel threatened, and when we feel secure we can let go of it more easily. Sometimes anger can be channeled into creative expression or social reform, and thus be transformed from essentially destructive into creative energy. Anger can also contribute to the destruction of old forms, thus making way for new forms. Since the breakdown of form at one level of organization can be the precursor of re-formation at a higher level of organization, taking responsibility for anger may be a trigger for initiating change. Learning to express anger appropriately can be particularly useful in the treatment of depression, but it is a painful state of mind to be stuck in, and is probably best regarded as a transitional phase in developing awareness of wholeness.

When suppressed anger and resentments pertaining to the past have been released, anger is less likely to be frightening or overwhelming. Furthermore, letting go of old grievances can contribute to a sense of emotional well-being insofar as it leaves one feeling relieved. Suppressing any negative emotion can constitute a heavy burden that contributes to a feeling of fatigue that may not be recognized until it has been released.

In addition to dealing with anger, emotional health requires a willingness to confront fear and guilt. Everyone tends to feel some guilt for things done or not done, as well as experience a sense of existential guilt for just being who one is and not being who one might be. Feelings of inadequacy or imperfection contribute to a sense of guilt that must be confronted for optimum emotional health. Guilt, like anger, is associated with fear, since belief that one is guilty is usually accompanied by an expectation of punishment, conscious or unconscious, justified or unjustified. Genuine freedom from irrational fear, in contrast to repression or denial, is a hallmark of emotional health.

Emotional health is also characterized by the ability to give and receive love, to forgive oneself and others, to trust and sustain both intimacy and autonomy in relationships. Writing on the value of love in psychotherapy, psychiatrist Scott Peck says it is essential for the therapist to love a patient, and the successful therapeutic relationship becomes a mutually loving one. He also maintains that any genuinely loving relationship can be therapeutic.[5]

Three basic steps for maintaining emotional health and releasing negative emotions are the following:

1. Learn to identify and differentiate feelings. Acknowledge and experience them.

2. Learn to communicate feelings effectively when they arise. Express feelings as fully as possible, preferably directly if it concerns a person with whom you have a close relationship. Otherwise a feeling can be communicated to a therapist or a friend. If this seems too difficult, express it to yourself in writing or drawing.

3. Learn to intensify and release feelings deliberately as necessary. When you pay close attention to a feeling, you can learn to intensify, release, or change it, if you are willing to take responsibility for it, rather than

being victimized by it. In other words, you have it, it doesn't have you.
For best results, this step must be preceded by steps 1 and 2.

Mental Health

The thought manifests as the word
The word manifests as the deed
The deed develops into habit
And the habit hardens into character.
So watch the thought
And its ways with care
And let it spring from love
Born out of respect for all beings.[6]

The term *mental health* is commonly used to refer to emotional as well as
mental states of well-being, but here the term will be used to refer specifically to those aspects of health that pertain to the mind and thought
processes. Healthy mental attitudes, beliefs, and thought processes
affect both emotional and physical well-being. For clarification of this
relationship, let us consider how thinking and perception can contribute to optimum health and wholeness.

Living in a time of unprecedented communications technology,
we are no longer bound to live in accordance with inherited beliefs.
More people than ever before have an opportunity to transcend early
conditioning and choose whether to accept or reject parental or cultural
values. Education offers the possibility of greater mobility and opportunity for attaining levels of psychological maturity associated with
responsible ethicality. Traditional values are being questioned and
re-examined on a broad scale. Religious beliefs are no longer taken for
granted, and awareness of a variety of approaches to the good life is
increasingly widespread. Descriptions of reality that were once assumed to be factual have been called into question,[7] and understanding the subjective nature of perception has led to increasing acceptance
of general relativity.

Perception itself may be recognized as a selective, differentiating
function based on subject/object dualism. Nothing can be perceived
without separating the observer, as subject, from what is observed, as
object. Moreover, perception is always partial, since focusing on one
particular object tends to exclude other levels of perceptual awareness.
When attention is directed to observing the mind in meditation, the
degree to which subjective states of consciousness distort perception

becomes apparent.[8] Perception is invariably influenced by conditioned patterns of thoughts, beliefs, and expectations, in addition to being colored by emotional states.

Perceptions and beliefs tend to be mutually reinforcing. When one believes something to be true, perception will selectively reinforce it. Thus, for example, when a teacher is told that a child is exceptionally bright, he or she will tend to notice behavior that reinforces this assumption and the child's performance will actually improve. This is known as the Pygmalion effect. If, on the other hand, the child is identified as a slow learner, the teacher is likely to notice evidence that supports this assumption. Such patterns of self-evaluation may be established very early. For instance, if a parent is impatient with a child developing motor skills, the belief that he or she can "never do anything right" may persist into adulthood.

The power of belief as self-fulfilling prophecy is often underestimated. In an essay entitled "Peace is Possible," Willis Harman says,

One of the most far-reaching of the findings related to consciousness has been dubbed "the self-fulfilling prophecy." More precisely, it is that our beliefs, conscious and unconscious, create the future in ways more subtle and more powerful than we ordinarily take into account.[9]

Everyone has been socially conditioned, but it is possible to transcend that conditioning to some degree. We know that the mind can be reprogrammed, but conditioned patterns of perception tend to persist in the absence of self-awareness and conscious intention to change.

American business provides many examples of success stories based on the power of positive thinking. It is often applied in sales training programs as well as in personal growth programs. Henry Ford has been quoted as saying, "Those people who think they can do something and those who think they can't are both right." From a psychological standpoint, the risk of applying the power of positive thinking to personal growth lies in the problems that can ensue from repressing or denying those aspects of oneself that do not fit with consciously chosen ideals and values. These values can be reinforced by techniques such as affirmations, which consist in repeating positive phrases that affirm desired qualities or outcomes. Although such techniques can be very effective, genuine mental health must also take unconscious wishes into account.

Healing and wholeness are more likely to result from acceptance and integration of both desirable and undesirable aspects of self-image. The persona, the acceptable self-image that one shows to the world, and the shadow, the unacceptable self-image that one attempts to keep hidden, must be reconciled, not split. Suppression of the shadow tends to generate a backlash. As we learn more about how the mind works and how it can be programmed, we find that when we ignore unconscious wishes in trying to comply with super-ego demands, we can expect the unexpected. Just when we think we have everything under control, we may find ourselves subject to some self-defeating behavior or inexplicable compulsion. Healing for the whole person must therefore be based on a balance and synthesis of opposites in the psyche, not on the repression, denial, or projection of what one does not like. Mental health depends on self-acceptance at least as much as on self-improvement.

A more effective way of taking responsibility for health at the mental level seems to lie in learning to observe or witness mental processes without trying to change them. When negative patterns are identified, awareness per se can bring about change in a desired direction. Sometimes therapeutic intervention can facilitate using mental capacities for positive change without negative repercussions, but the process of self-observation need not be limited to psychotherapy. Observing dreams and other expressions of unconscious mental life can contribute to maintaining mental balance and avoiding the problems associated with excessive conscious programming.

Dreams can provide a key to mental health by drawing attention to unconscious factors that might otherwise be ignored. As creations of the mind, dreams can be a source of important information for emotional and mental well-being. They can also be a source of meaning, insight, creativity, and guidance in everyday life. In addition to evoking intense emotional experiences, dreams can serve a compensatory function to conscious waking life that contributes to healing and wholeness. Different approaches to dreamwork are effective for healing at different levels of consciousness, but almost any ongoing, open-ended investigation of dreams provides a revealing mirror of the psyche. (See Chapter 8 for further discussion of dreams.)

Practicing self-observation at any level of consciousness—physical, emotional, mental, existential, or spiritual—enables us to see how every experience, whether waking or sleeping, is shaped by beliefs and attitudes. For example, when one has a critical attitude, one finds fault with everything, including oneself; when one is acquisitive, one selectively perceives only that which can be acquired for oneself.

Attention is unconsciously given to whatever is valued, often without awareness that it can be directed at will in any direction one chooses.

During early life, particularly in education, attention is directed primarily to the outer world. One is told what to do, what to learn, and how to think. Unfortunately the habit of taking directions from others often persists long after it has outlived its usefulness. Turning attention to inner experience, which allows one to know how one feels, what one thinks, and what one really wants, is often delayed until the pain of dissatisfaction with what one has taken on from others becomes unbearable.

Learning to pay attention to inner experience is an essential part of maintaining mental health. One gains autonomy and self-determination not just by being free from external constraints, but by consciously choosing goals and values and learning how to direct attention. The mind can be trained to think in any number of ways. The freedom to choose a direction can be ignored, but remains available to anyone who claims it.

Optimum mental health is based on recognizing freedom and assuming responsibility for thoughts, beliefs, and values. The power of thought cannot be ignored in healing at the mental level.

Existential Well-Being

When a person denies his potentialities, fails to fulfill them,
his condition is guilt.—Rollo May[10]

In addition to becoming aware of sensations, feelings, and thoughts, wholeness depends on facing all the realities of human existence. At this level neurotic anxiety is differentiated from the existential anxiety that is experienced as one faces such inescapable facts of life as aloneness, meaninglessness, and death.

At this level one becomes acutely aware of personal freedom and choice. The essential unity of mind and body as a total organism is recognized and attention is directed to fundamental concerns such as identity, authenticity, and the meaning of life. Well-being from an existential perspective means coming to terms with the finite nature of existence, accepting the inherent limitations of ego, and being willing to face things as they are, without self-deception.

Therapeutic approaches at this level may be either body-oriented (e.g., bio-energetics) or mind-oriented (e.g., existential analysis and logotherapy), but in either case the underlying concern is with the individual organism as a whole, as it exists in the world, and healing is oriented toward healing the split between mind and body, bringing thoughts, feelings and physical impulses into alignment in order to promote satisfactory functioning as a coherent whole.

A genuine confrontation with the truth of existence and being in the world demands authenticity and personal integrity. Authenticity implies consistency between inner experience and outer expression and congruence between beliefs and behavior. When thoughts, feelings, words, and actions are in harmony, when they do not contradict one another, one develops a sense of integrity and inner consistency that is essential to existential well-being. If, on the other hand, one thinks one thing and says another, or feels one way and acts in another, one creates internal conflict rather than coherence and experiences stress and disharmony or dis-ease.

The desire for a more meaningful and authentic existence may be experienced as a vague sense of longing that cannot be satisfied by the attainment of external ego goals. Once the transitory nature of egoic satisfactions has been recognized, whether they are in the realm of material possessions, personal achievement, or interpersonal relationships, attention may be turned to inner development in a search for deeper meaning.

Carl Jung suggested that the first half of life was appropriately devoted to external accomplishments and the development of ego, while the second half should be devoted to the inward journey and letting go of ego. Although healthy ego functioning may precede confrontation with existential issues in healthy human development, it appears that the process is not necessarily chronologically sequential. Ego development may be satisfactorily completed in early adulthood, and a call to inner development can be experienced at any age. It is no longer necessary to make a choice between devoting oneself exclusively to outer or inner development. On the contrary, it appears that optimum well-being demands both. Perhaps if the inner life were not so badly neglected in the educational system, there would be less need for remedial work in psychotherapy in order to redress the balance between inner and outer development. When inner experience has been ignored or repressed throughout adolescence and early adulthood, it can become a source of considerable pain, anguish, and existential despair. If, on the other hand, existential concerns can be acknowledged in conjunction with one's work in the world, one may discover inner resources for guidance, inspiration and deep satisfaction that transcend the boundaries of isolated individual existence.

Spiritual Well-Being

. . . . to transcend mind in Spirit is not to lose mind or destroy mind but merely to include mind in the higher-order wholeness of the superconscient.—Ken Wilber[11]

The medical model of psychiatry provides relief for certain biologically based conditions of mental illness, and behavioral psychology has developed a remarkable technology for the measurement, control, and prediction of behavior. Humanistic psychology provides an impressive array of techniques for emotional development, and cognitive psychology addresses the mental level par excellence. Existential psychotherapy deals with the problems of separate isolated existence, but the spiritual dimension of human experience has largely been ignored by traditional psychology and psychiatry.

Spiritual pursuits have often been considered escapist if not downright pathological. Yet the lack of a meaningful spiritual context in life has become the bane of modern society. Cut off from the wellsprings of authentic spiritual experience, modern men and women tend to feel trapped in perpetual alienation and despair. Today many people have rediscovered the validity and importance of spiritual experience through a variety of nonconventional approaches. The thirst for direct experience, in contrast to teachings about spirituality, is evident as increasing numbers of people participate in experiential groups, Eastern religions, meditation, wilderness vision quests, American Indian rituals, and mind-altering drug experiences.

The lack of authentic transcendent experience contributes to feelings of spiritual deprivation and malaise. Spiritual well-being cannot be derived from substitute gratifications. We know intuitively when we are out of touch with the underlying ground of the psyche. We also know when we are in contact with the truth, because truth is recognized, not learned. Learning to pay attention to inner experience, developing authenticity, and honoring inner truth are essential aspects of wholeness, but they fall short of spiritual awakening or self-transcendence.

Spiritual well-being does not require formal affiliation with a particular religion, but it does require an openness to transpersonal dimensions of experience. The spiritual quest is, above all, a search for truth, and in order to be at peace with oneself one must be willing to see truth as it is. Spiritual well-being is characterized by a sense of inner peace, compassion for others, reverence for life, gratitude, and appreciation of both unity and diversity. Healthy spirituality also implies qualities such as humor, wisdom, generosity, and a capacity for nonattachment, self-transcendence, and unconditional love.

Traditional spiritual disciplines require, at the outset, a period of purification for the spiritual aspirant. In some traditions, the seeker must demonstrate a strong desire to pursue spiritual goals before being accepted. Genuine spiritual growth is said to be attained only through a whole-hearted commitment to truth. Where duplicity and deception, which create conflict, constitute obstacles to the attainment of inner peace and spiritual understanding, spiritual well-being seems to depend on a commitment to the truth, which "will set you free." Truth can become a strong force for healing once the commitment is made. In psychotherapy, telling the truth about experience is an essential part of the process, but its relevance to spiritual well-being is rarely recognized. The more subtle properties of consciousness associated with spiritual practice tend to remain in the background in most psychological work, yet they can have a powerful influence on healing.

Figure 2 represents the five levels of consciousness discussed here that pertain to healing for the whole person. Obviously any two-dimensional figure representing levels of consciousness is inadequate as a map of multi-dimensional reality. These levels are mutually interpenetrating, but differentiation is particularly useful for bringing the more subtle levels represented by the outer rings into awareness. All five levels are potentially available to everyone and the inner levels are contained within the outer, but the more subtle levels may remain unconscious unless attention is deliberately turned to them. In the absence of training, attention tends to be dominated by the levels of consciousness represented by the inner rings. Consciousness becomes increasingly subtle as it differentiates physical, emotional, mental, existential, and spiritual levels. At each level one must learn to accept and observe. Each preceding level must be sufficiently quiet, or free from turmoil and pain, in order for the next, more subtle level to emerge in awareness. Although health or pathology at each level may appear to be independent of other levels, healing the whole person depends on awareness of well-being on all of them.

Conclusion

Health is traditionally defined as a state of perfect balance; and healing is that which brings about that kind of balance once again.—William McGarey[12]

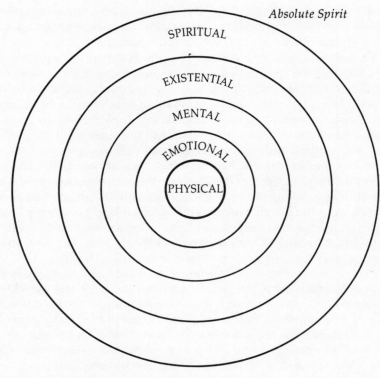

Figure 2.

When we consider the fact that every major threat to human survival today is human caused, we cannot escape the conclusion that the human race as a whole is in desperate need of healing. If the state of the world reflects the state of our collective mind, we seem to be facing a collective existential crisis, in which we must choose between self-destruction and self-healing. If we look at the way human beings treat each other from the perspective of family therapy, we must conclude that the human family is insane. But who will rescue us from ourselves? It is up to us, each and every one of us, to take responsibility for making the changes in our lives that will enable us to contribute to the well-being of the whole. Just as healthy individual cells make up a healthy body, everyone participates in the human condition. If we aspire to optimum health either individually or collectively we must learn to pay attention to all aspects of physical, emotional, mental, existential, and spiritual well-being. Effective self-healing depends on taking all of these into account.

It is sometimes argued that concern for nonphysical needs is contingent upon material affluence. Certainly basic physiological needs must be met for human survival, but what constitutes adequate material support is debatable. Affluent people are not necessarily happier than those who live more modestly. The capacity to give and receive love may be contingent upon having enough to eat, but it is not contingent upon conspicuous consumption. India, for all its material poverty, has produced some of the world's greatest spiritual teachers. Caring for physical needs seems to be a necessary but insufficient condition for healing and wholeness. Mother Teresa's work in Calcutta is a striking example of true healing work, which respects the dignity of the person and provides solace for the soul, in the care of dying bodies. Humanity is in need of healing at all levels.

Social needs, like individual needs, can be addressed from a perspective that includes a vision of wholeness. If we want to bring peace to the world, we must learn to create it in and among ourselves. We know something about how healing can contribute to creating the necessary conditions for peace in our personal lives. Perhaps, as we learn to stop doing violence to ourselves and each other, we can encourage others to do likewise.

We already have the requisite knowledge for healing and wholeness. In this age of communication it is not difficult to obtain information. What we need now is to learn how to apply what we know. I have learned from my clients and from my own experience that we *can* change and grow. We *can* learn to treat ourselves and each other more humanely; we *can* take responsibility for healing and wholeness, and share this learning with each other.

Experiential Exercises

Visualization: Health and Wholeness

Close your eyes, relax, and pay attention to your breathing for a few minutes until your mind is quiet.

Visualize yourself in perfect health, completely healed and whole. Notice your posture, the expression on your face, and your general appearance as you see yourself feeling radiantly healthy. Notice your surroundings. In what surroundings do you picture yourself feeling well?

Imagine that you are capable of transmitting this feeling of well-being to others. What would your family life be like if everyone felt well and happy? Imagine a sense of well-being extending beyond your family into your community and beyond.

2 Evolution of Self-Concept

As human beings we are made to surpass ourselves and are truly ourselves only when transcending ourselves.

—*Huston Smith*[1]

Definitions of Self

Everything we do can be seen as an expression of who and what we
think we are. For better or for worse, psychological theories and ideas
about the self often become commonly accepted assumptions about
human nature. As Gordon Allport said, "By their own theories of
human nature, psychologists have the power of elevating or degrading
that same nature. Debasing assumptions debase human beings; gener-
ous assumptions exalt them."[2] All mental illness involves some distortion of self-concept and psychological health is commonly associated
with a realistic assessment of self-limitations and potentialities. Since
self-concepts tend to become self-fulfilling prophecies, constricting
beliefs about the self can cripple human development. Definitions of
the self that expand awareness, on the other hand, can contribute to
healing and wholeness.

Definitions of the self are necessarily limited by personal experience and partial perceptions of the whole. These limitations are reinforced by unquestioned beliefs and assumptions. Furthermore, we
may often mistake the record of what we have been for a prescription
of what we can become.[3] Examining beliefs and self-concepts is therefore an important aspect of intensive psychotherapy.

Positive changes in self-concept can result from learning to pay attention to inner experience and differentiating direct experience from interpretations and concepts about it. When the sense of self becomes more authentic and encompassing and less constricted by conceptual limitations, change can be initiated more easily. In the light of growing awareness, the self continually expands, going through specific stages of development in the course of its normal maturation.

In Chapter 1 we described various levels of consciousness that constitute wholeness. Here we will delineate the stages that the self moves through as it grows into awareness of wholeness. It appears that the process itself can be facilitated and enhanced when it is clearly understood, hence the following descriptions may be useful for anyone participating in the adventure of consciousness.

Body and Emotional Self

At the stage where consciousness is identified exclusively with the body, the basic issue is survival. The more subtle nuances of feeling, thinking, and intuition as ways of knowing have not yet been differentiated. At the stage where consciousness is predominantly identified with emotions, a person is unconsciously driven by needs or desires and is often unable to tell them apart. Differentiation begins with the emergence of the verbal ego-mind.

The evolutionary journey of the self through various stages has been described in detail by Ken Wilber. He says:

Since the world of time is the world of flux, all things in this world are in constant change; change implies some sort of difference from state to state, that is, some sort of *development*.[4]

Wilber describes a process of differentiation, transcendence, and integration taking place at each stage of development.[5] In infancy the emergent self-sense first identifies with the physical body as it *differentiates* itself from the environment. When the infant has physically differentiated self from environment, he or she *transcends* identification with it, and henceforth can *act on* the environment and exert some influence on it.[6] At this point, the infant is *identified* with a physical and emotional self. Later, when the child learns language, the self-sense *transcends* exclusive identification with the body and emotions (wishes, desires) and expands to include identification with the verbal ego-mind. The child can then begin to *act on* the body and delay gratification by differentiating needs and desires. Gradually the child disidentifies from the body as he or she gains control over it.

With the use of language the self becomes increasingly identified with the verbal ego-mind. Wilber says, "As the mental-self emerges and differentiates from the body (with the help of language), it *transcends* the body and thus can *operate* upon it using its own mental structures as tools. . . . At the same time this allows a sublimation of the body's emotional-sexual energies into more subtle, complex and evolved activities."[7] Healthy evolution of self-concept rests on the *integration* of body and mind, whereas dissociation of body and mind leads to dis-ease and pathology. At a later stage, when transcendence of identification with the verbal ego-mind begins, health and wholeness still depend on the *integration* of former stages of identification.[8]

Egoic Self-Consciousness

Egoic self-consciousness is halfway between the subconsciousness of nature and the superconsciousness of spirit.
—Ken Wilber[9]

Questions of identity and self-concept loom large when the self is predominantly identified with the verbal ego-mind. At this stage one may be driven by the need to prove one's personal worth and engage in egocentric fantasies of heroism. In psychoanalytic theory, a strong, healthy ego identity is considered the hallmark of health. From a transpersonal perspective, this stage of identification is viewed as a necessary but transitional stage in the evolution of self-concept that is subsequently transcended in existential identity.[10]

The concept of ego identity[11] is familiar to psychologists, but they differ in their views about how we construct this identity and what its function is. The ego has been described by Wilber as a constellation of self-concepts and related images, fantasies, identifications, memories, sub-personalities, motivations, ideas, and information.[12] In other words, the ego can be regarded as everything we *think* we are. Like Descartes, the verbal ego-mind says, "I think, therefore I am," and becomes identified with thought. If I ask myself, "What am I?" every answer I can possibly give is just that: a thought about what I am. There is no way to talk about what I am except as a concept. In the process of searching for identity, one may become identified with a variety of thoughts or concepts that are essentially contents of consciousness. Thus responses to the question "What am I?" reflect limited perceptions and conditioned cultural beliefs.

If egoic identifications are regarded as essentially conceptual, ego can be defined as the self-sense that arises from identification of awareness with a constellation of thoughts about who and what we are. Characteristically, when awareness identifies exclusively with the ego as an independent entity, a separate and isolated self-sense is created. From the perspective of the verbal ego-mind, everybody exists as an isolated, individual entity subject to early conditioning that determines behavior. It sees itself existing precariously in a dangerous universe that threatens to overwhelm or obliterate it at any moment.

In order to transcend this stage, one must be willing to confront the existential realities of freedom, aloneness, and death. The self-sense that emerges in response to confrontation with these realities can be called the existential self. Coming to terms with the existential self is an important basis for further psychological and spiritual development.

Existential Identity

Logically as well as psychologically we must go behind the ego-id-superego system and endeavor to understand the "being" of whom these are expressions.—Rollo May[13]

The existential self demands authenticity and autonomy. As socially adaptable creatures identified with the verbal ego-mind, we can learn to present an acceptable facade to the world, but the price of adaptation may be a sense of loss of self, or a feeling of not knowing who one really is. A sense of being "real" is commonly associated with a commitment to authenticity and personal freedom. Where the egoic hero sets out to look for treasure and conquer the world, the existential hero sets out to look for truth and conquer fear. Authenticity, which implies free choice and inner directedness, is not conveyed by membership in a group. Personal integrity at this stage is not a function of either social conformity or nonconformity. A person who identifies with being a rebel or nonconformist may be dominated by collective role models just as much as the person who feels compelled to conform.

Studies of moral development indicate that capacities for moral judgment, like cognitive faculties, develop with maturity. Stages of moral development are broadly categorized as preconventional, conventional, and postconventional.[14] Preconventional morality is concerned only with personal survival and self-interest. Conventional morality is governed by societal rules. Postconventional morality is self-determined, based on personal integrity and awareness of interdependence. The morality of the healthy existential self is postconventional. No longer bound by social rules and roles, a person at this stage freely chooses ethicality as an expression of personal integrity.

Based on integrity that demands consistency between thoughts, words, and actions, the healthy existential self is experienced as a coherent, integrated whole. Recognizing the power of choice and intentionality, developing organismic wholeness and self-actualization is valued. A person whose self-concept has evolved to this stage is characteristically spontaneous and authentic. Behavior and communication with others is congruent with inner experience. Healthy existential identity implies self-esteem and self-referencing, rather than reliance on others for approval or direction.

Having come to terms with the facts of existence, the existential self squarely confronts aloneness and the inevitability of its own death. One is born alone and dies alone, and from this perspective there is no escape from isolation. The existential self may strive for longevity or the illusion of immortality through having children or creating works that will outlive its brief finite existence and prolong its memory.[15] However, since it is identified exclusively with the biological mind/body organism, its hold on life remains tenuous and temporary.

Belief in an afterlife, reincarnation, or other religious doctrine may serve as a consolation to the ego faced with the threat of nonexistence, but the existential self, with its commitment to authenticity, refuses to deceive itself. Eventually it must confront the threat of extinction. Awake to its own mortality, the existential self engages in competition with death as it seeks to prolong its independent existence, despite the inherent condition of suffering in its isolation in a meaningless world. Alienation is unavoidable for the self that perceives the universe and everyone else as other, unlike itself. There is no acceptable recourse for the existentialist, as escape from this condition of separation is believed to be self-deception.

Being willing to confront fear and the painful realities of aloneness and death, the existential self is committed to engaging reality exactly as it is. Its strength lies in refusing to gloss over suffering or pretend that things can get better. Unfortunately the preoccupation with death overshadows any transient joy. Hence the stereotype of an existential realist is morose rather than jovial. How can anyone delight in life's pleasures knowing they are temporary? The skull always grins at the banquet,[16] and everything gained must eventually be relinquished. Awareness of mortality and fear of loss thus permeates every experience and robs one of pleasure. Nothing lasts, everything changes, everyone must die, and love itself seems to be only a romantic illusion.

In the face of meaninglessness the existentialist attempts to create meaning through individual action in the world, but even the most heroic efforts cannot overcome ontological anxiety. From this perspective there is no way to overcome existential dread.[17] The separate self is always eventually overcome by death.

Approaching Transpersonal Identity

What treasure would I seek and find and keep that can compare with my identity?[18]

In order to transcend existential separateness one must be willing to question the assumption that the self is an independent, separate, self-contained entity. This does not deny the validity and importance of individuation and the search for existential identity any more than healthy mental development denies the importance of physical health. It does, however, recognize that wholeness includes, but is not defined by, existential identity.

A transpersonal view of healthy human development holds that as human beings mature, the sense of self expands.[19] When the self-sense, originally identified exclusively with the body and feelings, expands to include identification with the verbal ego-mind, social roles become important. This stage is characteristically conformist. Subsequently, the independent, existential self may emerge as a healthy self-concept based on personal experience of mind/body integration and organismic wholeness. Self-observation at this stage may differentiate the observer or inner witness from the contents of consciousness, i.e., images, thoughts, feelings, and sensations. Recognition of the interdependence of observer and observed, mind and body, organism and environment at all levels can lead to further expansion of self-concept.

Once again, transformation of self-concept proceeds through a process of differentiation, transcendence, and integration. Once mental, emotional, and physical representations of self have been differentiated, the self transcends or disidentifies from them. More inclusive representations of self include, in addition to these, the more subtle perceptions of spiritual consciousness. As this awareness develops, one may have experiences of illumination or intuitions of unity consciousness. Whereas identifications of self with partial representations of the whole are appropriate developmental stages, fixation at any stage is both limiting and pathogenic. Thus, while it is appropriate for a child to be exclusively identified with bodily feelings and for an adolescent to be identified with the verbal ego-mind, identifications that fall short of the whole spectrum of possibility can be regarded as a disturbance of healthy development. Thus, while mental and existential identifications represent essential stages of human growth, healthy maturation and wholeness require growing beyond them.

Consciousness cannot be confined to egocentric self-concepts. Existential identity is practical in terms of coping with the ordinary tasks of living in the world, just as Newtonian physics is practical for building bridges. However, exclusive identification with the existential self as an independent entity makes no sense in view of states of consciousness that transcend ordinary space/time limitations and operate in a reality that is more aptly described in the language of subatomic physics.[20]

Awareness that transcends ego boundaries may first be glimpsed in transpersonal peak experiences, or in deep meditation. Recent investigation of transpersonal states of consciousness suggests that disidentifying from egocentric self-concepts leads to the emergence of a more encompassing self-sense that can best be described as a transpersonal Self. Wilber says, ". . . at this point in evolution . . . the ego's task is done: it has served well to advance evolution from subconsciousness to self-consciousness, but now it must itself be abandoned to make room for superconsciousness."[21]

In transpersonal identity the self expands to include higher states of consciousness. Higher states may be defined as those states that include all the capacities of the ordinary waking state, plus additional ones.[22] From a transpersonal point of view, our normal waking state of consciousness is seen to be defensively constricted and early sub-optimal.[23] Although severe distortions of awareness are commonly considered pathological, the ordinary defensive distortions of projection, denial, and repression tend to be accepted as normal. Viewed from the perspective of transpersonal identity, however, the problems associated with defensive distortions of consciousness become apparent.

The process of relinquishing existential identity in favor of transpersonal identity can be facilitated by differentiating genuine transcendence or transpersonal states from regressive prepersonal states. Ken Wilber has called the confusion of the two the pre/trans fallacy. He says,

The essence of the pre/trans fallacy is easy enough to state. We begin by simply *assuming* that human beings do in fact have access to three general realms of being and knowing—the sensory, the mental and the spiritual. Those three realms can be stated in any number of different ways: subconscious, self-conscious, and superconscious, or prerational, rational, and transrational, or prepersonal, personal, and transpersonal. The point is simply that, for example, since *pre*rational and *trans*rational are both, in their own ways, *non*rational, then they appear quite similar or even identical to the untutored eye. . . . In other words, people tend to confuse prepersonal and transpersonal dimensions.[24]

Growing beyond ego does not mean regression to infantile oceanic oneness.[25] This misconception contributes to fixation at the existential level of identity and fear of transcendence. Sometimes a breakdown of boundaries and structures precedes reintegration on a more complex and inclusive level of organization. Just as the evolutionary chain from matter to plant to lower animal to mammal to human shows increasing complexity and awareness, so the self becomes increasingly capable of subtle distinctions as it evolves toward wholeness. Prigogine's theory of dissipative structures, which describes the way the structure of chemical elements breaks down and is subsequently reorganized on a higher level of complexity is sometimes cited as an analogy to this process, but the laws of chemistry do not always apply to psychology.[26] Clearly not every breakdown results in reintegration. It is therefore essential to differentiate a regressive disintegration of personal identity from transcendence that results in an expanded, more encompassing self-sense.

Similarly, in healthy personal growth early dependency evolves through independence to interdependence. It is not difficult to differentiate interdependence based on self-reliance from dependency, although neither is identical with independence. Thinking of the self as an open living system existing within a larger ecosystem can facilitate the shift from imagining the self to be a separate, independent entity, to recognizing its complete interdependence and embeddedness in the totality. Just as it is necessary for individuals to go through independence in personal development before arriving at healthy, genuine interdependence, existential identity must be established before it can be transcended.

Clearly differentiating transpersonal identity from prepersonal states allows the healthy integration of a whole range of states that transcend existential and mental identification. The shift from an existential to transpersonal perspective may be facilitated by viewing the self as an organizing principle or system, rather than as an object.

A systems view sees the world in terms of relationships, patterns of organization, and interactions, rather than as a composite of individual entities or structures existing in isolation, independently of each other. When the self is viewed from this perspective it may be perceived as existing as an open living system in an intricate web of mutually conditioned relationships.

This view recognizes both our biological and our psychological dependence on the environment. Although we may feel subjectively separate from nature and each other, we are actually interdependent and interconnected within the whole fabric of reality. We are conditioned by society and the environment at every stage in the evolution of self-concept. Yet we also shape the environment and co-create the social fabric that supports us. The complex web of relationships within which we exist involves a continuous flow of mutually determined interaction for which we can begin to take more responsibility as we understand our part in co-creating it.

The psyche that reflects the whole universe knows no boundaries other than those we impose on it.[27] Mental images and self-concepts can reflect only partial perceptions of this totality. Cherished beliefs thus become barriers to wholeness if we are unwilling to question them.

From an existential point of view, the self seems to grow like an organism, rather than being constructed by adding qualities or attributes like building blocks. It shows a remarkable degree of internal consistency, flexibility, and plasticity. Patterns of growth are discernable, but the process is not rigidly determined. Ostensible chains of cause and effect can be altered by choice. Feedback loops and information exchange reflect both creativity and reactivity in relational exchange at all levels. When consciousness is clearly differentiated from its contents, we realize that we can participate in programming the mind if we choose to learn how the process works.

When viewed as an organizing principle, the self is not exclusively identified with any particular stage or component of psychological development. It may be experienced in moments of unitive consciousness as being one with the larger whole of which it is an integral part. Whatever we think we are, we are continually engaged in a process of relational exchange at all levels of awareness: spiritual, existential, mental, emotional, and physical.

As an open living system the self is constantly participating in the co-creation of an interdependent world, consciously or unconsciously. When one stops defending separate mental and existential self-concepts and views the self as an open living system, transpersonal identity begins to emerge.

Open living systems are wholes whose specific processes arise from the interactions and interdependence of their parts.[28] If a living system is dissected into its separate parts, it is destroyed. Assuming that soma (the body) and psyche (the mind) form a natural living system, they cannot be dissected and must be studied as a whole. Yet consciousness, as an integral aspect of the whole, is not identical with any of its parts or its contents. Understanding who and what we are as whole beings therefore calls for integration not only of body and mind, but of consciousness as well.

Consciousness is difficult to observe and reductionistic attempts to analyze it can be destructive to its inherent properties. Consciousness is also colored and distorted by emotional states whose effects may be overlooked. Furthermore, states of consciousness in general are contagious and self-perpetuating. In clinical practice it is easy to see that fear, for example, is contagious. Even when the original stimulus is no longer present, anxiety persists and is easily communicated. Likewise, an angry person tends to make others angry, and a depressed person has a depressing effect on others. Taking responsibility for subjective states of consciousness is therefore essential for accurate observation in this domain.

Assuming responsibility at this level can have a liberating effect. When we are willing to look inside ourselves for contributing factors to present conditions, we can initiate change more easily. We tend to feel helpless when we believe the primary cause of any condition is in the past or in the external world. Lasting change often requires a re-examination of beliefs that perpetuate patterns of experience—and beliefs about the self and how change occurs are crucial. Beliefs and experiences reinforce each other. Healing wounds from the past and growing toward wholeness therefore depends, at least in part, on our willingness to question beliefs that perpetuate limiting self-concepts. In a healthy person psychological growth is a continuing process of changing and dying to former identifications.

When the self begins to let go of identifications it was presumed to be, the process can seem threatening to the ego. For example, a person in midlife in existential crisis is likely to resist embracing a radical redefinition of self even though it could provide a way out of what seems to be a dead end, no-exit situation. Letting go of a familiar self-concept can be experienced as ego death, and change may mean giving up cherished beliefs and assumptions about reality. It often means confronting the fact that things don't always turn out the way one thinks they should and facing the unknown.

Ultimately, identifications that are transcended are not lost, but subsumed in a more complex and inclusive organizational structure. However, the *exclusive* identification with a component part of the self as totality must be relinquished for continuing growth and fulfillment. Just as the child in transcending exclusive identification with the body must give up the desire for immediate sensory gratification, the adult transcending egocentric identifications must give up the desire for egocentric gratification. This does not mean being deprived, but it does mean learning to acknowledge desires without being driven by them. Ultimately, spiritual awakening calls for surrender of any claim to specialness or exclusive separate identification, while at the same time acknowledging all of it. Wholeness, after all, calls for an integration of both personal and transpersonal definitions of self.

When a person is ready to transcend exclusive identification with the existential self and expand the self-sense to include the more subtle realms of transpersonal consciousness, conceptualizing a higher self can ameliorate the fear of loss of identity. Psychological development beyond ego is not loss of ego, but transcendence of the verbal ego-mind and the existential self in a more inclusive, higher-order integration. Letting go of old constricting self-concepts is a necessary part of the process and healing and wholeness depend on it.

Conclusion

The diagram in Figure 3 represents the stages of evolution the self moves through on its journey to wholeness. Each level of consciousness corresponds to a specific stage of identity and has a corresponding worldview. The self-sense expands to become more encompassing as awareness develops. Originally identified exclusively with the body, the self gradually expands to include identification with the more subtle levels of consciousness. Each stage calls for a more refined sensitivity to experience and a different way of experiencing relationship to the whole.

In summary, the evolution of self-concept proceeds through distinct stages of identification with the five levels of consciousness discussed in Chapter 1. Basic orientations and worldviews are largely determined by specific identifications and each psychological theory tends to view the self from a specific perspective. For example, behaviorism focuses on the physical self, whereas psychoanalysis fo-

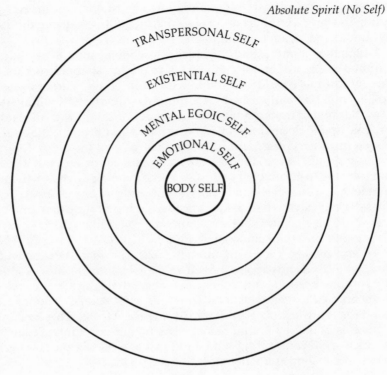

Figure 3.

cuses on the emotional self, and ego psychology on the mental self. Humanistic and existential psychology address the existential self, and transpersonal psychology brings the transpersonal self into view. Each school is limited by its beliefs about human nature and its self-concept, just as individuals are limited by what they believe about themselves. The most complete description of the whole self may be presumed to be one that transcends and includes all of them. It is this larger view of the self that we will now examine in more detail.

Experiential Exercise

Who Are You?

Make a list of all the answers you can think of in response to the question, "Who are you?"

Then close your eyes, pay attention to your breathing, and relax. Think about a long time. Think about an even longer time, and think about a time that is twice as long as that. And think about eternity.

Now think about your life and reflect on its finiteness. If you let go of all the thoughts about the roles you are playing in this life, what are you? Keep repeating this question to yourself and notice whatever responses your mind produces. Whatever you *think* or *say* cannot encompass all of it. The limits of conceptual thought are readily apparent when we attempt a stretch beyond our limited interpretations of what we are. "What you think you are is a belief to be undone."[29]

3 The Transpersonal Self

A person is neither a thing nor a process, but an opening or a clearing through which the Absolute can manifest.

—*Ken Wilber*[1]

The transpersonal self, or Self, as I will refer to it, is a self-sense that transcends the egoic and existential identifications described in Chapter 2, but is not yet Absolute Spirit. The term *transpersonal* means, literally, beyond the personal, but does not deny the validity or importance of individual uniqueness. "Transpersonal" can be distinguished from "transcendent" in that it refers to the transcendental as manifested in and through the person. Transpersonal psychology is therefore concerned with experiences and aspirations that lead people to seek transcendence, as well as the healing potentials of self-transcendence.

It is apparent that transcendence of existential identity does not result in the dissolution of a separate self-sense altogether. The transpersonal Self that transcends personal boundaries, remains as an *experiencer*, distinct from what is *experienced*. The transpersonal Self may first come into awareness with the awakening of the inner witness or observer of experience that remains distinct from the contents of consciousness such as thoughts, feelings, sensations, or images.

In analytical psychology, the Self as the center of the psyche is differentiated from the ego as the center of the conscious personality. This Self is defined as:

. . . an inner guiding factor that is different from the conscious personality . . . [it is known as] the regulating center that brings about a constant extension and maturing of the personality. But this larger, more nearly total aspect of the psyche appears first as merely an inborn possibility. It may emerge very slightly, or it may develop relatively completely during one's lifetime. How far it develops depends on whether or not the ego is willing to listen to the messages of the Self.[2]

This definition of the Self as an organizing principle is useful in mapping advanced stages of psychological growth and spiritual development. Awakening self-awareness at this level may be marked by a shift from personal, egocentric motivation to more altruistic, socially conscious values, or it may focus for a time on inner development. When attention turns to spiritual development, it may at first appear to be narcissistic and self-absorbed. But the shift in values inherent in genuine spiritual aspiration is reflected in behavior that is characteristically ethical, well intentioned, and concerned with the effects of one's actions on others. Healthy spiritual development is not bent solely on personal gain.

The transpersonal Self is discovered by turning inward, sometimes in the practice of meditation or contemplation. Self-knowledge cannot be attained by searching outside of oneself. The value of inner searching is affirmed both in depth psychology and in every major spiritual tradition. In Christianity: "The Kingdom of God is within." In Buddhism: "Look within, thou art the Buddha." In siddha yoga: "God dwells within you as you." In Hinduism: "Atman (individual consciousness) and Brahman (universal consciousness) are one." In Islam: "He who knows himself, knows his Lord." In the perennial philosophy, Self-knowledge is an essential stage on the path to transcendental wisdom and universal consciousness.[3]

In analytical psychology Carl Jung postulated an instinct or drive toward individuation or intrinsic wholeness. This autonomous force is constantly pushing us toward fulfilling our truest self.[4] Part of the goal of individuation is "to experience most deeply existential being as such, to accept and affirm it."[5]

However, on the journey of Self-discovery this too is transcended. Jung saw the egoic tendencies to identify with the Self as a potential danger. If the ego becomes mistakenly identified with the Self, pathological conditions are likely to result, usually in the form of ego inflation or grandiosity. From a Jungian perspective, the problem of ego inflation is one of the principle hazards of identifying with a transpersonal Self. The Self must therefore be clearly distinguished from ego. Jung writes:

The Self is something exceedingly impersonal, exceedingly objective. If you function through your Self you are not your-self—that is, what you feel. . . . As St. Paul expresses it, "it is not I that lives, it is Christ that liveth in me," meaning that his life is not his own life but the life of [the Self].[6]

Only when one has succeeded in observing thoughts, emotions, and sensations as contents of consciousness and seeing that one has them but is not identical with them, can one begin to know the Self. Transpersonal development is thus initiated through a process of disidentification from egoic self-concepts. Jung said,

Nobody understands what the Self is because the Self is just what you are not—it is not the ego. The ego discovers itself as a mere appendix of the Self in a sort of loose connection.[7]

The process of disidentifying from the ego is a transcendence of ego, not a denial of ego. Typically, the inner quest that begins as a search for meaning, on the existential level, leads eventually to disidentification from ego and to transpersonal awakening. As the process unfolds, it progresses through egoic stages of identification concerned with self-image and the existential search for authenticity. "Who am I if I am not what I appear to be?" A healthy egoic self-image grows out of the integration of the *persona*, the mask or positive self-image that one presents to the world, and the *shadow*, the repressed self-image or what one fears one might become. The mental egoic self-image must also be integrated with body awareness in order to become fully conscious of its organismic wholeness and existential freedom. When authentic existential identity is established, awareness of the transpersonal Self can be approached through disidentification from both mental egoic and existential self-concepts.

Disidentification can reduce the dangers of ego inflation, but if practiced prematurely it can contribute to denial or repression of the shadow. When this happens the split between the persona and the shadow may be exacerbated instead of being healed. From a psychological perspective, disidentification is therefore appropriately undertaken only after existential identity has been fully affirmed. Thus in Maslow's hierarchy of human motivation, self-transcendence lies above (or beyond) self-actualization.[8]

It is important to differentiate the transpersonal Self from the ego ideal. Although transpersonal awareness is the source of values such as love and compassion, the Self does not exist as a separate, independent identity to be attained by egocentric striving. It is, rather, an archetypal form to which no specific image can be attributed. Awakening to its presence is not a product of effort or achievement. Unlike ego ideals that are culturally determined and associated with social status or recognition, the transpersonal Self is a universal dimension of experience associated with subjective experiences of authentic transcendence in all cultures. An ego ideal may incorporate some of its attributes such as wisdom, truth, and beauty, but the transpersonal Self is not defined by personal aspirations or projections.

The transpersonal Self does not engage in making judgments or setting standards. It does not avoid or pursue anything. It simply is present to every experience, internal or external, viewing inner and outer as two interdependent sides of one reality. It can be described as holistic and ecological, recognizing the interrelatedness of all phenomena. As an integrated harmonious whole, it defends no boundaries and sees no separate parts. As limitless transcendental being, it partakes of infinite wisdom and compassion, understanding, allowing, and forgiving all things, without exception and without reservation. As a manifestation of absolute spirit, it is capable of unconditional love.

Qualities of the Transpersonal Self

One way of becoming more aware of the transpersonal Self is to differentiate it from the super-ego. This distinction is useful in avoiding the pitfalls of confusing the two in the desire for self-transcendence. It is sometimes easy to mistake what one thinks one *should* do for guidance from the transpersonal Self as a source of inner wisdom. The Self can be differentiated from the super-ego as follows:

Super-Ego	*Transpersonal Self*
Judgmental	Compassionate
Fearful	Loving
Opinionated	Wise
Intrusive	Receptive
Dominating	Allowing
Limited	Unlimited
Rationalizing	Intuitive
Controlled	Spontaneous
Restrictive	Creative
Conventional	Inspired

Anxious	Peaceful
Defensive	Open
Separated	Connected

In contrast to the super-ego, the transpersonal Self takes no position for or against anything. It is nonjudgmental and nonintrusive. It is not fearful or defensive and does not attempt to control or manipulate reality.

The transpersonal Self remains in the background of awareness until we choose to pay attention to it. Typically, the transpersonal Self as a context of experience is described as awareness or consciousness that is like a polished mirror, reflecting everything without distortion. The mind state is one of calm alertness. Perception is clear, accurate, and nonattached. The affect is joyful and loving, and the predominant emotion is gratitude. There is an easy flow of energy, clear vision, easily focused or diffused attention, and a sense of being connected to everyone and everything as an integral part of a larger whole. At the same time, this awareness can be described as being nothing special, or just a quiet letting-be. One need not become different in order to experience it.

The transpersonal Self is both an organizing principle and an embodiment of higher values. The basic characteristics of the transpersonal Self are wisdom and compassion. We know we are awake to the transpersonal Self when we feel at peace. The voice of the Self is the voice of truth. We know we are listening to this voice when it is harmful to no one.

When a shift from existential to transpersonal identity takes place, the changes that can be observed can best be described in terms of process. Although a sudden breakthrough may result in a reversal of thinking and a spiritual conversion experience, lasting change is more likely to be a gradual evolutionary development of personality traits and values associated with higher states of consciousness.

Personality changes occurring at this level tend to be away from positions of arrogance, judgment, and condemnation, toward humility, compassion, and forgiveness; from denial and repression to acceptance and integration of thoughts, feelings, and physical limitations; from defensiveness to openness; from fear to love; from victim to creator; from adversary to friend; from independence to interdependence; from a partial mechanistic worldview to a holistic organismic perspective; from isolated individualism to interrelated systems theory; from existential despair to transpersonal healing.

Commenting on a Christian perspective, Lex Hixon writes:

The limited self is the dimension of consciousness that has evolved from greed and fear and persists until we can affirm with our whole being that . . . *God is all in all*, that there is nothing to desire or fear. Even after we begin to live in this illumined affirmation . . . the limited self remains as an illusory phantom. . . . Self-indulgence or concern for our limited self springs from the illusion of separateness. As long as we remain ecstatically open at the level of Spirit, there is no separation between the self and the Christ nature. Paul explains, *What the Spirit brings is . . . love, joy, peace, patience, kindness, goodness, trustfulness, gentleness.*[9]

Awakening the Transpersonal Self

Awareness of the transpersonal Self can be approached through a practice of disidentification. However, disidentification is appropriately undertaken only after egoic identity is well established. Practicing disidentification from the contents of consciousness, one says, "I *have* thoughts, feelings, and sensations, but I *am not* my thoughts, feelings, or sensations." When one is able to differentiate emotions, experience them fully, and disidentify from them, one can learn to act on them appropriately. One may consciously choose to express or suppress them, attend to them or ignore them.

Once one is disidentified from emotions, one is no longer the victim of emotions over which one has no control. This does not mean one does not have emotions. On the contrary, the more one is willing to be fully aware of subjective experience the better one can see how it is actively created. When one is relatively unconscious and unaware of inner experiences, then thoughts, feelings, and sensations seem to just happen. As one learns to pay close attention to mental processes and take responsibility for them, one can exercise more freedom in creating those states that enhance well-being. Healthy disidentification implies mastery, in contrast to dissociation, wherein the range of available experiences is diminished and one remains confined to a very restricted portion of potential being, out of touch with both subjective and objective reality.

The expanded sense of Self that results from practicing disidentification is appropriately considered transpersonal, rather than impersonal, since it is manifested in and through the personal, and yet transcends it. The transpersonal Self thus serves as a bridge between existential self-consciousness and transcendental unity consciousness where no separate self-sense remains.

As an organizing principle, the transpersonal Self guides evolution toward wholeness, and awareness of it can be a source of healing and inspiration. Healthy transpersonal identity depends on self-knowledge, self-regulation and self-mastery, and a new experience of Self in which separate egoic and existential identifications dissolve. Experiences of the Self are acknowledged in Jungian analysis as being therapeutic, providing an influx of energy and vitality and contributing to more creative responses to life.[10] The healing potential of numinous transpersonal experiences was explicitly affirmed by Jung, who said, ". . . the fact is that the approach to the numinous is the real therapy and inasmuch as you attain to the numinous experiences you are released from the curse of pathology."[11]

Descriptions of the transpersonal Self always reflect values that transcend egocentric concerns and affirm participation in the larger whole. Despite authenticity and freedom, existential identity remains a dead end unless one *chooses* to transcend it. Perhaps a better understanding of the transpersonal Self can contribute to envisioning a future different from the past, in which human beings can recognize their interdependence and learn to live together more compassionately.

Increased awareness of the transpersonal Self can enhance the capacity for viewing reality in terms of relationships.[12] Consciousness awakened on the inward arc is reflected in the quality of every relationship. If one willingly surrenders separateness in accepting interdependence, one may become more accepting of others as they are. The awakened state of mind that transcends individual points of origin and personal history can be recognized by the presence of openness, truthfulness, and sympathetic joy. Becoming identified with the transpersonal Self means there is nowhere to go and nothing to do for oneself. Even the desire for enlightenment is transcended. When achievement and status goals are no longer perceived as meaningful and striving ceases, equanimity and liberation may result. This awakened state can bestow freedom from conditioning, freedom from fear, and freedom from unconscious conflicts.

Self, Soul, and Psyche

The transpersonal Self as conscious witness of existential, mental, emotional, and physical experience is not identical with the term *soul*. However, since the terms are sometimes used interchangeably, it seems appropriate to discuss the soul in relation to psychotherapy in order to differentiate it from the transpersonal Self. The term *soul* is commonly used to designate only the simple subject of awareness at any level of consciousness. The soul, as simple subject of awareness, may be identified with any level of consciousness, whereas the transpersonal Self as witness has disidentified from contents of consciousness and transcended former identifications. Although the term *soul* has religious connotations, some psychologists have suggested that the concept of soul should be reinstated as a primary object of attention for psychology. Bruno Bettelheim writes that Freud often spoke of the soul, but that his references to it have been excised in translation. He claims that English translations of Freud's writings cleave to an early stage of his thought, inclined toward science and medicine, while disregarding the more mature Freud who was concerned with broadly conceived cultural and human problems and with matters of the soul.[13]

Bettelheim claims that Freud himself insisted on thinking in terms of the soul when referring to the whole psyche. The term *I* (translated as *ego* in Freudian terminology) refers specifically to the conscious, rational mental life. The whole psyche also includes the "it" (translated as *id*), the unconscious drives that sometimes take over, and the "above I" (translated as *super-ego*). The totality includes both the conscience that imposes reasonable moral values and the irrational, demanding, and punitive aspects of introjected societal values.

Freud used the terms *psyche* and *soul* interchangeably as follows:

"Psyche" is a Greek word and its German translation is "soul." Psychical treatment hence means "treatment of the soul." One could thus think that what is meant is: treatment of the morbid phenomena in the life of the soul. But this is not the meaning of this term. Psychical treatment wishes to signify much more; namely, treatment originating in the soul, treatment of psychic or bodily disorders—by measures which influence above all and immediately the soul of man.[14]

For Freud the soul was not a religious phenomenon but a psychological concept meaning "that which is most valuable in man while he is alive." The soul was thought to be the seat of both the mind and the passions. In the absence of careful investigation one is likely to remain largely unconscious of the soul.

Psychology, as the study of the *psyche*, originally meant a study of the soul, but this original meaning has been lost in most Western psychotherapy. The word *therapy*, derived from the Greek word meaning healing, has also lost some of its original meaning. James Hillman, among other Jungian analysts, has argued that psychotherapy should indeed serve the soul.[15] If psychotherapy is consciously directed to serving the soul, it could conceivably transcend exclusive focus on physical, emotional, and mental healing and include a transpersonal perspective, but it does not necessarily do so.

How the soul is envisioned depends on the level of consciousness from which it is perceived. From a Jungian point of view, Hillman describes the soul as the anima, or inner feminine, in man. The soul may generally be considered feminine insofar as it is receptive in relation to Spirit, but in a woman it may appear as the animus, the inner masculine principle. In contrast, the transpersonal Self transcends gender distinctions.

In Christianity the soul is differentiated from body and mind, but does not necessarily subsume or include body and mind. Wilber says,

The soul-realm . . . refers to the realm of Platonic Forms, archetypes, personal deity-forms (Yidam, ishtadeva, archangelic patterns, and so forth). In the soul-realm, there is still some sort of subtle subject-object duality; the soul apprehends Being, or communes with God, but there still remains an irreducible boundary between them.

In the realm of spirit . . . the soul *becomes* Being in a nondual state of radical intuition. . . . In the soul-realm the soul and God commune; in the spiritual-realm both soul and God unite in Godhead or absolute spirit. . . .[16]

The transpersonal Self is further distinguished from the soul since its recognition implies a transcendence of egoic and existential self-concepts, the same self-concepts that are sometimes attributed to the soul as a subtle separate entity. So while the transpersonal Self includes *awareness* of the soul, it is not exclusively identified with it. Wilber points out that the task of the soul in this life is to remember itself, to discover its unity with absolute spirit:

The soul's duty in this life is to remember. The Buddhist *smriti* and *sati-patthana*, the Hindu *smara*, the Sufi *zikr*, Plato's recollection, Christ's *anamnesis*: All of those terms are precisely translated as remembrance.[17]

Awareness of the transpersonal Self, then, designates the specific stage of development wherein the soul remembers itself and its prior unity with the Absolute.

As a religious scholar, Jacob Needleman has discussed the need to "bring back the symbolic power of the idea of the soul, to recover it as a guide to the search for ourselves." He refers to the soul as the intermediate principle in human nature, occupying the place between Spirit and matter. He suggests that the power or function of the soul is attention, the development of which is considered equivalent to the growth of the soul. He says,

> . . . the soul is the name for that force or principle within
> human nature that can bind together all the intellectual, emo-
> tional and instinctual aspects of the human being through a
> mediating relationship to the highest principles of order and
> mind in the universe. Therefore, as it is said, "love nourishes
> the soul."[18]

Needleman goes on to make a distinction between outer-directed psychological love, inner-directed religious love, and ontological love, which he defines as a transmission from one person to another of the conditions that foster the growth of the soul. The great spiritual traditions may be understood as expressions of ontological love that breaks down into religious, psychological, and social expressions. From this perspective, the fulfillment of human possibilities depends on the core of ontological love that leads to the development of the soul.

In the English translation of the spiritual teachings of Sri Nisargadatta Maharaj, in the Hindu tradition, the term *psyche* has replaced soul as the link between spirit and matter. He says,

> It all boils down to the mental or psychological link between
> spirit and matter. We may call the link psyche (antahkarana).
> When the psyche is raw, undeveloped, quite primitive, it is
> subject to gross illusions. As it grows in breadth and sensitiv-
> ity, it becomes a perfect link between pure matter and pure
> spirit and gives meaning to matter and expression to spirit.
>
> There is the material world (mahadakash) and the
> spiritual (paramakash). Between lies the universal mind
> (chidakash) which is also the universal heart (premakash). It is
> wise love that makes the two one.[19]

In contrast to the transpersonal Self, neither psyche nor soul designates a particular stage of development. The term *soul* is commonly used to refer to the subtle separate self-sense that travels the spiritual path through various realms of existence. The term *psyche* is more often used to refer to the ground of psychological self-awareness at any level on the spectrum of consciousness.

At each stage of psychological development a well-trained transpersonal psychotherapist may assist the developmental healing process by eliciting awareness of the transpersonal Self. By reframing experience from this perspective, emergence of the next stage of identity can be facilitated. Each stage brings one closer to Self-remembrance, but it is when identity shifts from an existential to a transpersonal Self that the soul consciously remembers its unity with absolute Spirit. Even here, as long as the subtle separate self-sense persists, self-remembrance is incomplete.

Spirit, which is differentiated from soul in being both the ground and the goal of the process of human evolution, is all encompassing. It is already as it has always been. The spiritual journey is therefore described as one of eternal return, not to a prior condition in time, but to the awareness of unity in reality, despite the appearance of separation.[20]

The Transpersonal Shadow

The only devils in the world are those running around in our
own hearts. That is where the battle should be fought.
—Mahatma Gandhi[21]

The shadow is an evocative term used in analytical psychology to refer to unconscious aspects of the personality that have been repressed. The personal shadow consists of traits that are unacceptable to the ego and do not fit the image that one is consciously trying to present to the world. The shadow is what one is afraid one might become if one let go of defenses and controls. It is projected onto those who are envied, hated, feared, or despised. The shadow is thus the opposite of the persona or mask that one assumes in conventional social roles. The personal shadow is a dark, unexpressed aspect of the psyche. "The brighter the light, the darker the shadow," is a warning against being deceived by appearances. It can also be a safeguard against self-deception, especially when the inflated or arrogant ego regards itself as a shining light and assumes that it doesn't have a shadow. The shadow can be identified in dreams and in those members of the same sex that are feared or disliked. The personal shadow is the opposite of the ego ideal.

Beyond the personal shadow, however, lies the problem of the collective or archetypal shadow, represented by evil as it appears in the world at large. The problem of the collective shadow is a collective responsibility that cannot be ignored. It must be confronted in any attempt to heal existing conflicts. The magnitude of the collective shadow may be more than anyone is prepared to contemplate, yet it is always manifested through human beings. In medieval times, blaming the devil was an acceptable way of abdicating responsibility for human evil. Today evil is more likely to be projected onto other people.

Current human threats to planetary survival are basically psychological in origin.[22] For the first time in history, humankind has the power to destroy the world. This collective shadow of self-destruction must be faced. Unmasking it may be our only hope. As long as it is disowned, projected, or avoided, it constantly threatens to engulf us.

Evidence from psychotherapy suggests that the shadow cannot be faced alone. If one is fortunate to have a therapist who is not afraid to confront it, the shadow can be unmasked and its energy made available for creative integration.[23] In the development of healthy egoic identity, the split between the persona and the personal shadow must be healed. In healthy existential identity the whole organism faces the reality of biological death. The challenge to be faced in claiming transpersonal identity lies in healing the split between the transpersonal Self and the collective shadow. This task requires a joint effort. No one can do it for us and no one can do it alone.

With a little self-criticism one can see through the shadow—so far as its nature is personal . . . it is quite within the bounds of possibility for a man to recognize the relative evil of his nature, but it is a rare and shattering experience for him to gaze into the face of absolute evil.—C. G. Jung[24]

Vision of light and shadow as opposites permits an appreciation of their interdependence and the relative nature of what is judged to be evil. When darkness is described as an absence of light, the shadow itself may be perceived as substanceless. The transpersonal shadow is often projected onto the unknown. Our relationship to the unknown mirrors our assumptions about reality: to the extent that we embrace it we are free from fear; to the extent that we run away from it, it pursues us; to the extent that we fight it, we are in conflict.

In Tibetan Buddhism, the wrathful deities, the terrifying masks of God, threaten death to the ego.[25] What is most feared is the destruction of the separate self—which was only an illusion in the first place. The shadow, always associated with fear, is the inseparable counterpart of egocentric self-concepts. The shadow that mirrors the ego and threatens it with annihilation must be embraced with the emergence of existential identity. The archetypal collective shadow, as the polar opposite of the transpersonal Self, must also be unmasked and integrated in ultimate formless awareness.

From a transpersonal perspective, the wish to be separate and apart from what one fears perpetuates the illusion that the shadow is outside in the world rather than within oneself. As long as it is projected onto others, one remains victim of the terror it elicits. Healing, as a process of becoming whole at each level, occurs when the shadow is consciously differentiated, transcended, and eventually integrated in a more broadly encompassing self-concept.

Each one carries the light of consciousness within. The shadow, as the darkness, is the unknown that lies outside of awareness. The shadow resides in everyone, below the threshold of ordinary waking consciousness, yet within our ability to recognize. True vision does not ignore it, but unmasks it, understanding it as a part of ourselves that has yet to be accepted and integrated. It is a part of the Self we have abandoned, something our vision has not yet encompassed.

Discovering transpersonal identity allows us to see that whatever we see in others is a projection of the shared Self. When perception is subject to fear, anything can take on the threatening appearance of the shadow. Sometimes the terror of nonexistence is formless; sometimes it appears in the images that we create. But it does not lie in the world outside of the psyche. It is the very condition of existence of the separate self. Whenever the separate self is threatened by annihilation, it perceives its shadow. When the sense of separate self is transcended and no boundaries are seen, there is neither shadow nor fear. Wherever there is other there is fear. When nothing is perceived as other than Self, there is nothing to fear.[26] This state is attained only in awareness of absolute Spirit. Wilber, like Hegel, Aurobindo, and the perennial psychology in general, tells us that evolution is the process of the self-actualization of Spirit.[27] Awakening to the awareness of absolute Spirit is the culmination of the evolutionary journey to wholeness.

In analytical psychotherapy the psyche is seen as a self-regulating system that functions purposefully in the direction of wholeness and fuller awareness.[28] Wilber defines the Self system as the organizing principle that confers unity at any given level of development. It therefore cannot be exclusively associated with any one level of consciousness.[29] The transpersonal Self, then, can be understood as an integrating principle that operates at every level of development. Yet it is known only when recognized as the formless center of awareness that apprehends all objects and contents of consciousness but is itself nothing. As the eye cannot see itself, the Self cannot *be* objectified.

Awakening the transpersonal Self as a conscious disidentified observer, then, is one more stage in the process of evolution of self-concept, and this too may be transcended. Arthur Diekman says:

The basic difference between Western psychology and the mystical tradition lies in our assumptions about the self. We regard the self as a type of object, localized to the body and separate from other objects; mysticism considers that belief to be an illusion because it applies only to a limited aspect of human life. Mystics insist there is a Self, masked by ordinary consciousness, unbound by space and time, that can be both individual and universal—as with the wave that exists and then merges completely with the ocean from which it has never been separated and whose substance is its own.[30]

Thus Clement of Alexandria could say that he who knows himself knows God, and as Jung observed, the Self becomes indistinguishable from a God image.[31]

No Self

Beyond identification with a transpersonal Self that embodies archetypal qualities of divinity lies the realization of absolute Spirit or the unity of subject and object. When Self as subject knows itself as nothing, as emptiness or pure awareness to which no qualities can be attributed, it can no longer be called Self. Since a subject is only a subject in relation to objects that are perceived as separate from itself, when the subject is no longer objectified as an entity capable of perceiving that which is other, but remains cognizant of its all-encompassing awareness of everything as it is, it is no longer identifiable as anything. There is no *one* to identify or differentiate. There is only awareness.

In Buddhism this awareness is sometimes described as process. For example, when I hear the bell ringing, awareness is not separate from the ringing. The bell is an object only when I separate myself as a subject from hearing it. In awareness is only the ringing. The object can be known by a subject only when duality has been established, and it is my own concept of myself as an object, distinct from awareness, that creates the separation. In awareness there is only the ringing or only the hearing—there is no hearing apart from the hearer, no subject without an object.

Perhaps one may understand that the Self as a subject cannot be known without turning itself into an object, thereby separating itself conceptually from the whole, apart from which it does not exist. One may nevertheless persist in treating oneself *as if* one were a distinct separate entity looking for its true nature. Just as the eye cannot see itself, the Self cannot find itself. As soon as I see myself as an object, I have made myself into an entity which exists only as a concept in my mind. The ego, insofar as it is known or perceived as an object, becomes the object of an unknown and superordinate subject, namely the Self. This Self can be experienced, but cannot be known as an object.

Bernadette Roberts, a Christian contemplative, has described her experience of no self as follows:

It was a journey through an unknown passage-way that led to a life so new and different that, despite forty years of varied contemplative experiences, I never suspected its existence . . . because the self at its deepest center is a run-on with the divine, I never found any true self apart from God, for to find the One, is to find the other.

Because this was the limit of my expectations (and my experience), I was all the more surprised and bewildered when I came upon a permanent state in which there was no self, not even a higher self, a true self, or anything that could be called a self. Clearly I had fallen outside my own, as well as the traditional, frame of reference when I came upon a path that seemed to begin where the writers on the contemplative life had left off. . . .

Though the Buddhist notion of no-self struck me as true, its failure to acknowledge, or first come upon the wholeness of the self in its union with God, naturally left the Christian experience of no-self unaccounted for.[32]

The Buddhist teaching of anatta or self as no-thing states simply that Self as subject cannot be an object. As soon as I say, "I see," or "I get it," I have missed it, precisely because I cannot "see" or "get" anything without objectifying it. As absolute subjectivity there is nothing that can be said about the Self. There is no self as "it." There is only whatever is arising moment to moment. From this view, which is actually not a *point* of view but an all encompassing vision, there is nothing to seek and no one to do the seeking.[33]

But seeking continues. In subject/object separation, what is being sought is precisely that which is doing the seeking. Since I *am* my Self or "true nature" it cannot be found as long as I persist in the activity of seeking. The seeking apparently separates me from it, but the separation is illusory. The world of perception is therefore said to be illusory not in the sense that it does not exist in awareness, but in the sense that all objects exist only in relation to a subject and vice versa. There can be no subject without object, no object without subject. It is the separation of the two that is purely conceptual and therefore held to be illusory. Where there is no separation, no duality between subject and object, self and other, there is neither path nor achievement. About this final truth there is nothing to say.

The concept of a transpersonal Self, like any theoretical construct, is therefore considered an expedient or transitional teaching rather than a final teaching. As a center of awareness, the transpersonal Self encompasses both the conscious and the unconscious mind as codeterminants of experience. As a transcendental postulate, it seems psychologically justifiable. As a goal to be realized, it becomes an ethical postulate providing a link between the separate self and Atman or the God within. To pursue this dimension of identity is to embark on the spiritual path. But the person who sets out on the spiritual path never arrives at the destination, because who one thinks one is turns out to be only an illusion of a separate self that ultimately dissolves into the deity, or larger whole.

Once the illusory nature of all self-concept is perceived in the context of absolute subjectivity, the transpersonal Self can be perceived as an image of qualities one chooses to value, rather than a separate identity to be constructed. It may be considered as existing a priori as an embodiment of abstract ideals such as truth, goodness, and beauty (Platonic idealism) or it may be considered to have no existence apart from concrete expressions and manifestations (existentialism). Either way, identification with and expression of a transpersonal Self is an alternative to choose, an identity to seek, a value to create, and a reality to be experienced as long as one feels that one exists as a subject, separate from a world of objects.

Psychology, like exoteric religion, is an expedient rather than a final teaching. It can be applied to healing the mind, relieving suffering, and facilitating the evolution of consciousness. One naturally outgrows various identifications in the process of biological and psychological maturation. Each stage of self-development calls for letting go of previous identifications, and the process can be difficult, particularly if one resists and fears the next step into the unknown. When one has disidentified from existential self-concepts that appear to be isolated and separate from the rest of the universe, and awakened to the transpersonal Self that is interconnected to everyone and everything, one may begin to trust the process more easily. Eventually one may see that the part is never separate from the whole, and that all self-concepts are both stepping stones and obstacles to truth.

Experiential Exercises

Preparation for Experiencing the Transpersonal Self

The transpersonal Self can sometimes be experienced directly in meditation. When the mind is quiet and the endless inner monologue ceases, the quiet, open mind may experience the Self as source and context of all experience. In the practice of insight meditation, a practice in which careful attention is given to whatever predominates in the field of awareness,[34] attention is first concentrated on the sensation of the breath, breathing in and breathing out. After good concentration is attained, attention may be expanded to include other physical sensations such as muscle tension, pain, or subtle pleasure. When observed closely, all sensations are seen to arise in awareness and then pass away.

The same can be observed to be true of feeling states and thoughts. When all experiences are carefully observed, the meditator may begin to see the transitory nature of all phenomena. Everything arises in awareness and passes away. When the mind becomes engaged with a particular thought or fantasy and forgets to observe the process of arising and passing away, it gets lost in a dream, forgetting that it has chosen to focus on this particular aspect of experience while ignoring the rest.

The practice of self-observation need not be confined to formal meditation. It can be practiced continuously in any activity, but it is more easily learned when attention is withdrawn from the external environment and directed inward, keeping the body still and the mind alert.

Training attention or mindfulness has been described as a process of refining perceptual sensitivity and training the mind to observe itself.[35] Attention is usually focused first on observing the *contents* of consciousness, e.g., sensations, feelings, and thoughts that arise in awareness. A second step involves training attention to focus on the *process* whereby we choose to attend to one stimulus rather than another. This is a direct observation of selective perception. Psychologists know that perception is selective, but very few have learned to observe the internal process whereby attention can be directed to the mental events that precede focusing attention on a particular object or aspect of experience.

Finally, as awareness becomes more and more encompassing, the field of attention may include context as well as content and process. Optimum states of awareness could conceivably include all these aspects of experience—context, content, and process—simultaneously. But without first training attention to differentiate each aspect individually, attempts at this open focus may be too vague to provide a conscious experience of the transpersonal dimension of being.

Open choiceless awareness[36] can be a useful practice for discovering transpersonal identity. It implies free-floating attention that is alert and diffuse. No effort is made to focus on any particular object. Moment by moment, experience is simply noted. This practice may be undertaken by anyone who wants to learn to heal him or herself. The process of becoming whole means acknowledging all experience. In order to know oneself fully, it is necessary to temporarily withdraw attention from the outside world and turn inward for self-observation. This process need not be self-indulgent or narcissistic. It is just another type of education. It is part of learning how the mind works and how it can be used more skillfully to resolve conflicts and reduce suffering.

Self-healing begins with self-awareness, and transpersonal Self-awareness can be viewed as a source of healing within each one of us. When we are willing to pay attention to inner experience we become capable of conscious self-regulation. Without self-awareness, attempts at self-control are likely to be unsuccessful in the long run, and may even be damaging. We must know ourselves and accept ourselves before attempting to manipulate ourselves for the purpose of changes we think are desirable. To understand all is to forgive all, and forgiving ourselves for being just as we are is the first step to healing.

Dialogue with the Transpersonal Self

Each of us has within us a source of wisdom, compassion, and creativity that we can learn to contact.

Imagine that your transpersonal Self represents the highest qualities that you value. This image of your Self embodies all the positive qualities that are latent within you and that you might expect to find in an enlightened being. It embodies your intuitive knowing, your inner wisdom, and your loving kindness. If you were to visibly embody these qualities, how would you see yourself?

Let the image go now, and focus attention on your breathing. When your mind is quiet and your body relaxed, imagine that you are walking alone in a beautiful place where you feel perfectly safe. Reflect on your life as it is and consider any problem that may be troubling you. Pick one issue that you are concerned about and formulate a single question on which you would like to receive guidance.

Imagine now that your transpersonal Self has come to meet you where you are. Take a moment to imagine what it feels like to be in the presence of a being of total compassion. You can ask this being whatever you want to know. Whatever answer is given, listen and take time to reflect on it. It may be exactly what you need to know for the next step on your way. Trust your Self. Become your Self. Let go, say goodbye, and return to being here now in your ordinary waking state.

The transpersonal Self is always accessible, but is never intrusive. It is the context of personal experience, whether acknowledged or not. Once the choice to be aware of it has been made, it becomes increasingly available as a source of healing and guidance.

Affirmation

I am Spirit . . .
Safe and healed and whole.[37]

We will now turn attention to a more detailed discussion of how awareness of content and process can contribute to healing and wholeness at any stage of the evolutionary journey. Given the understanding that experience is always viewed through a particular lens of self-concept, according to the various stages of identification described here, we can facilitate healing and growth toward wholeness at any level.

4 Healing Awareness

Healing comes only from that which leads the patient beyond himself and beyond his entanglements with ego.

—*C. G. Jung*[1]

Healing awareness is a quality of attention that one can bring to experience when consciousness identifies with the transpersonal Self. The qualities of the transpersonal Self described in the preceding chapter are qualities that tend to promote healing. When identity is no longer exclusively invested in an isolated existential self and one has disidentified from mental and emotional states, one may observe not only *what* happens in the psyche, but *how* it happens. When consciousness itself becomes the object of attention, the necessary conditions for healing may become apparent.

When one attends to inner experience for the purpose of facilitating healing, one must be aware of the context and process as well as the contents of consciousness. This becomes easier with practice. At first it is enough to notice the quality of attention that one usually brings to experience. Most of the time the contents of experience are so engrossing that the state of consciousness of the experiencer is overlooked.

Healing awareness is an available option that can be consciously cultivated. It is a noninterfering attention that allows natural self-healing responses to take place. This awareness is similar to what Freud called free-floating attention. Fritz Perls, the founder of Gestalt therapy, maintained that "Awareness *per se*—by and of itself—can be curative."[2] Carl Rogers emphasizes the value of unconditional positive

regard in supporting personal growth, and Ken Wilber speaks of the
need for free-feeling attention in the natural unfolding of consciousness.

Healing Awareness in Psychotherapy

Awareness can be utilized in psychotherapy as a primary tool for healing. Ideally, all psychotherapists should learn to give clients their undivided, open, accepting attention in order to facilitate healing. Different
approaches to therapy focus on different contents of experience, i.e.,
some therapies focus on early childhood experiences and the emotional self (psychoanalysis), some on learning (cognitive psychology
and behaviorism), some on personal growth and mind/body integration (existential and humanistic psychology), and some on inner experience and spiritual development (analytical and transpersonal
therapy). Each therapeutic school may also offer a different method for
effective healing, but all of them bring to the process a certain quality of
focused attention that constitutes an underlying context for the work.

A psychotherapist needs to cultivate healing awareness for him-
or herself as well as for clients. Unfortunately, therapists rarely learn to
give themselves the unconditional positive regard or free-feeling attention that they try to provide for others. Feelings of deprivation and
burnout are therefore common among helping professionals. When
one cannot give oneself the necessary attention for self-healing, one
may try to get it from somebody else, and perhaps succeed temporarily. If it is unavailable, one may feel angry, hurt, or disappointed. Excessive self-criticism may also indicate lack of awareness in this area.
As a therapist, developing healing awareness in oneself can be a wel-
come relief from such self-criticism, and provide a favorable context for
self-healing and prevention of burnout.

More importantly, healing awareness can be evoked in others by a
therapist who consciously models it. Consciously or not, a therapist is
always modeling attitudes as well as behavior. What is less obvious is
that everyone is doing this all the time. If one is warm and compassionate, one is modeling these attitudes and can more easily evoke them in
others. If one is cool and aloof, these are the qualities that are demonstrated and, by implication, valued. Clients learn more from what a
therapist is and does than from what he or she says. When a therapist
or anyone else models nonjudgmental, free-feeling attention, others
learn to cultivate these qualities also. Qualities of consciousness seem
to be catching. One may easily be caught up in someone else's fear or

anger, for example. The same applies to positive states, and particularly to healing awareness.

Psychotherapy is only one possible avenue for developing awareness of the transpersonal Self and cultivating healing awareness. Awareness can be practiced anywhere, any time. It seems to work best when it is used consistently. If it is blocked or constricted, its healing potential is inhibited.

As healing awareness develops one learns to witness the content, process, and context of consciousness, without trying to evaluate, control, or modify them. As the self-sense disidentifies from physical, emotional, mental, and existential self-concepts, it becomes more open and available for free-feeling attention. When distortions of self-concept are corrected, healing and growth toward wholeness can unfold unimpeded.

Healing awareness can be brought to bear on any aspect of the psyche. Current psychotherapies can be differentiated according to the levels of consciousness they address, the interventions that are made, and the outcomes that are sought. Attention at any level may be directed to content, context, or process.

Biological psychiatry is an approach to treatment of mental disorders that focuses specifically on physical, biological interventions. Biological psychiatry treats mental disorders by chemical or biological interventions. It is a medical model in which cure is equated with adjustment to social norms. Some psychoanalytically oriented therapies focus exclusively on the emotional contents of consciousness. Some aim primarily at symptom relief and adequate functioning. Some brief psychotherapies use cognitive behavioral approaches for changing habitual ways of thinking, and reprogramming responses.

Many therapies that work exclusively on problem-solving and contents of consciousness do not address issues of process or context. Among humanistic and existential therapies, some focus primarily on process and aim at empowering the individual to take responsibility for both content and process of experience. These tend to emphasize choice and authenticity.

Transpersonal therapies that are concerned with liberation and transcendence are more likely to aim at developing a context of self-awareness within which the process unfolds. A transpersonal approach need not exclude the other types of work, but holds a broader perspective. In addition to the usual therapeutic techniques, this approach also questions beliefs about the nature of the self and reality, and thus establishes a favorable context for healing at any level.

Levels of Healing Awareness

Healing awareness depends on a willingness to acknowledge the truth about oneself at all levels. It is enhanced by cultivating qualities such as nonjudging attention, patience, compassion, understanding, and forgiveness; in short, by identifying with a transpersonal Self. When this kind of attention is genuinely available, it may be experienced as a peaceful presence. This attitude appears to facilitate healing in others as well as oneself. Others can help, but ultimately healing and wholeness must come from within oneself. The body and the psyche are continually engaged in self-healing and renewal. Yet we do not really understand how healing takes place. As a well-known medical researcher remarked, "If I cut myself shaving and the cut heals, I can't tell you how it happens although I have spent my life studying the process."

Although it is difficult to explain exactly how healing happens, we know that it can be facilitated by paying attention to all experience with healing awareness. Feelings, beliefs, and attitudes evidently affect the healing process at all levels: physical, emotional, mental, existential, and spiritual.

Physical Healing Awareness

At the physical level healing is facilitated by listening to the body and paying attention to physiological processes. One can be trained to regulate voluntarily such processes as blood flow, heart rate, and brain waves, which are ordinarily unconscious. The technology of biofeedback can speed up the process of learning conscious regulation of many physiological processes. This skill is not attained by willpower or conscious effort. It is most easily learned in a state of *passive volition*,[3] in which changes are first observed and then allowed. In physiological self-regulation we find that the harder one tries to do something, the less it happens. On the other hand, when one stops trying and allows it, it happens easily. For example, trying to raise the temperature in your hands, a method used for pain relief in the treatment of migraine headaches, works best when you visualize yourself holding your hands out in front of a fire and warming them, or immersing them in comfortably hot water, rather than making a conscious effort to control the temperature.

In addition to regulating physiological functions, mental imagery can be used to visualize healing in other areas as well. For example,

Carl and Stephanie Simonton have used visualization as an adjunct to traditional approaches to cancer treatment.[4] Whatever the form of visualization, effective use of imagery in healing requires maintaining an attitude of passive volition, or noninterfering attention that observes what is going on while images are introduced at will. Effective use of visualization in physical healing can be thus enhanced by developing healing awareness.

Directing attention voluntarily to different parts of the body is also important in learning to be sensitive to specific cues about what is needed for maintaining optimum health. Frequently the body is ignored unless it hurts. Only when one is willing to listen with healing awareness and attend to bodily needs for diet, exercise, and relaxation can optimum physical health be maintained.

In their pioneering research with biofeedback at the Menninger Clinic in Topeka, Kansas, Doctors Elmer and Alyce Green formulated the following psychophysiological principle that sums it up well:

Every change in the physiological state is accompanied by an appropriate change in the mental-emotional state, conscious or unconscious, and conversely, every change in the mental-emotional state, conscious or unconscious, is accompanied by an appropriate change in the physiological state.[5]

Accurate differentiation of mental and emotional states depends on consciousness. My body feels no pain if I am knocked unconscious. Pleasure and pain are differentiated only in the mind, and the more subtle distinctions between positive and negative emotional and mental states require clarity and alertness in order to be perceived accurately.

Emotional Healing Awareness

At the emotional level healing awareness implies recognizing both positive and negative feelings. Sometimes it may seem more difficult to acknowledge warm, tender feelings than angry, hostile feelings. It is often difficult to communicate deep longings and secret fears. Yet in the honest exchange of feeling the common ground of the human experience is discovered. Everyone experiences separation, birth and death, love and fear, hope and disappointment, success and failure, joy and sorrow, aloneness and relationship in some form. Learning to communicate emotions truthfully to another human being, either a therapist or a nonjudgmental friend, can be an important step in taking responsibility for self-healing and can facilitate a direct experience of healing awareness.

Emotional healing can take place in psychotherapy when the past is reviewed with healing awareness. One may willingly re-create painful experiences that have been repressed. Uncovering buried memories and re-experiencing the feelings associated with them can be facilitated by maintaining an attitude of healing awareness. A cathartic release of suppressed emotion can relieve depression, reduce anxiety, and contribute to feelings of inner peace. Emotional intensity can be more easily communicated in a climate of healing awareness.

For example, one may literally feel unburdened in letting go of guilty secrets from the past. Denying, projecting, or repressing guilt constricts awareness, whereas releasing it opens up new possibilities for genuine self-expression. As long as one holds on to something that one cannot tell another person, one carries a burden of guilt that asks for punishment. In the absence of healing awareness one is likely to punish oneself for it, albeit unconsciously.

Whenever one is experiencing pain, it may be useful to ask, "What could I be punishing myself for?" The more honest one can be, the more quickly and easily one can let go of the obstacles to healing that are inherent in anger, fear, and guilt. The willingness to allow awareness of emotions is a key to release. Fear of intensity, either positive or negative, can be more easily overcome when healing awareness is shared in an atmosphere of trust with another person. The necessity of acknowledging and expressing feelings does not imply license to attack or ventilate anger inappropriately. Attacking either oneself or another does not promote healing.

Becoming aware of feelings as they are, not as one wishes they were, reveals the inextricable connection between emotional well-being and overall health and wholeness. "I feel well," or "I don't feel well," is often said without differentiating specific feelings. Feelings may refer to physical, emotional, or mental states. If I am angry, for example, I am not feeling "well."

When it is assumed that feelings are caused by external events, the internal sources of feeling may remain unexamined. In the light of healing awareness, inner sources of conflict or stress can be identified more easily. The willingness to see, to acknowledge what is actually going on subjectively, is essential in this process. Sometimes one is afraid of what inner clarity might reveal. If one tends to be judgmental, one may suppress awareness of thoughts as well as feelings, preferring the fog of confusion to awareness of things as they are. When this is the case, the natural healing is blocked.

Healing awareness at the emotional level requires a willingness to face fear and confront the truth about oneself, just as it is. It is this truth that frees one from self-imposed limitations and fearful fantasies. Release from fear and anger depends on freedom from guilt, thus anything one tries to keep hidden tends to block the process. When one pays attention to inner experience and communicates it, one may also uncover patterns of thought and behavior that contribute to creating emotional stress as well as physical tension.

Negative emotions are always associated with fear in some form. When one is exclusively identified with the body, old age, disease, and death are fearful. Sometimes, when one feels needy and dependent, one may regress to a childish or infantile state. In contrast, when one feels well, one may eagerly seek new experiences, communication, exploration, and growth. Sometimes feelings are described as being light or dark and heavy. We speak of being lighthearted or being in a dark mood. Sorrow weighs on us. Regret, remorse, and resentment can be heavy emotional baggage carried from the past into the present.

A Buddhist teaching story tells of a young monk seeking enlightenment traveling up a mountain path looking for an old sage who lived high up on the mountain. On his way up the path, he met the old man coming down, and asked him to tell him about enlightenment. The old monk, who had been carrying a pack on his back, simply put down his burden for a moment. Then he picked up his burden again and resumed his journey down the path. The young monk understood and became enlightened.

Healing awareness can enable one to let go of emotional burdens from the past more easily. When one has identified grievances and resentments one is unwilling to forgive, the painful wounds one has not forgotten, one is likely to uncover guilt as well. Guilt and resentment are two sides of one coin. One may feel guilty at times for mistakes, in addition to feeling guilty for not living up to one's potential.

Feeling that one should do one thing when one wants to do another is a common experience. But "shoulds" can be changed to "coulds" and experienced as legitimate choices; then one can exercise freedom of choice. One can take responsibility for either fulfilling the "coulds" or letting them go. If one does not like the results of choices made in the past, alternatives can be explored. Becoming aware that free choice is available (at the existential level) enables one to recognize freedom and choose a better way.

Emotional healing lies in the identification, acceptance, and communication of true feelings. Wholeness is based on a balance and integration of opposites, not on getting rid of what we don't like. When we feel an inconsistency or conflict between inner experience and outer expression, between persona and shadow, fear and love, life and death, body and mind, or any other pairs of opposites, we experience pain and tension. According to the ancient Hindu scriptures, the *Upanishads,* wherever there is other there is fear, for fear is born of duality.[6] We can be released from fear only when we recognize the unity of opposites and learn to balance the polarities of emotional experience in a context of healing awareness.

Mental Healing Awareness

When the mind is viewed as the source of all pleasure and pain, then any pain can be considered an indication that the mind is in need of healing. Thus, when healing awareness is focused on the mind rather than the body, as it is in many forms of psychotherapy, physical symptoms may clear up spontaneously. Symptoms can be relieved by any number of interventions, but unless attention is given to the conditions or states of mind that contributed to the development of the symptoms in the first place, they are likely to recur, either in the same or another form. Healing the mind can result in healing of the body, but simply relieving physical symptoms does not heal the mind.

Suffering in any form—physical, emotional, or mental—may be unnecessarily compounded by denial and avoidance. Unfortunately, trying to suppress awareness of pain tends to make it worse. The first step toward healing, then, may lie in acknowledging that something is wrong and that the mind as the source of experience can be changed.

The mind is active all the time. Even at night when we are asleep, it is busy dreaming; and anyone who has tried to meditate knows how difficult it is to quiet the mind. Everyone experiences what Aldous Huxley called "the endless idiot monologue" that goes on interminably, undermining efforts to concentrate or be silent. At the mental level healing awareness means paying attention to thoughts as they arise, without trying to manipulate or control them.

Most people are willing to take responsibility for behavior, but many tend to deny responsibility for thinking. Thoughts seem to come and go of their own accord. Yet health may be affected as much by what we think as by what we do. Healing awareness can help identify beliefs underlying experience and enable one to recognize how often thoughts become self-fulfilling prophecies. This process can also facili-

tate the uncovering of hidden assumptions and interpretations underlying emotional conflicts. From this perspective emotions can be
viewed as the interface of mind/body interaction.

The idea that thinking creates experience may be disconcerting at
first. Who has not had thoughts they would rather not have, or feel
they shouldn't have? Thoughts seem to have a life of their own.
Thoughts of violence, hatred, and attack are deeply rooted in the collective psyche. One cannot read the morning newspaper without ex-
posure to multiple images of violence. Yet isolation or controlled expo-
sure to information does not extinguish such thoughts. In addition to
coping with the daily barrage of outside information, we continually
create violent scenarios in fearful dreams and fantasies. Even in relatively protected environments such as a meditation retreat, where external input is drastically reduced, thoughts and fantasies continue to
generate fear and anger. Living in a relatively benign environment
does not preclude experiencing anxiety. It is tempting to assume that
outer reality causes inner experience, but one can also assume that the
opposite may be true. Collectively as well as individually, the state of
the world reflects the state of the mind.

Examining beliefs and assumptions about the world and reality is
an important aspect of healing and wholeness. Uncovering false beliefs, including false accusations against oneself or others, can help
one see how unconsciously one creates conditions in life that one
doesn't like. If, instead of blaming others, one looks into one's own
mind for the source of pain and discomfort, one may be able to initiate
change in a desired direction.

The attitudes that seem most conducive to developing healing
awareness of thoughts and mental processes are curiosity, investigation, and understanding. A good sense of humor can also be a great
help. Just as we learn to listen to the body on the physical level in order
to discover what keeps the body well, paying close attention to feelings
and thoughts can help one see clearly what contributes to happiness
and wholeness. The attainment of inner peace may be contingent upon
recognizing the power of thought.

Existential Healing Awareness

In addition to coping with the uncertainties of everyday life, the existential self is plagued by the terror of extinction. Trying not to think
about death can mask fear, but does not make it disappear. In order to
escape the crippling effects of fear on the mind, death must eventually
be accepted. How clearly one thinks about it and what one believes

about it are choices. If one chooses to avoid it, there is a price to pay. When one tries to ignore it, it lurks in disguise behind every shadow in the mind and every symptom in the body. When one decides to come to terms with it, one can more easily bring healing awareness to every aspect of experience and thus reduce the defensive distortions of repression, projection, and denial.

Defenses ostensibly protect the ego from what it perceives as threatening. The unwillingness to examine defenses and the beliefs that maintain them tends to constrict awareness, and one may be caught between avoiding fear of death on one hand and fear of life on the other. When mortality is denied, freedom is curtailed and self-expression is inhibited. Consequently one lives with a pervasive existential dread and a constriction of awareness that contributes to feelings of guilt for not living fully.

Optimum health demands healing awareness and responsibility at all levels. At the existential level one can learn to take responsibility for beliefs, thoughts, and feelings, as well as behavior, and thus gain authenticity, autonomy, and freedom. Eventually one may claim whole-hearted responsibility for personal experience.

Spiritual Healing Awareness

Spiritual healing awareness may awaken slowly or suddenly, consciously or unconsciously. Awareness of transpersonal dimensions of experience may be precipitated by spontaneous mystical experiences, a spiritual relationship, a confrontation with death, a psychedelic drug, or any intense experience that lifts the veil of conditioning to reveal hitherto unsuspected dimensions of reality that seem more real and meaningful than the more constricted perceptions of ordinary consciousness. Such experiences can have a liberating and healing effect on the psyche. Spiritual awakening calls attention to the fact that everything in this life is transitory and that one cannot impose permanence, or hold on to anything for long. Full development of healing awareness depends upon recognizing both transpersonal identity and absolute Spirit. An experience of self-transcendence, or a glimpse of no self, can enable one to view any personal melodrama from a broader perspective.

Although self-awareness is widely recognized as a therapeutic tool, the value of spiritual awareness is seldom acknowledged in Western psychology. As one grows toward wholeness, healing awareness provides a context within which both the dark and the light side of oneself can be accepted. A sense of wholeness may be attained only by consciously accepting all of oneself, including transpersonal identity. Attitudes that are most conducive to expanding awareness at this level are love and gratitude. When one is willing to love oneself and express appreciation for all that one is, one can open more fully to transpersonal identity as Spirit.

In spiritual practice, liberation from the delusion of a separate self-sense through the attainment of transcendent insight may be perceived as a goal of practice. When the spiritual aspirant fully recognizes the insubstantial nature of all phenomena and awakens to the realization of no self, freedom from suffering is meant to ensue. From a Western psychological perspective it appears that insight and cognition may be necessary but insufficient conditions for wholeness and stable psychological well-being. To see through the veil of illusion is one thing; to live in that awareness is quite different. Even when a person has a profound realization of transcendent insight in connection with spiritual practice, he or she returns to ordinary states of consciousness in which the separate self-sense appears once again to have objective reality. With continued practice such flashes of insight may become an abiding light of mindfulness that permeates all experience, but the process often takes time, and in this *process* of awakening, psychotherapy can be useful.

From a transpersonal perspective, one might say that to heal the self is to transcend the self. Wholeness lies in recognizing the illusory nature of all self-concepts and holding them all in healing awareness. Improving self-concept, then, may be considered an expedient teaching in which one illusion is exchanged for another, judged to be better, or more "realistic." However, since all separate self-concepts are misperceptions of reality and hence some form of delusion, they all tend to perpetuate suffering. As long as one remains attached to a separate self-sense, dualistic polarities that generate conflict remain an integral part of experience. Only in complete disidentification and transcendence can the psyche be whole or fully healed.

Spiritual healing awareness facilitates letting go of constricting self-concepts and attachments to what one thought one was supposed to be, in favor of becoming what one can be. When one has let go of pretenses and self-deception at the existential level, it may be easier to surrender to self-transcendence and discover inner peace, which can provide optimum conditions for healing. At this stage it is not a matter of doing more, but of allowing healing to happen. Carl Jung writes,

The art of letting things happen, action through nonaction, letting go of oneself, as taught by Meister Eckhart, became for me the key opening the door to the way. We must be able to let things happen in the psyche.[7]

Healing happens more easily through us when we allow it to happen in us. In this way the wounded healer who, at the existential level, identifies with the pain and suffering of those he or she attempts to heal, becomes the healed healer who, being grounded in emptiness and compassion, can facilitate healing more effectively. By perceiving Spirit not as a realm apart from others, but as the ground or being of all realms,[8] healing awareness may be established as the context of any interaction, and any situation may become an opportunity to heal.

Experiential Exercises

Accessing the Inner Healer

The psyche has within it a powerful source of self-healing. This inner source of healing may be identified as the transpersonal Self. It is a source of wisdom, compassion, strength, insight, and inspiration. Access to it can be facilitated by joining with another person who can help us establish a context of healing awareness.

Reflect on your own life and remember a time when you were significantly helped by another person. What were the qualities in that person that seemed helpful?

Whatever qualities you saw in that person, you can find them now in yourself. Having recognized them in another, you can also experience them in yourself. Whatever qualities you have found helpful in others, you can cultivate in yourself. As you give attention to those qualities in yourself, they gradually become more available for self-healing and facilitating the process of healing for others.

Affirmation

Clients in therapy tend to improve when they take responsibility for themselves at each of the five levels of consciousness we have discussed. Repeating the following affirmation of responsibility can facilitate a shift in attitude and contribute to developing healing awareness:

I am responsible for what I see.
I choose the feelings I experience,

and I decide upon the goal I would achieve.
And everything that seems to happen to me
I ask for and receive as I have asked.[9]

If I choose to view what happens to me as something I have asked for,
I can probably learn something from every experience. Instead of com-
plaining about events in my life, I may begin to see how choices in the
past have contributed to present circumstances and hence become
aware of how choices I am making now are shaping the future.

If I accept this affirmation as if it were true, it tends to become true
in my experience. In assuming responsibility I become responsible.
Furthermore, I am more alert to options and opportunities when I have
a clear goal in mind. The more I exercise my intentionality, the more
effective and powerful it becomes. When I am ready to grow into
greater autonomy, authenticity, and wholeness, this affirmation can
help me do so. When I am free from preconceived expectations I may
envision a future different from the past, in which healing is easily
accomplished.

Whatever may have happened to me in the past, I can now choose
to see my experience from a new perspective, focusing on my part in
creating it rather than blaming others. If I desire change, I know I can
change. If I have a specific goal in mind, I can initiate changes in a desired direction. Taking responsibility for my creative participation in
experience can be the beginning of becoming a conscious healing agent
in my own life.

If saying the affirmation brings up resistance, notice your objec-
tions and use them as feedback regarding obstacles that need to be
acknowledged. As you repeat the affirmation you may start to notice
some occasions when you genuinely feel responsible for your perceptions and reactions, and some when you do not. Remember that you
do have the freedom to set your own goals and intentions, whatever
your present circumstances may be. At the existential level, "If I cannot
choose my fate, I can nevertheless choose my attitude toward it."

Integration

Becoming whole means learning to accept all of ourselves and heal the
splits between shadow and persona, thinking and feeling, mind and
body, and ultimately between subject and object. Some of these dichotomies may become apparent when you notice what you like and dislike
about yourself and others. Make a list of all the things you like about
yourself and all the things you dislike. You may find that many of them

turn out to be pairs of opposites. For instance, if I pride myself on being responsible, I will probably dislike myself for any lapses in responsibility, and also dislike anybody else that I consider irresponsible. My task, then, is to accept the fact that I am both responsible and irresponsible, without condemnation.

I may say that I want to be more responsible, that I am trying, or that I intend to be. My good intentions, however, will probably not have much effect unless I am willing to explore my resistance to owning both sides of the split. Exploring resistance means listening to the shadow part of myself that does not want to be responsible; the part I do not acknowledge as a legitimate part of who I am. It may seem easier to excuse myself by saying, "Well, at least I'm more responsible than some people." I then project my own tendencies of irresponsibility onto someone else and pass judgment or get angry about that person's behavior, while continuing to ignore the part of me that wants to be less responsible. Taking the position of other and role playing whatever is the opposite of what I think I should be can be useful. The willingness to do this can be an important step toward self-healing.

If one is unwilling to integrate the shadow, it is likely to be projected unconsciously onto others. One then finds fault with everyone except oneself, pretending personal innocence, seeing what is disliked only in other people. On the other hand, one may also project positive potentials onto others, not seeing anything good in oneself, admiring those who seem to be better in some way. Developing healing awareness means learning to accept both the dark and the light side of oneself and letting go of comparisons and condemnations. The process enables one to appreciate better both the shared commonalities of human experience and the unique individuality of what one can be.

Choice

A simple process for changing perception of "shoulds" to "coulds" is to take an inventory of all your "shoulds," i.e., identify them, and change them in your mind to "I could, and I have a choice." For example, "I should be more loving" becomes "I could be more loving, and I have a choice." Notice any tendency to be judgmental, to judge yourself for not being already free of guilt, or for feeling discouraged. Take time to feel it all with healing awareness.

If you feel deprived, ask yourself, "How am I depriving myself in this situation?" The answer may not be apparent at first glance, but if you persist in the asking, you may discover something that you *can* change.

Healing the split between body and mind means being willing to confront such intense emotions as fear, hopelessness, and despair. No amount of denial, repression, or wishful thinking will relieve the secret fears one tries to hide. Accepting the necessity of sharing deep feelings and thoughts with another person can be the first step toward unburdening oneself and resolving the conflict inherent in trying to get rid of fear, while trying to conceal it.

5 In Pursuit of Happiness

God, being Love is also happiness.
And it is happiness I seek today.

—A Course in Miracles[1]

The perennial pursuit of happiness is based in part on the American dream that assumes happiness is possible, and that if one is unhappy, something must be wrong. A better understanding of the nature of happiness and the problems of pursuit may provide some insight into motivations for choosing the spiritual path instead of the secular pursuits that are more widely accepted. Sometimes the relentless pursuit of happiness, ever elusive and disappointing, can itself be a strong motivation for turning attention to the inner journey of the Self.

Awareness can be tuned to any dimension of experience. For example, a therapeutic bias that assumes problems need to be solved tends to focus awareness on psychological problems. There is never a shortage of real or imagined conflicts to be resolved, or needs to be fulfilled. But as Carl Jung observed, the most important problems of life cannot be solved, but only outgrown, and this outgrowing requires "a new level of consciousness."[2]

Awareness may be trained in psychotherapy to observe the process of outgrowing problems, but is seldom trained to observe happiness. As one goes through the various stages of development one naturally outgrows some problems and some desires; and ways of seeking happiness change both with age and with levels of consciousness. In adulthood the specific shape of the pursuit of happiness is largely determined by the stage of psychological development of the person. In other words, who and what we think we are tends to determine where we look for happiness.

Thus symbols of pleasure and status in the form of material possessions may be ardently pursued when one is exclusively associated with the body-ego. When one gets in touch with feelings, emotionally satisfying relationships tend to become increasingly important. The mental egoic self tends to pursue personal accomplishments. When existential identity is paramount, the transitory nature of sensory pleasures, relationships, and accomplishments is recognized and happiness itself may be perceived as illusory. Truth may then replace happiness as the object of pursuit.

At the transpersonal level, ideals of selfless service, often in the form of teaching and healing, may take precedence over other motivations. This is exemplified in the bodhisattva vow, in which personal liberation is renounced until all sentient beings become enlightened. The bodhisattva chooses to remain in this reality in order to relieve suffering and help others become enlightened. One who takes this vow consciously renounces personal happiness as a goal. This commitment to service cannot be attributed to the pursuit of happiness in the usual sense, yet it may still be subtly operative if one feels virtuous about it. Only when the exclusive concern with the separate self is transcended are giving and receiving perceived to be the same. Selfless service may then become a genuine source of joy.

Reflecting on what gives one pleasure and where one looks for happiness can mirror how one sees oneself in the process of growing toward wholeness. Each stage is characterized by attraction to certain types of pleasure. Higher forms of pleasure are those that are more satisfying and enduring. Thus spiritual teachings encourage people to seek peace and love rather than material pleasures. Buddhism teaches that peace is the highest form of happiness, and some Christian teachings equate happiness with love. *A Course in Miracles* says, "Happiness is an attribute of Love. It cannot be apart from it."[3]

Yet the search continues, and many have faced personal pain and existential dread before finding an inner source of peace and love, not in blind faith or illusion, but in the light of understanding and Self-knowledge.

Unhappiness is attributed to different causes in different systems. In psychoanalysis unhappiness may be attributed to inevitable conflict between personal desires and social necessities, i.e., between the drives of the id and the demands of the super-ego. In behavioral psychology unhappiness may be attributed to faulty learning, inappropriate conditioning, and environmental influences. A Marxist might attribute it to social injustice and oppression. In humanistic psychology, Maslow saw unhappiness as a function of the failure of self-actualization. He wrote, "If you deliberately plan to be less than you are capable of being, then I warn you that you'll be deeply unhappy for the rest of your life."[4]

Gerald May points to the hazards of becoming preoccupied with personal happiness and assuming that unhappiness is a psychological defect. The expectation that being holy will make you happy he sees as a dangerous assumption that contributes to spiritual narcissism. He makes a crucial distinction between happiness and joy:

Happiness has to do with Freud's old pleasure principle: the satisfaction of needs and the avoidance of pain. Joy is altogether beyond consideration of pleasure or pain, and in fact requires a knowledge and acceptance of pain. Joy is the reaction one has to the full appreciation of Being. It is one's response to finding one's rightful, rooted place in life, and it can happen only when one knows through and through that absolutely nothing is being denied or otherwise shut out of awareness.[5]

In Buddhism the root cause of unhappiness in human life is said to be desire, clinging, and attachment. In a world of constant change, where nothing lasts and everything is in flux, the desire to hold on to anything is inherently frustrating. In Christianity unhappiness may be attributed to original sin or separation from God. Fear of loss or fear of punishment, coupled with feelings of helplessness, lead easily to hopelessness and despair. In the Hindu tradition, Sri Nisargadatta says, "Everyone creates a world for himself and lives in it, imprisoned by one's ignorance."[6]

The problem inherent in any search for happiness is rooted in ignorance. Whenever one perceives a lack that gives rise to desire, one feels deprived. When one discovers that fulfillment of ego desires never gives lasting satisfaction and that new desires arise the moment any one of them is satisfied, one may turn from secular to spiritual pursuits in hopes of finding a more lasting source of happiness. Motivation at the outset of the spiritual quest is often mixed, but a genuine commitment to inner work can help eradicate self-deception.

Once a person has made a commitment to a spiritual path, escape from suffering may be sought in transcendence. The goal then becomes liberation from desire and the illusion of a separate self. Peace seems to be obtainable only in a state of egolessness. Given appropriate training, one may learn to cultivate calm and equanimity. To a Westerner this may seem like disengaging from life. Some meditative practices do aim at eradication of desire through asceticism and suppression of impulses to seek satisfaction in the outside world. A faulty assumption that may be associated with such practices is that suffering is not only inevitable, but that it is good for you, hence the more the better. But suppression is not transcendence, and worldly desires are often replaced by equally strong desires for spiritual merit, high experiences, or subtle mind states.

Western paths leading to relationship or identification with the deity (religion) or Self (psychology) and Eastern paths of disidentification both offer alternatives to the frustrations of everyday life, but they are not the same. Both assume a problem and offer a solution, and both work with the mind in a particular way in attempting to escape from the pain of existence. The existentialist, on the other hand, chooses to live in the pain rather than attempt what seems to be an illusory escape. Even in hell, when the jail door opens in Jean-Paul Sartre's play *No Exit*, the protagonists do not choose to leave. An existentialist tends to view happiness as self-deception. Seeing the tragic side of life, he or she has little patience with superficial happiness.

The pursuit of happiness, like the pursuit of spirituality, can contribute either to suffering or to healing, depending on the outcome expected. A rejection of happiness in the name of authenticity is reminiscent of puritanical attitudes toward pleasure. Pleasure, like happiness, cannot be grasped, but it can certainly be experienced. It is as much a part of human experience as pain. Social taboos that engender feelings of guilt associated with any form of pleasure can contribute to unconscious avoidance, and to feeling "safer" when one is unhappy or in pain than when one is happy. It is a truism to say that one cannot have pleasure without pain, yet no one questions that it is possible to have pain without pleasure. Although such pairs of opposites are inextricably interwoven, one may lose sight of the positive side of this polarity. Today those who are inclined to overlook pain are called idealists, while those who overlook pleasure are called realists.

Fear of pain, presumed to be the inevitable result of pleasure, may inhibit enjoyment of even simple pleasures. Guilt about pleasure can also constrict happiness. Pleasure cannot be equated with happiness, but happiness includes the ability to find pleasure in ordinary experience. Examining attitudes toward pleasure and happiness with healing awareness can deepen the appreciation of delight, satisfaction, peace, and joy in every moment.

Expanding the Pleasure Principle

Satisfying the sensory desires cannot satisfy you, because you are not the senses. They are only your servants, not your Self.— Yogananda[7]

Much activity that is presumably pleasure seeking, when consciously examined, may be found to actually deliver very little, not only because it is transient, but because one fails to appreciate it while it lasts. Both happiness and a full appreciation of pleasure demand freedom from fear, guilt, and conflict. A healthy self-actualizing person who responds to life as an opportunity for discovery and creative self-expression may find pleasure and happiness in a wide variety of activities. Such experience can be welcomed and enjoyed. On the other hand, its absence is not necessarily interpreted as cause for suffering.

The pursuit of happiness takes different forms at different stages of development. When basic physiological needs are satisfied, a wide variety of pleasures are available, but enjoyment may be severely constricted. Becoming conscious of inhibitions can be a first step toward releasing them, but psychotherapy may be needed if early conditioning has been harsh.

Guilt inhibits the enjoyment of pleasure, no matter how innocent or innocuous. For example, sexual pleasure is often inhibited, even when sanctioned by marriage. For some people, any leisure activity that is not goal-oriented can induce guilt. If one values having and doing above being, it may be difficult to stop compulsive activity. For example, leisure time may be devoted to competitive sports or home improvement projects. People who enjoy being in nature often set goals, such as learning botany, collecting driftwood, or hiking to distant places. On the spiritual path meditation can become task-oriented in the effort to control the mind. When goal-oriented activities are collectively sanctioned, doing nothing can be highly anxiety-provoking. The value of free time that allows healing, happiness, and creativity may be difficult to accept. Giving oneself the privilege of doing nothing for a time in order to allow a deeper sense of Self to emerge may demand a struggle with one's own resistance. Yet it is clearly necessary, not only for personal happiness, but for relevant social action as well. Sri Nisargadatta says:

Only those who know the self, who have been beyond the world, can improve the world. . . . What is in the world cannot save the world; if you really care to help the world, you must step out of it.[8]

A good example of this is Mother Teresa of Calcutta, whose work with the destitute and the dying earned her the Nobel Peace Prize. For her, the need to withdraw, to be alone with God, is as important as her work.[9]

Personal freedom lies in choosing the goals one wants to pursue. It does not guarantee satisfaction or happiness, but conscious choice can have a liberating effect. What is pursued changes with time. In Dante's description of hell in the *Divine Comedy*, sinners were required to endure forever the pleasures they had once coveted.[10] What is pleasurable at one stage of development is of no interest at another. What was important at age ten does not matter at twenty, and what was attractive at twenty may not be appealing at forty. Folk wisdom says we should be careful about what we want in our twenties, because we are likely to get it in our forties. Clearly the egocentric pursuits of money, power, and status that dominate the lives of many Americans become empty and meaningless in the face of death. Existential concerns with meaning and purpose may become equally meaningless in an experience of transcendence. From a perspective of unity consciousness, such as that expressed in Zen Buddhism, nothing is more important than anything else. Everything may be enjoyed, although everything is ephemeral.

Unfortunately, the pursuit of pleasure or happiness, like the pursuit of enlightenment, tends to interfere with its enjoyment. But rather than trying to abandon the pursuit altogether, identifying different types of pleasure and happiness can facilitate the process of letting go of attachment to them, while freeing the mind, as the source of all pleasure and pain, to enjoy and share more possible forms of happiness.

Sensual Pleasures: Sex, Money, and Achievement

The most familiar and often-pursued pleasures are sensual and material pleasures, such as the intense pleasure of sexual orgasm, the sensual delights of a hot bath and massage, or the refined flavors of fine

French cuisine. For drug addicts the drug of choice is probably the only source of pleasure in their lives. Health food fans find pleasure in fresh fruits and vegetables, sports enthusiasts think of swimming or running or gliding down a ski slope on a sunny day. Homeowners find pleasure in redecorating their houses, young drivers in owning a new sports car. The pleasures of buying new clothes, staying at luxurious resorts, drinking fine wine, and enjoying good entertainment are sensory pleasures, the pursuit of which supports multi-billion-dollar industries.

The fact that such pleasures are fleeting at best does not deter the pursuit. A lot of hard work goes into earning the money required to buy them. They can provide moments of delight, but these symbols of pleasure contribute little to happiness. The nature of desire is that something is wanted until it is obtained. Then, almost immediately, other desires emerge. Sometimes novelty itself becomes the object of pursuit.

When desire for material or sensory pleasures has been gratified to some extent, continued satiation may seem flat or superficial. A person who feels lonely, alienated, or insecure finds little solace even in the best form of material or sensory gratification. More rewarding sources of satisfaction may be sought in personal achievement. The pleasure of winning a competition, breaking a world record, or making a successful business deal easily takes precedence over simple sensual pleasures. Sensual gratification may readily be given up for the purpose of attaining some desired goal, such as winning an Olympic gold medal. When achievement is valued, sensuality may be considered hedonistic self-indulgence, and treated as an interference or distraction. Rather than including sensuality as part of an integrated self-image that is open to such experience without being dominated by it, desire for sensual pleasure may be repressed and projected onto others who may then be perceived as misguided, inferior, or evil.

Both physical and mental disciplines demand forgoing immediate pleasure for future gratification that is presumably more satisfying. A runner training for a race or a meditator training his or her concentration willingly suffers bodily discomfort in order to gain what is valued more highly. Everyone chooses, more or less consciously, what pleasures to forgo and what to pursue.

Emotional Pleasures: Relational Exchange

Pleasure that is derived from relationship (e.g., communication and cooperation), pertains to the emotional level of consciousness and includes empathy and joining with others in any type of interpersonal exchange. For some people, the pleasure of shared work, of team building, and accomplishing goals that require leadership and organizational skills may take precedence over individual accomplishments. Feeling effective in communication with groups and establishing rapport with others may be a source of satisfaction that is more gratifying than personal recognition. Sharing ideas and feelings may be, in itself, a source of pleasure. When it is mutually enjoyable, it may be called happiness.

Happiness is closely associated with a well-developed capacity for love. If one "loves" someone or something, it sometimes means that one is addicted to it and wants to possess it. It could mean, however, that one finds pleasure in its existence without desiring to control or change it. Love itself is not possessive, but the fears and fantasies that are sometimes associated with it can engender clinging and attachment that easily become a source of pain rather than happiness.

The experience of falling in love is a pleasure that is sometimes relentlessly pursued throughout life. Unfortunately, like other pleasures, the experience of being swept away by another person is always temporary. Loving can continue indefinitely, but the thrill of falling in love depends on novelty and is enmeshed with unconscious projection. Popular love stories cater to the universal desire for this experience. Everybody loves a good love story, real or imagined. Romance is often marred by envy, jealousy, or cynicism, but the attraction is universal.

Love in personal relationships is necessary for healthy emotional development. When the need for affection and intimate communication is unfulfilled, other forms of pleasure seem pale by comparison. Some satisfying relationships may predominantly be a source of emotional intimacy; others may include physical, emotional, mental, and spiritual levels of relational exchange. Intimacy can develop at any or all of these levels. Ideally, falling in love is presumed to be intimate on all levels, but it often turns out to have been based largely on fantasy and projection. Romantic disillusionment, like other difficult emotional experiences, can contribute to self-healing if one is willing to consciously examine the process in the light of healing awareness.

Emotional intimacy is sometimes confused with sexuality, but can be clearly differentiated. Either can be experienced without the other. Sex without emotional intimacy is common, but seldom associated with happiness. Some people feel sexual pleasure depends on emotional intimacy. Others who are emotionally inhibited may only allow themselves sex without intimacy.

Emotional intimacy without sex (e.g., the phenomenon of transference in therapeutic relationships) can be a healing experience. Emotional intimacy tends to develop naturally when inhibitions are released. This was a discovery that fueled the encounter-group movement in the sixties. It feels good to be with people with whom one can be totally oneself, revealing the feelings that are hidden when one is worried about approval.

Intimate relationships such as marriage are enhanced when partners enjoy both physical and emotional intimacy. With rising expectations, marriage partners today tend to demand satisfaction of both these levels of pleasure. The current popularity of sex therapy reflects the widespread concern with giving and receiving physical pleasure. Marriage counseling is more likely to address emotional issues. Thanks to Freud, it is now widely accepted that sexual gratification contributes to emotional and mental health. It is often assumed that if these levels of exchange are operating satisfactorily, one will be happy—all evidence to the contrary notwithstanding.

An enhanced capacity for sexual and emotional pleasure may indeed contribute to health and happiness, but like any pleasure that depends on external stimulation, the pursuit absorbs large amounts of time, energy, and attention, and is never fully satisfying. One might infer from psychoanalytic theory that other forms of pleasure are only substitutes for sex. Yet sexual pleasure is often pursued as a substitute for love. Once sexual and intimacy needs are both satisfied, other desires tend to emerge.

The pleasures of intimate communication (mental), self-determination (existential), and transpersonal (spiritual) joining can be a source of relational pleasure for people who have, as well as for those who have not, satisfied physical and emotional needs. These pleasures may be experienced even in the midst of physical or emotional pain, and can have a healing effect on the persons involved. When defenses crumble and façades are dropped, genuine contact with another person at a transpersonal level may be experienced as deeply meaningful. This may open a dimension of happiness that is not found in object-oriented pleasures.

Psychologically sophisticated people are well aware of relationships as a source of pleasure in everyday life. Yet many who know that buying another house or a different car will not give lasting happiness still believe that if they could only find the right relationship, the pursuit would be over. Eventually, when the pursuit of happiness through a specific relationship seems utterly hopeless, when one no longer expects someone else to provide the happiness that is sought, one may despair, become cynical, or one may begin to look inward for other sources of pleasure.

Mental Pleasures: Creativity and Communication

The pleasures of creativity include and transcend aesthetic sensitivity evoked by artistic excellence. Art as a form of communication bypasses logic and reason. It can be inspiring and can change perception of the world or the way we see things.

Self-expression through art can be a source of great pleasure and satisfaction. Many artists are willing to forgo not only the accumulation of wealth or possessions, but personal relationships as well, in pursuit of the muse. An artist is more likely to view his or her work in terms of authenticity than pleasure, but cannot be happy without it. Dissatisfaction with other pursuits may be expressed in restlessness or inspiration for new work.

Of course, one need not be an artist to appreciate the satisfaction of self-expression. Whatever the form— visual arts, movement, music, or words—the pleasure of self-expression is available to anyone who tries it. Freedom is essential to any form of genuine self-expression, and freedom in this context means not only freedom from external oppression, but freedom from internal repression as well. Creativity cannot be enjoyed when one is laboring under internal inhibitions or external constraints that demand conformity. Artists are typically non-conformist and relatively free from ordinary social conventions.

Creativity in any field can be intrinsically satisfying, but meaningful communication adds another dimension of satisfaction. If one's work has meaning for others, that tends to be highly valued. Delight in creativity can also be expressed in an intellectual exchange of ideas. Here clarity, insight, originality, and elegance can be sources of intrinsic satisfaction to a thinker, just as the aesthetic quality of a painting is satisfying to a painter. Communication, however, is essential for a sense of completion. The process of discovering or creating meaning in life can also be a shared creative endeavor.

Humor is another creative source of mental pleasure. It involves a playful use of mental abilities to provide a fresh perspective that breaks out of the ordinary way of seeing things and invites laughter. Laughter can be a rich source of pleasure and enjoyment, as well as a favorable context for healing. The ability to laugh at our own foibles can be a powerful aid to self-healing. Humor, like words themselves, can be used in many ways. It can be used aggressively, as in scathing sarcasm, but it can also be an instrument of healing, as it was for Norman Cousins,[11] who claims to have restored his own physical health through humor. It is particularly useful in breaking up rigid mental sets and confronting beliefs and assumptions. Humor can be meaningful or meaningless, but good humor is associated with wholeness and happiness.

Existential Pleasure: Intrinsic Wholeness

Pleasures that pertain to the existential level of consciousness tend to be associated with authenticity and the integration of physical, emotional, and mental pleasures.

Reflecting on childhood, few people say they felt happy as children. It is commonly assumed that childhood is a time of simple pleasures and that others were happy in childhood. But growing up is never free of emotional pain. People who seek psychotherapy tend to think that their painful childhood memories are exceptional. They may see their own childhood as difficult or deprived, imagining that socialization was easy for others. This misconception may be cleared up in groups, when participants share how they felt about themselves when they were starting school or entering adolescence. Adolescence is often a time of conflict, both internal and external, and may entail a struggle for independence.

People tend to feel better about themselves in their twenties than in their teens, but this period can be fraught with troublesome existential questions of identity. Young adults may feel pressured to prove themselves and decide what they are going to do with their lives. Some become outer-directed achievers identified with social roles, others embark on an inner-directed quest for identity. Some fulfill parental expectations, others refuse or rebel, still others fail. Happiness during these years is usually perceived to lie in the future, when one may expect to have a mate and a family, make more money, and buy more things. The search for the right relationship is often a dominant theme. It can also be a time of self-searching. Whether finding a place in the adult world seems easy or difficult, young adults tend to focus on the future. In healthy development, hopes for finding personal happiness in the future tend to outweigh fears of failure or annihilation.

Approaching midlife is often a time of disillusionment and existential crisis. When goals attained have not proved satisfying, and distractions that were once entertaining lose their appeal, depression may set in. When activities that were once a source of pleasure become boring, life seems meaningless. Typically, midlife is a time of questioning the meaning of ego goals, regardless of success or failure in meeting them. Some may begin the inner journey long before midlife, others may put it off indefinitely; but it often begins at this time, and is marked by the recognition of the transitory nature of pleasure and the ephemeral nature of happiness.

At any age an exclusive focus on any one type of pleasure could be perceived as an imbalance. From an existential point of view, growth toward wholeness (intrinsic individual wholeness) may be perceived as the highest form of happiness. However, as mentioned earlier, happiness itself may be eschewed in favor of "reality" as perceived from the perspective of the separate self.

Disillusionment with the pursuit of happiness is typical of this level of consciousness. Satisfaction is sought not in happiness but in the pursuit of meaning and the truth of existence. If one persists in this pursuit and ends up on a spiritual path, a totally different perspective on the pursuit of happiness may emerge.

Open communication at any level—physical, emotional, mental, existential, or spiritual—tends to enhance pleasure and contribute to happiness. Meaningful communication at the existential level can open the door to communion and love. Love contributes to happiness, healing, and wholeness at all levels. A Christian psychiatrist, Scott Peck, considers genuine love to be volitional rather than emotional. He defines love as "the will to extend oneself for the purpose of nurturing one's own or another's spiritual growth."[12]

Spiritual Pleasure

Spiritual pleasure is usually associated with qualities such as love and inner peace. The joy of illumination, the ecstasy of mystical states, and absorption in blissful meditative states are all pleasurable. In Buddhism, the pleasure of the concentrated mind is said to surpass all sensory, aesthetic, or intellectual pleasures. Yet advanced meditators say that this is not the highest form of pleasure derived from training the mind. When a person has learned to maintain one-pointed concentration and has overcome the hindrances of negative emotions or mindstates, inner peace and purity of mind are said to prepare the mind for equanimity, compassion, and sympathetic joy—the ability to experience pleasure in the joy of others.

Training the mind to maintain these states of consciousness may be compared to training the body to peak performance. Just as a healthy body can be a source of pleasure and satisfaction at the physical level, a quiet, balanced mind becomes a source of pleasure from a transpersonal perspective.

Pleasure at this level may also be derived from intuitive insight. Whereas psychological insight tends to focus on contents of consciousness, process, and patterns of perception, pure intuitive insight takes as its object the domain of Spirit. Common "Aha!" experiences that reveal obvious but previously unnoticed relationships, for example, can give the impression that when we know enough everything falls easily into place. The "Aha!" experience, however, may be either a genuine illumination or a more limited cognitive understanding. Insight into the relationship of consciousness to happiness can itself become a source of pleasure and satisfaction. But even the most profound insight is still concerned with the mind and its objects. The greatest spiritual pleasure, commonly called bliss or ecstasy, is found not in insight, but in transcendence of duality, in the realization of unity consciousness.

The spiritual life, which affirms and includes all experience in awareness, tends to manifest joy that radiates from an inner source. It cannot be found by searching in the outer world, but when the source within is awakened it is reflected in all things. In the words of Kalu Rinpoche, a Tibetan Buddhist teacher, "When you practice the Dharma the clouds of sorrow will drift away and the sun of wisdom and great joy will be shining in the clear sky of your mind."

Pleasure at this level may be described as rapture, joy, or pure light. The happiness that results from healing the mind at this level is impossible as long as one feels fragmented or conflicted. Peace is a necessary condition for this form of happiness. In its attainment all other forms of happiness pale, but are not excluded.

Experiencing spiritual happiness is contingent on awareness. In growing toward wholeness, awakening to the reality of Self as spirit can generate spontaneous joy. At first the possibility of this level of happiness is only glimpsed or intuited. In time it may become a pervasive feeling of well-being. It is not a separate state to be acquired or added to a repertoire, but can be expressed in communication at any level of consciousness. Happiness that results from healing the mind is impossible when we feel fragmented or conflicted.

Balance and Wholeness

Restoring the balance between pain and pleasure requires healing awareness. Attachment to pain can be as much of a trap as attachment to pleasure. A willingness to examine attitudes toward pleasure and pain can free one from compulsive, repetitive patterns of experience that seem to be beyond conscious control. Sometimes pain is preferred to pleasure out of fear and guilt; sometimes pleasure is sought as an avoidance of pain. Neither one contributes to happiness. Authentic happiness associated with wholeness and the awakened mind may depend on acceptance of the full spectrum of consciousness.

Since everything in the world is constantly changing, including our states of mind, nothing can guarantee lasting happiness. Only with the relinquishment of illusory self-concepts can the conditions for happiness be established. Happiness may then be perceived as an attitude that depends on wisdom and healing awareness.

Once upon a time an ancient king asked a wise man for the secret of happiness. The sage gave the king a ring with this inscription: "This too will pass." The realization of the inevitability of change and the transitory nature of life and all human experience can lead to a deeper appreciation of the potential for choosing happiness in each moment. The promise of liberation is not found in the future or in the past. Nor does it exist somewhere else. It is, rather, a condition or state of mind that can be chosen, moment by moment. The freedom to choose it, however, is contingent on freedom from want, from fear, and from guilt.

It is nonetheless possible to experience moments of pleasure and happiness even in the midst of suffering or pain. An experience of healing, for example, may be felt as a pleasurable sensation of warmth. The pleasure of feeling close to someone who is loving and caring can have a healing effect at all levels. Physical, emotional, and mental health can all benefit from moments of genuine pleasure and happiness, however short-lived they may be.

In the absence of inner freedom, happiness remains elusive. Even the best of spiritual pleasure may be haunted by the spectre of impermanence. Only when the separate self no longer clings to its independent identity can one be free from fear. Fear always interferes with pleasure and precludes happiness, and wherever there is perception of other, there is fear.

The Spectrum of Pleasure

Pleasure is available at any level of consciousness. Sensory pleasures can be enjoyed in spite of being devoid of meaning, and pleasures of relationship, creativity, and insight can be perceived as significant and meaningful. Happiness cannot be found in pleasure alone, but can become a conscious choice as one develops a capacity for pleasure at higher levels of consciousness. The higher one goes on the spectrum, the deeper and more lasting is the form of pleasure associated with it. Higher pleasures, like higher states of consciousness, do not preclude other levels, but include them in a larger perspective. Thus, a person devoted to creative work can certainly enjoy sensual pleasures. In fact, enjoyment of any pleasure is enhanced when it is not sought as an end in itself, but is simply enjoyed when available. When the mind is acknowledged as the source of all pleasure and pain, the necessity of healing the mind for the relief of human suffering becomes apparent.

Assuming healthy psychological development, tastes in pleasure change with maturity. Physical and sensory delights that are compelling to the young become boring in themselves and require refinement or increased intensity for satisfaction. In healthy development one does not outgrow the enjoyment of food or sex, but they find their place in a larger spectrum of possibilities. When a specific pleasure becomes an addiction and is pursued exclusively, it becomes a source of pain. Burnout, restlessness, and frustration tend to accompany satiation and the persistent search for novelty and stimulation.

Delight in nature, good company, and such simple pleasures as drinking a cup of tea or watching a sunset, on the other hand, can grow to be more fully appreciated with time. The attraction of activity and excitement may be balanced by the desire for harmony and inner peace. At any age enjoyment may be either constricted to a narrow band or expanded to the whole spectrum. A healthy person would presumably be open to experiencing a broad range of pleasures, without undue attachment to any one.

Conventional morality considers pleasure to be a transient, superficial experience unworthy of pursuit. Yet the pursuit of happiness is endorsed as an inalienable right. The implied promise of lasting satisfaction is part of the American dream of human perfectability. It is rarely associated with psychological health, maturity, and generativity. But it seems evident that happiness cannot be separated from self-actualization and transcendence. The secret of happiness is revealed by the wisdom that sees the play of opposites and does not attempt to impose permanence on any one aspect of the totality.

If one listens to the wisdom of the Self in the process of changing, growing, and understanding more about human experience, one may discover that happiness is inseparable from the fulfillment of a unique function in the world. When one responds to an inner calling, following truth and authenticity at every level, one may taste happiness in the process of becoming whole.

Happiness is not inherent in pleasure, but the capacity for happiness includes the capacity for pleasure at all levels. The ability to experience pleasure in any passing moment is based on the willingness to give undivided attention to what is present. Letting go of expectations of people, situations, and life itself, seems to be a prerequisite for expanding the capacity for happiness. As long as one looks to the future for the attainment of happiness, whether it be projected onto the next job, the next relationship, or the next spiritual awakening, one is deprived of the experience in the present. The joy of communion, for example, whether with nature or a person or God, can only be experienced in the moment.

As long as one persists in searching for happiness one is like the hungry ghosts described in Buddhism, beings with huge bellies and tiny throats, doomed to craving and dissatisfaction. Whether one craves intimacy, knowledge, or material possessions, it is the condition of craving that precludes the possibility of pleasure, happiness, or satisfaction in the present. Thus whatever takes attention away from the present into the future, pursuit of any kind, diminishes one's capacity to experience fulfillment of desire.

Just as Alice in *Alice Through the Looking Glass* had to move away from something when she wanted to get closer to it, in order to find happiness one must relinquish the pursuit. One must learn to experience it now, despite all obstacles, real or imaginary. The state of mind that allows satisfaction and happiness cannot be purchased or obtained from anyone else. It does not result from an effort to eliminate negativity and count blessings. It is, rather, a state of consciousness that allows everything to be exactly as it is. In desiring to make reality into what one thinks it should be, one misses the opportunity to appreciate it as it is. There is nothing one can *do* to *get* more pleasure or happiness, yet one can choose to *allow* more of it at any time.

The Conditions for Happiness

He that binds to himself a joy
Doth the winged life destroy.
He that kisses the joy as it flies
Lives in eternity's sunrise.—William Blake[13]

As long as happiness is the object of pursuit, one separates oneself from it and it remains unattainable. Prescriptions for happiness that stress the power of positive thinking may be useful up to a point, but they are often superficial and ineffective. Psychologists are familiar with the negative effects of too much conscious programming. Conscious manipulation of thought that ignores emotional factors can lead to denial and suppression of impulses toward healing and wholeness. More effective prescriptions for happiness seem to be based on training awareness to remove the obstacles that seem to prevent the experience of happiness in the present.

As long as men and women believe that someone or something outside them can make them happy, they usually fail to make the changes that can contribute to more pleasure and happiness in everyday life. The changes that actually do increase enjoyment and satisfaction are changes in perception, attitude, and consciousness. Taking responsibility for subjective states of mind can be the beginning of change in a desired direction. The yearning for intimacy, for inner peace, and for a sense of meaning and purpose may be forms of "divine discontent" that prompt one to keep growing toward wholeness, to risk evolving beyond ego and to surrender to the Self.

The genuine desire to experience the full spectrum of pleasure, to give and receive love, to find a satisfying mode of self-expression, and to contribute to the well-being of others are shared longings that may be difficult to acknowledge. However, when one admits openly what one really wants, one is well on the way to finding it. Dissatisfaction with symbols of pleasure at any stage can be interpreted as a message from the Self. Divine discontent is a call to transcendence. As long as happiness eludes us, the search continues. We can never be completely happy with less than total Self-awareness.

As long as we are busy making judgments, pursuing conscious goals, and allowing the more subtle aspects of present experience to escape our notice, happiness eludes us. Only when we change our attitudes to pleasure and pain and learn to quiet the endless inner monologue can we begin to see truth, freedom, and joy in every moment. Hopes and fears, desires and expectations, judgments and perceptions can be distractions that prevent the recognition that we exist embedded in an incredibly rich and complex ecosystem that we did not engineer.

Happiness may not be found in material sufficiency, approval, or achievement. It does not come from purely intellectual knowledge, but from how we live. Understanding this may be a first step to its discovery, but knowledge or insight alone does not heal or make us happy.

The fundamental condition of lasting happiness is Self-awareness, but even that remains incomplete unless it is shared. Its expression in the world is not an impossible ideal. In fact, it may be a necessary condition for human survival. When one despairs of finding happiness in the external world and consciousness becomes the focus of attention, the inward arc unfolds. The spiritual path begins when we attend to what we truly want.

Experiential Exercise

Reflections on Pleasure

What is your favorite pleasure?

What gives you pleasure on a daily basis?

Are there some activities you do every day that are sometimes pleasurable, sometimes not? What is the difference?

Has your capacity for experiencing pleasure expanded or deepened in recent years?

What sources of pleasure have you not noticed? What pleasures do you reject?

Reflections on Happiness

Take a few minutes to recall the happiest times in your life. What do they have in common?

What is a source of happiness in your life now?

What might be a source of happiness in the future?

6 Mapping the Spiritual Path

> We are manifestations of Being, but like the cosmos itself, we are also in the process of Becoming—always growing, changing, developing, evolving to higher and higher states that ever more beautifully express the perfection of the source of existence.   —*John White*[1]

The spiritual path represents the process of becoming whereby the soul remembers itself and the Self discovers its true identity as Spirit. The spiritual journey can also be perceived as a healing journey that is completed in the recognition of wholeness. Every spiritual tradition offers a map for the seeker. Each metaphorically depicts a journey of the soul from darkness to enlightenment, or from ignorance to knowledge. We have already explored some psychological maps of development that point in this direction. We will now look at some of the traditional ways of mapping the journey through various levels of consciousness and stages of Self-remembering.

I. Christian Metaphors: The Heroic Journey

Evelyn Underhill described five stages on the path of Christian mysticism: awakening or conversion, self-knowledge or purgation, illumination, the dark night of the soul, and union or the unitive life. In the unitive life inner and outer are no longer seen as separate but simply as differing aspects of the One Great Truth of Existence.[2] The unitive life is lived in the world but is not of it, hence it eludes human attempts to quantify it. The unitive life is not lived apart from humanity. On the contrary, having at last come to full consciousness of reality the circle of being is completed in returning to fertilize those levels of existence from which it sprang. The mystic is portrayed here as a pioneer of humanity, an activist among the saints, a practical and intuitive person. The attainment of the unitive state depends on having traveled the path through each of the preceding four stages and having come at last to self-surrender or transcendence. In the unitive state the self has triumphed over the dark night, the existential confrontation with nonbeing, and fulfills its destiny in the total disappearance of selfhood in the divine.

At the beginning of the fourteenth century, Dante Alighieri wrote *The Divine Comedy*, in the form of an autobiographical narrative. This is a classic allegory depicting the journey of the soul through hell and purgatory, arriving finally in paradise. At the outset, on the night before Good Friday, Dante awakens to find himself lost in the middle of a dark, wild forest. He is rescued by the ghost of Virgil who, as his rational guide, informs him that his only escape lies through the center of the earth, traversing the realms of hell. Here sinners are condemned to endure forever the punishment of their addictions. Having inspected the various realms of hell and conversed with some of the inmates, Dante emerges, with Virgil's help, on the other side of earth on the shores of the mountain of purgatory on Easter Sunday. On the upper slopes of the mountain repentant souls are doing penance, or discipline, for the seven cardinal vices. Below, on the lower slopes are those who are not yet admitted to the disciplines. In purgatory Dante meets those who once were famous and are now aware of the "empty and transitory nature of human glory." At the top of the mountain is the Garden of Eden. Eventually, when the goal of purgatory is reached, Virgil informs Dante that his function as guide is now discharged. Dante, having recovered from the dire effects of the fall of man, is now free to enter paradise. He has no further need of external or institutional direction. He is now "king and bishop of himself."[3]

Reason is an essential guide through the realms of personal history that encompass physical, emotional, mental, and existential levels of consciousness. But reason does not enter into paradise. In the upper realms it is Beatrice, representing Love, who becomes Dante's guide. Beatrice, as an anima image that embodies transpersonal qualities, leads him up through the revolving heavens into the eternally motionless heavens of God. The climax is the vision of God. In contemporary language, Dante, inspired by love, transcends reason and moves beyond existential anguish to unity consciousness.

Dante's allegory of the journey is Christian, but the three levels of reality—the lower, the middle, and the upper world—are universal symbols that reflect levels of consciousness. A shaman, for example, learns to travel in all of them on healing journeys. Hell, purgatory, and heaven are part of human experience on any spiritual path.

If, in contemporary life, one awakens to find oneself lost in a confused and frightened state of consciousness, one may indeed get help from traditional psychotherapy. The process of healing often does involve going through hell—facing all the painful consequences of previous choices that were perhaps made unconsciously. As one begins to see the way out, to climb the mountain of purgatory, discipline may be necessary and helpful. An effort must be made to take responsibility for oneself before one can aspire to the higher states of illumination and unitive consciousness. The soul is instructed by reason, an excellent guide in the lower and middle realms. The higher realms that are inaccessible to reason may be attained by opening the heart to love and forgiveness.

The grail legends of Western Europe also symbolize the journey of the soul in search of the truth. Here the theme of romantic love is carried into the battlefield. The knights fight for the sake of love and honor, attempting to set right the wrongs of the world. Loyalty in service to love is portrayed as the ideal motivation for action.[4] The legendary hero always goes alone. He confronts the unknown when he enters the dark forest and is required to battle various forms of evil along the way. When a dragon is slain, a maiden is liberated. The culmination of the journey may be finding the treasure or achieving union with the goddess. When the journey is complete the hero returns with the treasure to his homeland, bringing peace, prosperity, and renewal to what he left behind. In *The Hero with a Thousand Faces* Joseph Campbell writes:

The hero ventures forth from the world of common day into a region of supernatural wonder: fabulous forces are there encountered and a decisive victory is won: the hero comes back from this mysterious adventure with the power to bestow boons on his fellow man.[5]

The hero may manifest as a warrior, lover, ruler, prophet, saint, redeemer, or sage. Whether Christian, pre-Christian, or non-Christian, the heroic journey is always an adventure in consciousness. It is a universal theme that appears in all cultures.

From a psychological perspective the heroic journey can be viewed as a metaphor of psychological development. We all experience a personal version of this journey when we outgrow egocentric identifications and engage the world from a new level of consciousness. The heroic journey can be interpreted as representing the journey of the separate self seeking actualization, or the journey of the soul beyond ego, culminating in transcendence.

Specific images encountered on the path are culturally determined. Universal symbols appear in different forms in all cultures, sometimes with a variety of meanings. For example, light may represent illumination or enlightenment, fire may represent transformation, purification, or creative consciousness. The snake appears as a symbol of healing or of differentiated consciousness.

When symbolic images become familiar we tend to forget the meaning they can convey. It is therefore not uncommon for people raised in one religion to find another more meaningful, or more intriguing. One may tend to feel defensive in relation to symbols associated with guilt and restriction. Even the image of a path or a ladder may be experienced as linear restriction on consciousness. A multidimensional metaphor such as a web or a sphere may be more appealing. However, the spiritual path is the universally acknowledged metaphor for the inward arc of human development in the major religious traditions.

Campbell writes,

The modern hero, the modern individual who dares to heed the call and seek the mansion of that presence with whom it is our whole destiny to be atoned, cannot, indeed must not, wait for his community to cast off its slough of pride, fear, rationalized avarice, and sanctified misunderstanding. "Live," Nietzsche says, "as though the day were here." It is not society that is to guide and save the creative hero, but precisely the reverse. And so every one of us shares the supreme ordeal—carries the cross of the redeemer—not in the bright moments of his tribe's great victories, but in the silences of his personal despair.[6]

On any spiritual path the psyche comes to know itself and the world in a new way. Progress on the path leads from self-consciousness to superconsciousness, or transcendent insight. When the goal of the path is attained, the separate self-sense is transcended. Thus the hero who sets out on the spiritual path does not complete the journey, because who one thinks one is when one sets out on the path turns out to be an illusory self-concept that is transcended in the realization of no self.

Bernadette Roberts, a contemporary Christian contemplative, writes,

The knowledge of individual wholeness and unity realized before the journey began, is akin, though not identical to, the wholeness that remains when the journey is over, or when there is no self. Once we pass over the line, it becomes possible to realize a greater wholeness than that of individual being, which is the wholeness of all that Is. The unity of the self has disappeared, disintegrated, and given way to a wholeness that has no parts and therefore cannot be said to be integrated. Nevertheless, it was the initial integration that constituted the necessary preparation for the journey, and without it, I do not see how the passage could be made. To have no self, there must first *be* a self—a whole self.[7]

Experiential Exercise

A Metaphoric Journey

With watercolors or crayons draw a picture that represents where you have come from. Draw a second picture representing where you are now, and a third representing where you are going. Each picture should be drawn quickly, taking only about three minutes to allow any abstract image or color or shape to emerge. Do not think about what you are drawing. Do not try to interpret it.

After you have finished all three drawings, place them in sequence—past, present, future—and make up a story about a hero or heroine traveling through them. Reflect on your story and see if there is anything about it that you would want to change.

For example, one person's story went like this:

A hero sets out on a journey, uncertain of his destination. He enters a forest and meets a demon on his path. The hero tries to kill the demon, but when he thinks he has killed him he discovers that the demon reappears in a different form. The hero continues to do battle and becomes so engrossed in trying to win he forgets about the journey.

Sometime later another hero comes along and the demon again appears to threaten him. This time the hero decides to learn what he can about the nature of the demon and tries to get to know him. He begins to role-play, acting like the demon, and soon becomes indistinguishable from the demon. He even learns to enjoy harassing other heroes on the path who think they are going somewhere. He lives for some time among the demons, who come to regard him as one of them and he, too, soon forgets the journey.

Sometime later a third hero traveling this path encounters a demon who tries to block his passage. This hero has a single purpose: to continue the journey. He manages to trick the demon by distracting him, while he passes by unharmed. When the others who had remained among the demons, either pretending to be like them or doing battle with them, see him passing through, they remember their own journeys. The first lays down his arms and sets his mind to continuing on the path. He no longer feels compelled to do battle. The second drops his disguise and remembers who he really is, and he too turns his attention to continuing the journey. He knows the demons now. He is no longer afraid of them. They continue their respective journeys up the mountain and come at last to the heaven realms where they join in consort with the goddesses. In time each one feels drawn by compassion for the suffering of the world to return again to show others the path.

Demons can symbolize any obstacle encountered on the inner journey. For one person they may represent fear, for another resistance. For another they may represent external obstacles rather than internal ones. What is important for each person is to identify the obstacles and recognize the traps one tends to fall into along the way.

II. Chakra Symbolism: Levels of Consciousness

The journey passes thru the seven valleys, the seven kingdoms, the chakras, the planes of consciousness, the degrees of faith. Often we only know we've been in a certain place when we pass beyond it. . . . —Ram Dass[8]

Different traditions portray the spiritual path in different ways, but all posit a potential end state of full realization or enlightenment. In this section we will review the levels of consciousness associated with the seven chakras in the Hindu tradition from a psychological perspective.

In yoga psychology, the seven chakras are defined as centers of psychic energy located in the human body. The chakras are discussed in various traditions, but not all agree on their precise location, the exact number of them, or what they represent. Tibetan Buddhism, for example, identifies five chakras or levels of consciousness associated with specific locations in the body,[9] while Hindu sources identify seven.[10] Variations are also found among different teachers influenced by Hinduism, such as Sri Aurobindo, Swami Rama, and Swami Radha, with regard to what each one represents.

In an essay entitled "Are the Chakras Real?" Wilber points out that awareness of the chakras is not mandatory on the journey to liberation, but physiological changes in the body associated with opening the chakras in kundalini yoga can be viewed either as cause or effect of changes in consciousness.[11] Although many scholars consider such physiological changes irrelevant to spiritual growth, the chakras appear to be real to the separate self that perceives obstacles on the path to the realization of unity consciousness. The chakras are said to be open when obstructions to transcendent bliss have been removed. Opening of specific chakras may be accompanied by distinct physical sensations of varying degrees of intensity. In general, opening is associated with becoming aware of the subtle levels of consciousness they represent.

Localization of the chakras in specific areas of the body corresponds to the universal tendency to localize certain feelings in specific bodily regions. Body therapies confirm this general topography. For example, orgasmic ecstasy and sexual bliss in normal adults is centered in, though not necessarily limited to, the genitals, while the joy and vitality of the life force seems to emanate from the abdomen. The heart region in the chest seems to contain and radiate universal love, while the head region is associated with insight and intellectual bliss. The crown of the head is associated with the spiritual ecstasy of samadhi. When the chakras are open, bodily feelings of transcendent bliss may be experienced in each area of the body.

Each chakra also symbolizes a specific stage in the evolution of consciousness. Self-realization as mapped on this path involves not only a physical sensation of these centers, but also awareness of the various levels of reality they represent. In the ordinary waking state, consciousness, symbolized by a serpent representing kundalini energy, is said to lie coiled at the base of the spine in the root chakra.

The image of the Uroborus, the snake biting its tail, is a universal symbol of unconscious wholeness. Eric Neumann says, ". . . existence in the Uroborus was existence in *participation mystique.*"[12] This means that no egoic self-sense has yet developed. At the level of the first chakra, consciousness is relatively undifferentiated, concerned mainly with food and survival. As consciousness evolves, the kundalini serpent energy awakens from its slumber and rises up the spine, opening each chakra on the way.

Enlightened beings are therefore depicted with snakes poised above the head in religious iconography, indicating that the kundalini energy has reached the highest level. The Hindu deity, Lord Vishnu, for example, is portrayed with seven serpents forming a halo or crown above his head. In Buddhism, the sage Nagarjuna is similarly portrayed.[13]

Like the snake in the Garden of Eden that enticed Eve to eat the fruit of the tree of knowledge of good and evil, the awakening of consciousness at the first chakra is the beginning of differentiation. Distinctions between good and evil, being and nonbeing, consciousness and unconsciousness, mark the beginning of the journey of human evolution. The serpent itself takes on a dualistic nature. Joseph Campbell tells us:

Wherever nature is revered as self-moving, and so inherently divine, the serpent is revered as symbolic of its divine life . . . in the Book of Genesis, where the serpent is cursed, all nature is devaluated . . . In Christian mythology, . . . the serpent is normally identified with Satan.[14]

The serpent can thus be viewed as a symbolic representation of dualistic consciousness that perceives itself as separated from its source.

In the course of spiritual practice, consciousness eventually encompasses all seven centers. This journey of awakening is generally portrayed as proceeding in a hierarchical manner, moving from the lower to the higher chakras, although there may be some distortions or exceptions. Each lower level of consciousness is subsumed or included in the one above it, so the process does not eliminate or discard lower levels, but includes and integrates them in the larger perspectives of each higher level. As the evolutionary process unfolds, earlier stages are subrationed, i.e., evaluated as incomplete or less than optimum.

In psychological terms, the opening of the first three chakras corresponds to ego development. The first chakra represents the domain of the simplest sensations and perceptions pertaining to the physical, material world. It is associated with survival instincts and behavioral patterns of stimulus and response. The second chakra, associated with sexuality, can be considered the domain of Freudian psychoanalysis. The third chakra, associated with personal power, can be related to ego psychology, or the will to power in Adlerian theory.

The fourth chakra, the heart center, representing altruistic values of love and compassion, is often associated with the psychology of Carl Jung, who thought it represented humanity's highest development to date. Jung noted a correspondence between the archetypal images appearing in the visions of his patients in the process of individuation and the symbolic images representing stages of psychological development in the chakra system.[15]

Transpersonal development as defined here would begin at the fourth chakra and come to completion in wholeness when all seven chakras are open. Each chakra also represents a particular context or framework through which reality is interpreted. As consciousness evolves from the lower to the higher centers, healthy psychological development could be expected to bring them all into full awareness.

Muladhara

The first chakra, the *muladhara* (translated literally as "root support"), physiologically localized in the perineum, is associated with survival and is represented by the element of earth. Healthy development at this level could mean successful accomplishment of materialistic goals, earning a living, and satisfying basic needs for safety, food, and shelter. This can be viewed as the most basic level of self-awareness, popularly called "me" consciousness.[16] The dominant reality is material and the self is identified with the body. Consciousness has differentiated the body from the environment but remains identified with the body rather than the mind. Once differentiated, the body-ego begins to act on the environment and manipulate it to its own advantage. The infant at this level asserts ownership of objects; "me" and "mine" are favorite words. In the adult, pride of ownership, identification of self with material possessions, and pleasure derived from accumulating things are characteristic of this level of consciousness.

Societies at this level tend to exploit both natural and human resources, and to seek expansion at any cost. The desire for domination over nature extends to domination over other people. The predominant motivation is the desire for safety, and concern for personal survival outweighs other values. Change is generally experienced as threatening, and fear of death tends to be repressed. Causality is attributed to external circumstances rather than oneself, and unacceptable impulses are projected onto others. Magical thinking is evident in attempts to control the external world.

At this level, religion tends to be literal and superstitious. Prayer is petitionary, and ethical behavior is contingent on fear of punishment or hope of reward, either in this life or another. Belief in supernatural miracles is common. Accumulation of merit may replace material consumption, but remains motivated by the desire for personal gain.

In the world of the first chakra, fear is the dominant emotion. It could manifest as fear of loss of physical health or material possessions. Attack on others is presumed justifiable, as in "the best defense is a good offense." People at this level appear to lead normal lives, but attention remains narrowly focused on basic needs. The Self, asleep at this level, seems to be the victim of unconscious impulses and outside circumstances. The gods, too, seem to be asleep and inefficient, if not totally powerless. The strength and inertia of this worldview is represented by the image of an elephant. It is difficult to dislodge and sometimes runs amok.

Escape from the banal, mundane reality of the first chakra is not impossible, despite the strength of its hold over ordinary consciousness. A break with this reality may be precipitated by a psychological crisis that upsets the ordinary equilibrium of life, or by the realization that lasting satisfaction can never be attained from possession or manipulation of external objects.

When the kundalini energy that lies sleeping at the base of the spine in this chakra is awakened, it may be profoundly disturbing and disruptive. Jung likens the kundalini energy to the anima, the spirit of adventure, the divine urge. In the absence of crisis, it may be experienced as divine discontent that pulls one out of the mundane concerns of everyday life and pushes one to embark on the inward journey of Self-realization.

Svadhisthana

When attention is given to understanding unconscious psychological processes, we reach the domain of the second chakra, or *svadhisthana*. This chakra is associated with sexuality or general life-expansiveness, and is represented by the element of water. It may be described as "you and me" consciousness in which relationships are given a higher value than material possessions.[17] Motivation at this level is predominantly based on the desire for approval and love from another person, be it a parent, lover, or teacher. The desire for love at this level has strong elements of fear in it and loss of love tends to be equated with loss of life. Ethicality is maintained in order to ensure survival and social acceptance or to avoid rejection by a love object who is simultaneously feared and hated. Self-esteem depends upon external validation by others, and this dependency is deeply resented.

Relationship issues dominate personal preoccupations at this level. Typically, a compulsive interest in new sexual conquests or, conversely, a preoccupation with what other people think, might be attributed to this level of consciousness. Identity is now invested in relationship, perhaps in addition to being invested in material possessions, or as a substitute for it. Women in traditional gender roles are susceptible to remaining at this level, seeing their identity only in terms of relationship, as somebody's daughter, somebody's wife, or somebody's mother. Developmentally, this level is appropriately associated with learning to behave in a socially acceptable manner and stages of conventional morality. Emotional maturity at this level implies ability to establish stable and satisfying personal relationships. Healthy integration of this level receives considerable attention in Western psychology, but may be bypassed in spiritual systems that consider it a distraction from higher goals and aspirations. This can have detrimental consequences, from a psychological perspective, as either suppression or avoidance can result in emotional disturbance.

At this level of consciousness sex and spirituality are differentiated and tend to be experienced as conflicting opposites. Intense involvement or immersion in one tends to generate repression of the other. Psychoanalysis, for example, emphasizes the importance of bringing sexual impulses to conscious awareness for psychological health, and consequently tends to repress spirituality, interpreting the desire for mystical union as regressive, infantile wishes for union with mother. On the other hand, repression of sexuality is not uncommon in spiritual disciplines that emphasize the importance of elevating consciousness to higher levels.

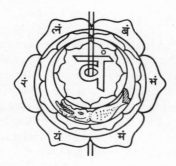

Symbolically, the dangers of this level are depicted as a sea serpent, the monster in the depths of the unconscious that can devour us. The passage through the depths of this world is portrayed cross-culturally in the symbolism of baptism and rebirth. Initiation rituals depict this transition as an awakening of new consciousness. Personal freedom at this level may be won by slaying the dragon of social or parental constraints and releasing sexual energy. Only by becoming conscious, by confronting the demons one fears to face, can the dangers of this level be overcome and the next level of consciousness attained.

Manipura

The third chakra, the *manipura*, meaning "the fullness of jewels," is associated with power, will, and intentionality, and is represented by the element of fire. It is localized physiologically in the solar plexus, or upper center of the abdomen, under the diaphragm. The image of the sun (not shown here) appears as a symbol of the solar ego. The initiate who has gone through baptism at the level of the second chakra is now brought into relationship with the sun, as eternal light. In Christianity, for example, baptism symbolizes being reborn in the spirit, the Christ. At this stage, the initiate may become identified with God, as part of the eternal, in possession of an immortal soul. The figure of the ram here symbolizes the ability to scale the highest peaks. In the religious symbolism of ancient Egypt, the journey through the underworld precedes riding through the heavens with the sun-god Ra. Jung sees the third chakra representing the great wealth of the sun and the abundance of divine power that is symbolically attained through baptism.[18]

Jung's psychological interpretation of this passage suggests that if one dreams of baptism or going into water (a symbol of the second

chakra), it means going into the unconscious for the purpose of cleansing and renewal. Afterward, there can be a connection with the *manipura* as a source of energy. Once the inward journey is underway and one gets in touch with unconscious forces, the fire of emotional passion can be released. Fears of desire running rampant and fears of sex and power are common when repression begins to lift, and the fullness of one's uninhibited emotional nature is acknowledged. The unleashing of storms of emotional passion is literally experienced as fiery: one burns with desire or with rage. This level can be painful and full of conflict, but it is also a source of energy. When this emotional energy is mastered, one feels powerful in the world.

Centered in this chakra, however, one is not free. One is still caught in suffering, still run by emotions, still driven by ambition and desire. Repression has lifted, and energy has been released, but conflict continues. Behaviorally, conflict may be manifested as impulsiveness on one side and compulsiveness on the other.

Personal power at this level may be sought out of fear of domination, as compensation for feelings of inadequacy, or simply for the satisfaction of personal dominance. However, an element of fear is always present, together with an underlying desire for control in order to have things be the way one wants them to be. At this level, a person is likely to have strong opinions and an egocentric investment in being right. Conflicts arise when others do not agree with a particular point of view, as one feels threatened by differing perspectives and dissenting opinions. The self at this level tends to be identified with a mental egoic self-concept.

Consciousness at this level has been called "we all" consciousness, characteristic of persons who want to ensure support for a particular position or ideology.[19] Such people make good administrators. They tend to place high value on logic and reason and on running things smoothly. Motivation is predominantly geared to achievement. Self-esteem is based more on the accumulation of status symbols (e.g., honors, titles, positions of power in organizations) than on the acquisition of personal possessions or sexual conquests.

At this level the heroic ego has struggled with unconscious forces and won the battle of independence. This is a stage of triumph over nature and instinctual forces that engenders law and order in society and patriarchal values such as logic, reason, and conceptual understanding. Problems and distortions tend to arise when the two previous levels are suppressed rather than integrated. Continuing healthy development depends on the integration of all levels.

When ego goals and power drives are no longer compelling, the Self differentiates, disidentifies, and transcends, and the egoic self fears annihilation. The summit of ego development leaves one at the level of the third chakra, where one eventually burns out. Few psychological guidelines are currently available for encouraging ego transcendence. Successful integration of the first, second, and third levels can form a healthy base for transcendence, and voluntary surrender of egocentric control is facilitated with the dawning awareness of fourth-chakra values.

Anahata

Above the diaphragm, in the region of the heart, lies the fourth chakra, or *anahata*, symbolized by the element of air. In Jungian terms, this represents the discovery of something impersonal after the passage through the fires of passion associated with the third chakra, and release from the struggle between will power and unbridled emotion. Symbolically, the diaphragm corresponds to the surface of the earth, and in the *anahata* we are lifted above it.[20] The opening of this chakra may be experienced symbolically, in dreams for example, as a passage through fire. Fire, like the sun, can be both creative and destructive. It can also be purifying. The inner calm and quiet that can be experienced after an emotional storm has run its course affords a taste of the peace of mind that becomes available when consciousness shifts from identification with passion to the subtler emotions associated with the heart center, namely love and compassion. At this level one becomes aware of the subtle energies of spirit, symbolized by air or wind or breath, as inspiration.

Psychologically, one is lifted above the stormy conflicts of emotional functioning associated with the third chakra by the use of higher reason. One begins to reflect on the nature of desire, the futility of competition, and the endless pursuit of pleasure and power that invariably entails suffering. At this point, cooperation may be valued above competition. For the first time, one may experience the divine nature of the Self, distinctly differentiated from the heroic ego that undertook the journey through the first three chakras.

In Wilber's terms, this is centauric consciousness, where wholeness is perceived as the integration of body and mind.[21] He suggests that the image of a centaur represents mind/body unity, in contrast to the image of a dominant human rider (or hero) on a horse. The horse here would represent instinctual, emotional/sexual vitality. When this integration is successfully completed, one identifies with the organism as a whole, existing in relationship to other wholes. This level of development corresponds to existential/humanistic psychological perspectives that emphasize the unity of body, emotions, and mind. Psychology at this level is often referred to as being holistic, although it does not include the transpersonal levels of the fifth, sixth, and seventh chakras.

In order to complete the process of body/mind integration at this level, one must die to former identifications, i.e., one must accept the death of ego.[22] The prospect of ego-death can be terrifying when one has been exclusively identified with egoic self-concept. Furthermore, the systematic classification of all non-ego states as pathological has effectively discouraged any psychological development beyond ego.

At this point on the ladder of levels of consciousness the ego's task is done. It has served its purpose in advancing evolution this far, but in order to proceed from here, Self must differentiate and disidentify from ego, transcend, and integrate in higher, more complex levels of consciousness. The ego remains intact, just as the body remains intact when identity, exclusively invested in the body in childhood, detaches from it when language is mastered and instead becomes invested in the verbal ego mind. When the ego is successfully transcended, it does not disappear, but the Self is no longer exclusively identified with it.

The inward arc of human development may begin at the level of the heart chakra when passion, appropriately guided by reason, is transformed into higher values. Both Wilber and Jung point out that awareness of levels beyond this point is rare in present-day society. On the inward arc the transpersonal Self awakens to discover its Buddha-nature, Christ consciousness, or Atman. At this point personal goals and achievements, either worldly or spiritual, may be superseded by a willing surrender to divine wisdom. The oneness of all beings is intuited, and values shift accordingly in the direction of compassion, cooperation, and selfless service.

In personal relationships individual satisfaction may be accorded less importance than family, community, or humanity as a whole. Love is no longer sought for personal gratification, but is offered out of gratitude for the fullness of an inner source. Individuals at this level are likely to be sensitive to subtle human needs and tend to be effective as priests, teachers, and healers.[23] Transpersonal psychotherapists who guide their clients on the inward arc may be conscious of working at this level.

The heart represents higher feelings. We say that we "take heart" when we feel encouraged, and that we "have no heart" if we lack feeling. We take things "to heart" when we feel they are important. In some traditions, one is advised to choose a path with the heart. The importance of feelings becomes clear when emotional values are recognized as compelling forces in life. In the heart center, according to Jung, we recognize the power and substantiality of the physical world.[24] In Tantric yoga, it is in this center that the *purusa,* or divine essence of being, becomes visible. This is the first inkling of a being within us that is not who we think we are. It represents shared consciousness that transcends individuality and has an entirely psychical existence. In Tibetan mysticism, the heart center is the organ of the intuitive mind and all-embracing compassion.[25]

One of the powers attributed to opening the fourth chakra is the power of invisibility. This means that one must have given up the desire to be noticed or to be the center of attention. Swami Radha, a Western teacher of kundalini yoga, points out that it is other people's preoccupations that render one invisible.[26]

Another power attributed to opening the heart chakra is the ability to enter another's body. In psychological terms this could mean the ability to take the place of another, to empathize, to walk a mile in another person's shoes. Training to be an effective therapist or healer calls for development of these powers. A therapist must be willing to give a client full attention while remaining relatively invisible; being present as the "opening or clearing through which the Absolute can manifest."[27] He or she must also be able to enter fully into the experience of the client, to know him or her from the inside. A good therapist learns to experience the world of the other as if it were his or her own.

The movement of consciousness and energy that opens the chakras is a process of transformation in which awareness becomes increasingly subtle as it reaches higher levels. The process is represented by the elements, moving from earth to water to fire to air in the first four chakras, and to ether, symbolizing intangible subtle awareness, at the fifth chakra. The idea of transformation of elements from gross to subtle is one of the oldest constituents of Hindu philosophy. It is also found in medieval alchemy.[28] Between the third and fourth chakras, in Jung's words, we cross the threshold from visible, tangible things to invisible, intangible things. Air and ether, as feeling and thought, become the focus of attention.[29] In many cultures, the soul or psyche is identified with the breath of life. The breath is also associated with inspiration, and inspiration for creativity comes from an integration, not a separation, of heart and mind.

Visuddha

Jung's commentary on kundalini yoga does not provide a psychological interpretation beyond the fourth chakra. He notes, however, that the fifth chakra, the *visuddha*, is the ether center and suggests that ether, being a substance that was believed to be more volatile than air, penetrates everywhere and yet can be found nowhere, and is not matter but concept. It is subtle, transparent and powerful. Here, beyond the four elements, one reaches a level of abstraction beyond the empirical realm, in the mental realm of human experience. It is literally ethereal. The element of ether could also be thought of as prana, the Hindu term meaning "life force," or in popular psychological language, as energy. In any event, at the level of the fifth chakra, we enter a world of psychical reality.

The elephant appears again at this level, but now it is white, representing a spiritual orientation in ordinary life. It is also smaller in size, to indicate the overcoming of unconscious, instinctual drives. When control of the mind and emotions is achieved, peace of mind ensues. One sees past, present, and future in the light of forgiveness, free from greed, malice, and pride.[30]

Jung felt that insofar as humanity is convinced that psychical things have some value, it is beginning to acknowledge the fifth chakra. He maintained that experience teaches one to believe in psychical reality, and that all great movements of history could be seen to occur for psychical reasons. However, he saw the common distrust of psychical realities as evidence that humanity as a whole had not yet reached the level of the fifth chakra.[31]

At this level, material reality is perceived to be a world of appearances or illusion, while abstract ideas and values become palpably real as the source of experience. The all-encompassing Self is perceived as ultimate reality. Concepts and thoughts are seen to have substantive reality and far-reaching effects. But concept is powerful here as an expression of experience, not as an abstract intellectual construct. Furthermore, one can arrive at this point only through experience, not through logical deduction, speculation, or blind faith.

The fifth chakra, located in the area of the throat, is associated with sound, and its opening emphasizes hearing. Training at this level means learning to listen internally to oneself and externally to others. In order to listen, one must learn to be quiet. Both speech and internal chatter must therefore be controlled.

This can certainly be an asset to healing at any level. Psychotherapy, commonly called a "talking cure," might be more appropriately called a "listening cure." As one young man commented, "My therapist doesn't say much, but when he listens I learn a lot!" The art of attentive listening to oneself and others can be of value in every walk of life.

The ability to hear and the ability to maintain silence are necessary for effective communication at all levels. Developing the skills associated with the fifth chakra seems particularly relevant to our current communication age. If one aspires to understanding and clarity in communication, one must first learn to listen with healing awareness, free from internal or external distractions. In this way the opposites can be brought into balance and one may hear more distinctly the subtle messages of the Self, whether audible or inaudible.[32]

This level seems to represent the current growing edge of human evolution. While there have always been individuals who attained higher levels of awareness, today increasing numbers of people are recognizing the possibility of advancing psychological growth to this level and perceiving the necessity for doing so. Becoming aware of the creative power of consciousness associated with the fifth chakra means taking responsibility for thought as well as behavior. All thought may be perceived to create form at some level, and the dynamics of self-fulfilling prophecies become evident. In the words of the Buddha:

We are what we think.
All that we are arises with our thoughts.
With our thoughts we make the world.[33]

Ajna

The sixth chakra, the *ajna*, physiologically localized in the region of the third eye, just above and between the eyebrows, represents the realm of ideal perception. In the sixth chakra, the God that was dormant in the lower chakras is fully awake. This center is the place of union with the deity, where one knows the Self as psyche. Opening of this chakra is associated with the development of psychic powers. It provides direct experience of the non-ego reality of the Self, at one with all creation.

The two lotus petals symbolize the dual functioning of the mind in manifest and unmanifest levels of reality. In the West, hearing (associated with the fifth chakra) is said to be the subtlest of the five senses. In Eastern thought the mind is regarded as a sixth sense that apprehends truth directly through intuition. A golden dot, representing essence of energy, symbolizes detachment from the body by either

male or female. Mind at this level is more subtle; more spiritual gifts are bestowed as it awakens. Fears are dispelled by personal experience. Control of imagination allows the discovery that all experiences are the creation of the mind.[34] In meditation at this level all colors, lights, and images disappear and the mind rests in the white light of the void. In this way the door to the seventh chakra is opened.

Sahasrara

Beyond this, at the level of the seventh chakra, or *sahasrara*, located at the crown of the head, the sense of Self disappears altogether. This is the realm of Absolute Spirit, the realm of nonduality, where all distinctions are transcended and one ceases to exist as a separate entity. This level remains a philosophical concept beyond experience until one reaches enlightenment, whereupon all levels are seen to be manifestations of this one. This ultimate state of consciousness is not something apart from other states, but is intrinsically present in all states. Thus it does not cancel the waking state, but is expressed through it.[35] As consciousness evolves and the waking state is refined and developed, it becomes an expression of this awareness.

The journey of consciousness becoming aware of itself, symbolized by the ascent of the serpent through the chakras, does not necessarily proceed in an orderly, linear fashion. Sometimes sudden revelation can precipitate an emotional crisis, and in the absence of appropriate guidance can block healthy development and integration of higher levels of awareness. Sometimes informed therapeutic intervention can prevent destructive distortions and misinterpretations. At each level, problems of imbalance, repression, and misperception may be encountered as obstacles on the path that must be surmounted if wholeness is to be attained.

Familiarity with a map can be useful for the person looking for a path, but it should not be mistaken for traversing the territory. In the following section we will consider the journey from a different perspective, as stages of self-awareness on the way to transcendence and enlightenment.

Experiential Exercise

Chakra Visualization

Sitting in meditation posture, either cross-legged on a pillow or on a chair with feet flat on the floor and spine straight, close your eyes and take a deep breath. Exhale completely and allow your body and mind to relax.

Visualize a light at the base of the spine in the region of the first chakra. Say these words silently to yourself in your mind as you inhale: "I activate the first chakra." As you exhale slowly say: "I am at peace." Visualize the light moving up the spine to the region of the second chakra and repeat the same phrases silently: "I activate the second chakra" on the inhale; "I am at peace" on the exhale.

Once again visualize the light moving up to the region of the third chakra and repeat the same phrases while inhaling and exhaling. Repeat the processes for the fourth, fifth, sixth, and seventh chakras. When you have completed the exhale on the seventh, holding your attention on a point of light visualized at the crown of the head, visualize the light returning to the base of the spine and say to yourself, "I am activated for a normal flow of energy throughout this day and every day."

This process may be repeated, visualizing the colors of the spectrum corresponding to each chakra. Red corresponds to the first chakra; orange to the second; yellow to the third; green to the fourth; blue to the fifth; violet to the sixth; and white (containing all colors) to the seventh.

Give yourself at least five minutes, more if you wish, to sit quietly and rest after this visualization.

Awareness of what each chakra represents will be helpful in deepening awareness of the spectrum of states of consciousness that are available at any time. This visualization can thus enable you to exercise more freedom with respect to subjective states. First one learns to move from one to another at will. With practice all can become more available, grounded in the underlying condition of peace.

If you experience any disturbing sensations, feelings, or images during this exercise, discontinue the practice until you are able to find an experienced teacher who can provide appropriate guidance.

III. The Ox-Herding Pictures: Stages on the Path

To study Buddhism is to study the self.
To study the self is to forget the self.—Dogen[36]

Every culture has its own symbolic representation of the spiritual path. In Zen Buddhism stages of self-awareness on the inward arc are depicted in a series of ten ox-herding pictures that originally evolved in twelfth-century China. A man is portrayed searching for, finding, and taming an ox, probably a water buffalo. The ox-herding pictures constitute a map that can help us see the spiritual path in perspective. It can also provide checkpoints and guidance at each stage along the way.

As a symbol a map always points beyond itself to meaning that is both concealed and revealed by its representational form. Thus a map can encourage a beginning seeker to explore transpersonal realms in more depth. This particular map points to direct experience, and offers multiple levels of meaning. Since interpretations always reflect the perceptual limitations of the interpreter, the commentaries offered here do not pretend to be authoritative or final. They naturally reflect a psychological bias.

As noted in Chapter 3, self-concepts tend to evolve through a sequence of identifications toward ultimate unity consciousness in which any separate self-sense is eventually transcended. In Buddhist terms, this unity results "from the profound knowledge that the conception of 'self' and 'not-self,' 'I' and 'not-I,' 'own' and 'other,' rests on the illusion of our surface consciousness."[37] Any map, then, appears to be relatively real, existing within the illusion for the purpose of guiding the seeker to liberation or enlightenment.

In an eloquent discussion of this process, Lex Hixon writes:

Enlightenment is not an isolated attainment of ancient or legendary sages but a process flowering through members of every culture, a process in which our consciousness gradually becomes transparent to its own intrinsic nature. . . .

The seeker of Enlightenment must become as close an observer of consciousness as the Eskimo is of snow conditions.[38]

When attention is turned inward to observe consciousness, even the observer may become an object of attention. As awareness becomes increasingly refined and subtle, a question arises, "Is there a watcher, or only the process of watching?"

According to Buddhist philosophy there is no permanent, unchanging entity which can be considered a separate self. Consciousness does not exist independently of the conditions out of which it arises.[39] All self-concepts are therefore equally illusory. A distinction is made, however, between the discursive, thinking mind and the intuitive mind that knows its universality. This awareness may be experienced in meditation "when the discriminating mind is quieted and the intuitive mind is liberated and identifies with the Universal Mind."[40] D. T. Suzuki says:

> The self or ego that has been constantly eluding our
> rationalized scrutiny is at last caught when it comes under
> *prajna*-intuition which is no other than the self. . . . The
> egolessness of things cannot really be understood until they
> are seen with the eye of *prajna*-intuition.[41]

In this context intuition refers to the knowing faculty that takes the spiritual realm as its object. Prajna is defined as transcendental wisdom.

Ten Stages of Enlightenment

The ox-herding pictures[42] correspond to ten stages or "seasons of enlightenment."[43] At the outset the ox, symbolizing the intrinsic nature of consciousness, is roaming wild in the rain forest.

1. Seeking the Ox
The first ox-herding picture marks the beginning of the inward arc or the spiritual path. The person has become aware of the possibility of

enlightenment, and sets out to look for it. Having realized that the external world will never give lasting satisfaction, the seeker turns attention to consciousness. At this point the seeker is likely to be confused by the maze of paths purported to be the way to liberation. Every path seems to say "Follow me if you want to find yourself, be free from suffering, and attain enlightenment." A sense of exhilaration and excitement often accompanies the change in values when worldly desires are replaced by spiritual ambition.

At this stage enthusiasm for the process of seeking may obscure the object of the search. The seeker is not aware that all seeking is based on a dualistic view of separation between subject and object that must eventually be transcended. One's true nature cannot be found and the search leads inevitably to disillusionment and disappointment. Thus at the beginning the seeker encounters paradox and confusion. Although all paths lead nowhere, the seeker must nevertheless begin the journey by choosing a path and undertaking some form of practice.

Initial attempts at spiritual development therefore involve some kind of external searching. When ordinary ego goals no longer seem important, one may feel drawn to seeking satisfaction from spiritual pursuits. Reflection on the transitory nature of existence can give a sense of urgency to the desire for more meaningful goals in life. Thus one may begin to question assumptions and try to learn something about consciousness. For some the search begins with reading, for others with the practice of meditation or some spiritual discipline. Some search for a teacher who can provide instruction and guidance in unfamiliar realms. Others may try analysis or some other form of psychotherapy in order to gain a deeper understanding of themselves. One way or another, the journey begins with searching for a goal that is envisioned in the future.

Today it is not unusual for a seeker to try many paths. Spiritual materialism[44] has become a cliche as the accumulation of spiritual experiences becomes increasingly popular. Seekers of spiritual renewal are not free of elitism. Many who embark on the spiritual quest consider themselves to be committed to the highest goal and doing the only work worth doing. They may also be disdainful toward those who follow a different path and separate themselves from others considered to be asleep or unaware of this dimension of experience.

2. Finding the Tracks

The second ox-herding picture represents the seeker who has begun to study the wisdom teachings—in this case, Buddhism. This stage in the quest involves intellectual knowledge. The seeker becomes a serious

student and may feel certain that he or she has found the right path.

Proselytizing is not typical of Buddhism, but may be found among any students on a path trying to convince themselves by convincing others that they have found the right way. Convincing others of the validity of a point of view can be a powerful influence on one's own thinking. One tends to learn what one tries to teach, and the task of recruiting new converts to a spiritual group is sometimes assigned to new students at an early stage as a means of reinforcing belief and reducing doubts. This stage of open display of spiritual concerns and attempting to persuade others of the value of one's efforts is not necessarily reprehensible. Testing ideas with others and discussing beliefs is an essential part of learning on the spiritual path. It becomes objectionable only when it is self-righteous and dogmatic.

The seeker at this stage becomes a finder, but has not yet realized that the tracks lead nowhere. The tracks are said to represent the wisdom teachings that all phenomena are the light of the one mind. Everything is seen as a manifestation of this one elusive source, but the illusion of duality persists in the finding as well as the seeking.[45]

In psychological terms, this stage can be viewed as a beginning of disidentification from ego, coinciding with initial awareness of the transpersonal Self. Through special conditions imposed by a teacher, the process of disidentification from the independent, self-sufficient, existential self-concept can take place. Wilber notes that when the subtle self begins to disidentify from body and mind, union with a guru and a traditional lineage is sought.[46] The possibilities of illumination and release are apprehended but not yet realized, and the desire for union draws the student deeper into spiritual practice.

3. First Glimpse of the Ox

The third ox-herding picture represents a shift of attention from esoteric teachings to direct experience. The source is found to be present in everyday sounds and activities, and in the six senses. The student at this stage has become a practitioner who is consciously enlightened, no longer seeking or following tracks. The ox is known to be all paths, as well as the seeker and forest itself. This is a stage of insight which requires further discipline for stabilization. Enlightenment has been glimpsed but requires further work to be developed into an abiding light.[47]

Psychological anxiety may arise at this stage, focusing first on fear of loss of self. Wilber points out that the obliteration of the self by light or bliss is not the same as identification with light or reabsorption into it. When this fear is overcome, fear of losing the light or access to it may still block further development.[48] The Third Zen Patriarch cautions: "Even to become attached to the idea of enlightenment is to go astray."[49] The dark night of the soul still threatens to engulf the practitioner who has glimpsed the true nature of the one mind. Despair and depression can seem even more overwhelming after the light of higher states of consciousness has been experienced than before. Separation and alienation can seem even more unbearable when the possibility of transcendence is known, not only intellectually, but by direct experience. At this stage the futility of further searching and striving may become painfully apparent.

4. Catching the Ox

In the fourth ox-herding picture the ox is stubborn and unbridled, and

filled with wild strength. The practitioner must practice self-discipline in every aspect of life. The release of energy at this stage can be both creative and destructive. Containment is necessary, and the practitioner is advised to practice truthfulness, compassion, and nonviolence.[50]

In psychological terms, this can be interpreted as the necessity for integrating spiritual discipline with daily life, and learning to sustain spiritual insight under any conditions. Problems occur when spiritual ambition leads to pushing too hard. The practitioner may find him- or herself overwhelmed by archetypal energies. For example, if kundalini energy is aroused in one who is unprepared for it, severe disturbance may result. Another danger at this stage is arrogance, stemming from egoic identification with the subtle transpersonal Self. Since this is an extraordinarily high-order self, it is easily mistaken for Atman or ultimate awakening.[51]

Evidence of this distortion may be seen in cult leaders who demonstrate psychic powers, yet also function in ways that are self-serving and egocentric. Any overt claim to enlightenment is likely to reflect this stage of development, since according to this tradition truly enlightened sages make no claim to specialness. Claims to esoteric knowledge, coercive demands for obedience from followers, and manipulation of others by fear can also indicate misuse of powers attained at this stage of development. In Jungian terms, the danger is of ego inflation, which could indicate that transcendence of ego is incomplete. This inflation frequently involves other people. There is no shortage of seekers who can be persuaded to follow such would-be gurus in their eagerness to attain to those levels of subtle development that clearly transcend their own. Disidentification at this stage can be difficult, since the person must let go of attachment to bliss and light if he or she is to continue to the next stage of enlightenment.[52]

5. Taming the Ox

The fifth ox-herding picture is a stage of advanced training in which an effortless friendship is established with one's own true nature. The advanced practitioner lets go of disciplines learned at an earlier stage, and even the discriminations between truth and illusion are transcended. Discrimination between spiritual life and ordinary life is no longer useful, and one makes friends with the limitations of ego. The ox becomes a free companion, and movement is balanced.[53]

Practitioners who have successfully integrated the experiences of the subtle transpersonal Self have arrived at this stage. Healthy development is indicated by a relinquishment of specialness, and a subtle infusion of spirituality into every facet of existence. The intuitive flashes of insight have mellowed into a sustained awareness of the nature of existence, and attachment to any one stage of consciousness is no longer compelling. This is the attainment of those who have mastered the low subtle realms, without getting sidetracked by developing psychic abilities. Consciousness has differentiated itself entirely from the ordinary thinking mind, and hence is called Big Mind,[54] or supermind,[55] since it transcends mental forms and intuits its oneness with that which is prior to mind.

6. Riding the Ox Home

This drawing depicts the sage riding easily on the ox. "The struggle is over, 'gain' and 'loss' no longer affect him." At this stage the sage radiates enlightenment, and actions are characterized by simplicity, naturalness, spontaneity, and tranquility. The sage blends with the

ordinary flow of life, but the subtle illusion of the ox as a separate entity persists.[56]

This stage corresponds to the realm of the high subtle in Wilber's map of transpersonal development. It is the realm of high religious intuition and inspiration, symbolic vision, higher presence, and dhyani-Buddhas. All of these are higher, archetypal forms of Self that initially appear as "other."[57] Such phenomena are not discussed or sought after in the Zen tradition, being considered a distraction from higher goals. They are, however, characteristically associated with a specific stage of the journey. Understanding the universality of these phenomena is also useful in differentiating healthy transpersonal development from pathology masquerading as spirituality.

7. Ox Forgotten, Self Alone
In the seventh ox-herding picture, the two have become one. The

seeker has returned home. The sage now regards Self as the full expression of true nature, and no longer needs concepts or practice. Solitude and serenity are enjoyed in the absence of distinctions.[58]

At the peak of the high subtle realms of transpersonal development, the soul becomes one with the Deity. It dissolves into that Deity of which it has been an expression all along. This is the archetype of the highest Self. Now there is no duality. The two are one. This is the final integration of the subtle realm, and identification with the transpersonal Self. At this stage one is no longer concerned with the world, having let go of any attachments or desires. One simply is.

8. Both Ox and Self Forgotten

The eighth ox-herding picture, an open circle, is associated with the *dharmakaya*, the causal realm in which consciousness remembers its prior unity as no-thing. There are no theories or holders of theory in the dharmakaya. Illusory barriers have evaporated, and a profound state of emptiness is open to the fullness of life.[59] The idea of enlightenment itself is transcended. Individual consciousness disappears into that from which it originally sprang. Wilber points out that this is not to be construed as a loss of consciousness, but an intensification at the causal level. At this level form is emptiness, emptiness is form. This realization may be perceived as a goal of Buddhist practice. Popular notions of nirvana, cessation, and obliteration of the separate self-sense are commonly associated with emptiness or nothingness. Some people therefore assume that Buddhism is antilife or escapist. Although a superficial reading of the teachings can lead to this interpretation, this map does not leave us here. Mahayana Buddhism, as represented here, points to the next picture depicting renewal.

9. Return to the Source

In the ninth ox-herding picture formless awareness grows back into form without losing its formlessness. It was necessary for form to dissolve into emptiness before it could become the source. Now emptiness melts into spring. There is no need to strive. Everything is observed to be endlessly changing.[60] The process of creation is always in motion, arising and disappearing, moment by moment.

Evolution completed, involution becomes apparent. From the void of undifferentiated potential the wellsprings of creation unfold. The enfolded potential of consciousness, having completed the evolutionary journey, is here fully realized in its manifestation of transpersonal oneness.[61] The Self as no-thing has become everything.

10. Entering the Marketplace with Helping Hands

The tenth ox-herding picture obliterates oneness as well as twoness. Here the sage is depicted returning to the human world of everyday life as a bodhisattva, one who has renounced personal liberation to help others. Open hands represent perfect emptiness, and no attempt is made to follow earlier sages. The enlightened one cheerfully manifests enlightenment and follows no path. He or she is full of life energy and compassionate love and "even the wisest cannot find him." The sage has gone beyond the path and has now returned completely to the human world. This suggests that the sage is, to all appearances, perfectly ordinary, indistinguishable from others, but motivated only by selfless service. In contemporary society he or she might be anybody.

Returning to the world with good humor and helping hands, the bodhisattva transmits enlightenment to others. "By being perceived as intrinsically Buddhas . . . all human beings in the marketplace of desire are swiftly brought to bloom."[62]

Finally, the whole series of ten pictures represents the *svabhavi-kakaya*,[63] or realm of absolute being which includes the process of becoming. In Wilber's terms, "development simply continues until there is only unity and the soul stands grounded in that Source and Suchness which formed the [purpose] of the entire sequence."[64]

The journey has ended where it began. It is a journey without distance to a goal that has never changed, yet its effects are universally acknowledged. "The end of all our exploring," as T. S. Eliot said, "will be to arrive where we started and know the place for the first time."[65] True mastery is invisible, but its presence can be experienced and intuited. The enlightened one is to all appearances perfectly ordinary, but awake and aware of the intrinsic transpersonal nature of all beings. Life then can become a lighthearted dance of selfless service, not in a spirit of suffering and sacrifice, but in the Spirit of joy and freedom.

Conclusion

Words or pictures describing the spiritual path can take us only to the threshold of experience. They do no more than point the way to enlightenment in nonduality. Since words belong to the mental realm of logic and discourse, they can only point to transcendence. They can never be a substitute for direct experience. Any commentary is thus necessarily limited and incomplete. However, wholeness presumes familiarity with all stages of development.

Reflecting on stages of the journey that can be intuited long before they are completed, one can easily make the mistake of thinking one understands the process without actually experiencing it. The egoic self may be eager to find an interpretation that avoids the demands of arduous practice. As one becomes aware of the vast range of potential development beyond ego, one gains a deeper appreciation of the process involved, and may begin exploring this domain experientially. In practice the apparent contradiction between the Buddhist teaching of no self and the concept of a transpersonal Self may be easily resolved when each is appreciated in the context of wholeness.

Experiential Exercise

Sitting Meditation

Meditation is probably the most direct route to experiential learning on the spiritual path. There are many ways to practice. One form of Zen practice is simple. It consists of assuming the traditional Buddhist meditation posture with legs crossed in the half lotus or full lotus position, left foot on right thigh and right foot on left thigh. Keep the spine straight and hands resting on the heels, left hand on top of right hand with the middle joints of the middle fingers together forming an oval with thumbs touching lightly. Eyes are lowered in a soft gaze directed at the floor approximately three feet in front of where one is sitting or at a blank wall. One may assume the posture and just sit. The objective is to remain still, alert, and relaxed. *The Zen Teaching of Huang Po* advises:

When you practice mind-control, sit in the proper position,
stay perfectly tranquil, and do not permit the least movement
of your mind to disturb you.[66]

This simple practice has been called the straight and narrow path that can lead to a direct experience of no self. Suzuki Roshi says:

Enlightenment is not some good feeling or some particular
state of mind. The state of mind that exists when you sit in the
right posture is, itself, enlightenment. If you cannot be satisfied with the state of mind you have in zazen, it means your
mind is still wandering about. Our body and mind should not
be wobbling or wandering about. In this posture there is no
need to talk about the right state of mind. You already have it.
This is the conclusion of Buddhism.[67]

7 Guidance on the Path

The path is not as yet the goal and Spirit does not reach the goal without having traversed the path.
—*Hegel*[1]

A person who understands the importance of actually traversing the spiritual path rather than remaining an observer will, sooner or later, choose a path and a teacher. How can one choose an appropriate path? How does one recognize a teacher? What distinctions should be considered? In this chapter we will address some of these questions for the purpose of seeing more clearly the alternatives that are available. We will then review some of the characteristics of spiritual mastery and the factors to be considered in making choices.

Choosing a Path

Each level of consciousness—physical, emotional, mental, existential, and transpersonal—offers specific approaches to self-knowledge and the spiritual path. Each has its unique requirements, stages of development, and characteristics of mastery. Each emphasizes a different type of attainment or realization.

1. Physical
Hatha yoga is a well-known example of a path that begins by focusing on training the body. Karma yoga, the yoga of work, is also a path that is oriented to physical action in the world. Roman Catholic liberation theology, with its emphasis on social action, could be another example. In any case, rigorous discipline is required for progress on this type of

path. Any physical path, one that requires mastery of the levels of consciousness associated with the first three chakras, demands strength, stamina, and personal power. How this power is handled may indicate degrees of progress on any path oriented toward concrete physical achievements. Mastery is evidenced in self-discipline and effective action. Objectives are likely to be concrete, visible accomplishments that can be touched and measured.

Personal mastery on a physical level may also be demonstrated by wealth, power, and influence in the world. The archetypal image of a person on a physically oriented path is the hero/warrior. Symbols of value are gold, jewels, or treasure. Masters who are emotionally, mentally and spiritually evolved can make a significant contribution to society. Service is the predominant expression of Self-awareness on this path. Those who master a physical path know that what they dream of having in the world can be attained. Insofar as training the body also involves training the mind, they may also attain such attributes as inner peace, loving kindness and discriminating wisdom. These are gifts of the spirit, the rewards of practice, faith and devotion on any path.

2. Emotional

A typical example of an emotional path is bhakti yoga, the yoga of devotion, the way of love. Christianity tends to be viewed by Easterners as a bakhti path, since it teaches that God is love, and that people must learn to love one another, to love their neighbors as themselves. The life of Jesus is an example of a person for whom this path was a way of transcendence.

Any path of the heart is an emotional path that pertains to the domain of the fourth chakra. It is represented by symbols of communion, such as the chalice, or the holy grail. This type of path tends to emphasize the importance of relationships. Self-awareness is expressed through devotion. The archetypal image of a person on this path is the healer. Mastery on this path is evidenced by compassion and a capacity for healing. Love is the healing power, par excellence. Some therapists and peaceworkers are on this path, but doing such work does not necessarily mean that one is consciously on a spiritual path.

3. Mental

The path of jnana yoga that emphasizes the skillful use of intellect is a good example of a mental path that requires rigorous mental discipline. A mental path is predominantly associated with the throat chakra, but ideally subsumes other levels. Mastery of this level may be expressed in scholarship and creative thinking. A symbol of this path is the sword of discriminating wisdom. On this type of path, attention is directed to control of the mind and creating experience at the level of thought.

Ideologies and cosmologies may be formulated on this path. Degrees of mastery may be attained by monks, scholars, or policymakers—those who influence history with ideas that shape human destiny, e.g., Plato, Hegel, and Marx. Even today wars are sanctioned in the service of ideologies. The archetype of this path is the philosopher king who rules with discernment and wisdom. One who would attain mastery on this path must train the rational mind, but mastery of the intellect alone is not an indication of spiritual illumination. The Buddha represents spiritual realization through mastery and illumination of the mind.

4. Existential

An existential path is one of reason and mind/body integration. Devotion to physical, emotional and intellectual honesty is coupled with a willingness to confront the absurdity of existence and being in the world as it is. At this level all paths are seen as leading nowhere. An existential position is one that refuses to be seduced by illusory constructs of reality that cater to human weakness and the desire for meaning and immortality. It is a *via negativa* that affirms nothing and negates the possibility of transcendence. It is perhaps best represented by the Tower of Babel or an image of destructuring that questions all assumptions and attempts to be free of beliefs that perpetuate illusion.

Mastery on this level is evidenced in freedom and responsibility. The courage to be and the courage to create in spite of fear is what is valued.[2] It is a path of struggle and no hope. It is a commitment to no commitment and a willingness to engage in life to the fullest, despite the belief that it is a dead end.

Perhaps this approach can only be considered a spiritual path when atheistic existentialism is transcended in choosing commitment to spirituality or God as the ultimate expression of freedom (e.g. Gabriel Marcel).[3] But insofar as it is a genuine search for truth, existentialism can be characterized as a *via negativa*, a way of negation that attempts to strip away illusions that prevent us from facing truth.

5. Transpersonal

Paths that emphasize intuition are commonly regarded as transpersonal. Examples of this type are sahaj yoga and shamanism. A shaman seems to have supernatural powers that transcend time/space limitations and transform negative influences into positive possibilities. Intuition may be represented by a wand, as in the Tarot cards, as a symbol of transformation. As a psychological function, intuition apprehends truth, gives form to formlessness, operates on the frontiers of knowledge and mediates our relationship to the unknown.[4] Understanding the relationship between intuition and creativity can contribute to awareness of how one participates in shaping experiences on the spiritual path.

Mastery on this level operates at the more subtle level of consciousness associated with the sixth chakra. Mastery of intuition includes mastery of dream consciousness, i.e., lucid dreaming and awareness of dreams in all states. Mastery on this path presumes psychic development. It requires a leap of faith that transcends reason, in addition to knowledge of the laws that govern this nonphysical domain of subtle energy awareness. On the intuitive paths, as on the physical paths, power may be attained through discipline, but does not necessarily indicate spiritual realization or Self-awareness.

Each path has its methods of teaching and learning, and human beings have the potential for mastery on all of them, although a life devoted to one may exclude the others. As we learn to think inclusively rather than exclusively, we begin to see that wholeness calls for balance and awareness of all paths.

Each path can be a way to transcendence, illumination, and Self-realization, but each one can also be a trap if it becomes an end in itself. Mastery on any one of them does not mean that the master is either a saint or a sage. Furthermore, a saint or a sage may or may not have attained the specific powers that are associated with mastery on any of them. To the awakened mind that is aware of Self as Spirit, any or all paths can be a means of Self-expression. To the seeker that is not yet aware of Self as source, any one of them offers opportunities for Self-development and awakening.

When a person demonstrates mastery on one of these paths, it is often mistakenly assumed that he or she is a highly evolved spiritual person who has also mastered the others. Yet examples of imbalance abound. The successful athlete who has attained a degree of mastery in the physical domain may be out of touch with his feelings; the devoted mother who is consciously on a devotional path may be incapable of making her own decisions; the brilliant intellectual with highly developed mental abilities may be wrapped up in his or her own ideas and out of touch with people; the existentialist who has attained organismic integration and the courage to be in the face of death may be denying his or her own intuitions of transcendence; the intuitive who has well-developed psychic abilities may be flighty and ungrounded. These stereotypes exemplify some of the problems associated with overemphasis on one aspect of development to the exclusion of others.

Each path has its characteristic strengths and weaknesses. Each calls for a particular form of commitment and a particular type of discipline. When a path is unfamiliar it tends to be idealized, feared, or pathologized. Thus a thinker may be suspicious of a person who is predominantly oriented by feelings or intuition, and the practical, physical person may be mystified, awed, or terrified by the intuitive. The intuitive, on the other hand, may attain mastery of the inner world and still have difficulty gaining credibility or being effective in the outer world. Wisdom may be erroneously projected onto one who has attained a degree of mastery on any of these paths. Perhaps the most common error is the projection of spiritual realization onto the person who has attained a degree of intuitive mastery or psychic power. However, power on any level is no guarantee of ethicality or spiritual Self-realization.

Pitfalls on the Path

All paths lead nowhere.—Carlos Castaneda[5]
Truth is a pathless land.—Krishnamurti[6]

In addition to the difficulties associated with overemphasis on one path to the exclusion of others, each path presents certain pitfalls to the unwary traveler. In each case, the virtue of the path may also be its liability.

One of the traps of a physical path, for example, is the exclusive identification with the body. Physical well-being may be pursued to the detriment of other aspects of health, as when diet or weight control becomes an obsession. In social terms, excessive concern with physical well-being could manifest in compromising ethical values for money or security, despite feelings of mistrust or intuitive misgivings.

The ideal of selfless service as an expression of spiritual awareness can easily become a form of self-sacrifice and a guilt-inducing martyr complex. Philanthropy as service can also become a way of buying dispensation for feelings of guilt or compensation for lack of self-worth. The person who consciously wants to give material support to those less fortunate may also fall into the trap of condemning others who do not share the same values.

A similar trap on the emotional path is exemplified by the devout Christian who may feel consciously dedicated to loving service, but may also be guilt-ridden and thus tend to'induce guilt in others, even when ostensibly practicing forgiveness. In the psychologically healthy person, forgiveness means letting go of the past and release from guilt. It does not mean judging others as guilty and oneself as virtuous for forgiving them.

A person on an emotional path should also be aware of the pitfalls of self-inflicted martyrdom and false humility. The mother who always gives unending service to her family and never takes anything for herself exemplifies this problem. When devotion becomes dependency the devotee becomes a burden and a liability rather than an asset to the person who is the object of devotion. Typically, hysterical personality types who are attracted to becoming devotees of cult leaders run the risk of exacerbating neurotic dependency needs on this path. The devotee is prone to accept whatever the teacher or guru says as gospel truth. "My guru, right or wrong!" could be a slogan describing this trap. Anyone outside the in-group of devotees may be seen as inferior, ignorant, or unenlightened. The split between self and other is thus reinforced by a socially sanctioned split between us and them.

A disciple on a mental path who may value discipline more than devotion runs a greater risk of becoming a zealot. Discipline can sometimes become harsh and controlling, and when it does it is seldom limited to oneself. What is deemed good for one is generally assumed to be good for others and may then be imposed autocratically. Obsessive compulsive personality types tend to be attracted to discipleship and run the risk of exacerbating their neuroses in the name of rigor, excellence, or purification. Would-be masters of this path run the risk of falling into the trap of authoritarianism.

The spiritual aspirant intent on attaining personal liberation and enlightenment through self-discipline may be willing to work hard but can easily become attached to evidence of attainment or spiritual progress. Self-control may then become self-congratulatory, with an accompanying "holier than thou" attitude that disdains those who aspire to liberation through grace rather than effort, i.e., those on emotional paths. When life is seen only as suffering, the desire for deliverance may be exacerbated by additional self-imposed suffering. Any escape may then seem desirable, leading to a denial of the value of earthly life. This trap is a pitfall encountered by practitioners that idealize the state of cessation or nonbeing, as some do in Theravada Buddhism.

Those who follow a path that emphasizes the power of the mind are particularly susceptible to repression of the shadow and denial of undesirable psychological traits. The risk on mental paths is that psychological imbalances may be ignored or exacerbated and subsequently erupt in disturbing ways. This problem can be observed among groups that emphasize the power of positive thinking as well as among those that attempt to control mental factors.

For those on intuitive, transpersonal paths, the emphasis on transcendence of reason can deteriorate into a glorification of the irrational, and ostensible surrender to higher guidance can become surrender to ordinary impulses or egoic desires. The leap of faith required to go beyond reason can also become a trap when it entails unquestioning obedience to authority.

The intuitive adept is also susceptible to spiritual specialness or inflation when he or she has mastered psychic abilities. This power is frequently accompanied by a proclivity to meddle in other people's lives, attempting to change or influence them in a direction that is believed to be "good for them." The pitfalls of imbalanced achievement in this domain are the theme of various teaching stories, such as the one about the sorcerer's apprentice who gets into trouble after unleashing powers that he does not know how to control or use wisely.

This particular path can also breed addiction to the "high" of subtle energy awareness. The taste of bliss can be very seductive, and seeking the thrill of subtle orgasmic experiences can easily become a self-defeating end in itself. Practitioners of kundalini yoga sometimes fall prey to this particular pitfall.

Addiction to unusual experiences can be a trap on any path and is referred to as spiritual materialism. The insatiable desire for experience commonly attributed, rightly or wrongly, to Californians who try one path after another can be viewed as a manifestation of insecurity, escapism, or just plain greed. What becomes evident in time is that any experience, being transitory, is never completely fulfilling. Genuine spiritual development is reflected in how one lives one's life, not in the attainment of special experiences, psychic or otherwise.

Another potential pitfall on any spiritual path lies in judging one state of consciousness to be better or more desirable than another. The very discussion of traps or pitfalls within a particular path indicates a set of expectations that one may fail to meet. Naming pitfalls presumes certain values and standards of discrimination. Pitfalls may also be described hierarchically, since what appears to be a pitfall at one level may not be a pitfall at another. In some contemplative traditions almost anything that arises in the mind can be considered a pitfall. In this case the very preoccupation with pitfalls can be a trap.

In Zen Buddhism, the concept of pitfalls is considered a trap that perpetuates the illusion of separate egoic identity. However, the opposite point of view, espousing the philosophy that anything goes, that there is no sin and everything is an illusion, can also be used to justify behavior that is detrimental to personal well-being in addition to being conventionally immoral and unethical. Thus the belief that there are no traps can also be a trap.

Every pitfall is rooted in egoic fear and desire. The separate egoic or existential self is afraid of failure, damnation, karma, etc. It also desires mastery, self-realization, salvation, enlightenment, or liberation. It is the egoic or existential self that worries about pitfalls and loss of control.

A useful distinction to bear in mind, one that can provide some perspective, is the difference between expedient teachings and final teachings. Expedient teachings work within dualistic, egoic self-consciousness to relieve suffering, improve the quality of life, and facilitate the evolution of consciousness. Final teachings remind us of the underlying oneness of Spirit that is always already expressed through all being, in all activities and all forms. Examples of this final teaching are found in Zen, Mahamudra, Vedanta, and *A Course in Miracles*.

Paradoxically, every path can become a pitfall. The way itself becomes a trap for the way-seeking mind. Yet living with awareness of duality we do experience better and worse, light and dark, love and fear, pleasure and pain, joy and sorrow, and all the rest of the opposites. When we become aware of choice we can change values, perception, thinking, feeling, and behavior. We can re-examine beliefs and re-evaluate priorities. In spite of the pitfalls, each path also offers opportunities for creative possibilities for healing and wholeness.

Leaders and Followers

Power is one of the most seductive pitfalls for those who attain a degree of mastery on any spiritual path. Those who are willing to take responsibility for positions of leadership inevitably confront the potentially corrupting influence of wielding power. "Power corrupts and absolute power corrupts absolutely" is a nugget of wisdom that is not to be taken lightly by those who either seek power or find themselves unwittingly drawn into positions in which they might exercise it. Learning to handle power skillfully for the benefit of one and all is a major challenge for anyone who is ambitious. Achieving success is only half the story. Handling success without being corrupted by it is a continuing challenge. Power is therefore called an enemy that a person of knowledge must overcome.[7]

Perhaps the best safeguard against abuses of power devised to date is the one that was built into the U.S. Constitution, namely a system of checks and balances. Among professional psychologists this is known as peer review. Unfortunately, peer review seems lacking among spiritual teachers. Few teachers get feedback from equals. Some spend all their time with followers; some are devoted to practice or service. Ongoing contact with people of equal power that can be trusted to question, confront, and encourage one when one becomes inflated or discouraged is invaluable, yet seems in short supply.

Everyone needs to check assumptions from time to time, and everyone needs to point out blind spots and offer alternative ways of viewing things. I do not know of any better safeguard against the pitfalls of self-deception than a community of trusted friends who can be counted on to give honest feedback and who are not afraid to challenge the wisdom of a choice. A therapist or teacher can serve this role for a time. However, each individual is responsible for choosing people whose opinions are valued and asking for their views. Peer relationships may be essential to developing responsible leadership qualities.

Whatever the path, masters and teachers may find themselves surrounded by people who put them up on a pedestal and want something from them. Followers may be genuinely desirous of learning, but they can also be a burden. Five types of followers can be easily distinguished: the sycophant, the devotee, the student, the seeker, and the disciple. Any of them may be found on each path, but certain types tend to be drawn more to one than another, and they correspond roughly to the five paths discussed above.

1. The Sycophant

This is a person who likes being in the presence of a master and enjoys basking in reflected glory. He or she is primarily interested in power and likes to feel important. This is the stereotypical groupie or flatterer whose seductive overtures are designed to entangle and cater to the ego of the master.

2. The Devotee

This person also wants to be physically close to the master, but he or she wants love rather than power. He or she will gladly sacrifice him or herself for love, and lives for moments of communion. The devotee may hope to get something for nothing, and feels empty when alone. The devotee wants to feel filled up by the master's presence, the guru's grace. What he or she offers in return is gratitude, devotion and dependency.

3. The Student

This is one who wants to learn from the master. He or she desires wisdom and may be eager to demonstrate what he or she has learned. A student wants verbal exchanges with a master at the mental level. He or she is often dissatisfied and may also be a dilettante, wanting to cover all possibilities. A student embodies the way-seeking mind, and typically tries to engage a master's attention by asking questions. He or she is willing to work to satisfy curiosity and gain understanding.

4. The Seeker

This person may be like a free-floating sponge on the spiritual path, and may value his or her own judgment more than anyone else's. He or she may be determined to do his or her "own thing" but tries to absorb as much as possible from any available master. This type may avoid commitment at all cost, but still be greedy for new information and experience.

5. The Disciple

This is one who desires spiritual realization and is willing to be disciplined by the master in order to attain it. The disciple, like the student, is more willing to work than either the sycophant or the devotee. He or she is willing to discipline him or herself in accordance with the master's wishes in order to advance on the chosen path.

Teachers on the Path

To teach is to demonstrate.—*A Course in Miracles*[8]

Teachers are essential on any spiritual path. Everyone can benefit from guidance, and the wisdom of the great traditions offers valuable information on spiritual development. How one finds a teacher may be either a matter of chance or of conscious choice. It is also a matter of individual taste. Some spiritual teachers work within established religious traditions, others do not. Some are authoritarian, others are not. Some require obedience, others are non-directive. Some that are highly visible, charismatic, or flamboyant tend to be controversial. Others that are more low-key or self-effacing go unnoticed by the media and the general public.

A spiritual teacher can facilitate the inner journey in many different ways. Whereas traditional psychotherapy tends to be oriented toward remedial work on the emotional and mental level, a spiritual teacher is presumably experienced in providing guidance in transpersonal realms. When one is inexperienced and looking for guidance, however, it may be difficult to differentiate genuine spiritual masters from false teachers, or those who claim mastery without having completed their own development in a healthy way.

Although there are no definitive rules for choosing a teacher, there are some guidelines that travelers on the spiritual path should consider before making formal commitments of loyalty or obedience to a teacher.[9] Maintaining a healthy balance between autonomy and surrender and making sure that the type of practice and community with which one seeks affiliation is appropriate to one's specific needs and goals can be challenging tasks. Not all teachers demand such commitments. One might ask whether a commitment ostensibly designed to help students and seekers may actually be serving the teacher or the system rather than the student.

Everyone encounters teachers on the path, regardless of whether or not one is formally affiliated with a church, a school, or a group. Lacking experience, it may be difficult to make an informed choice, but in the absence of valid criteria one cannot evaluate claims of mastery of levels of consciousness that are unfamiliar. One must be willing to take a leap of faith and suspend judgment if one is to taste the fruit of the vine and participate in spiritual practice. (A more detailed discussion of genuine mastery and how to discriminate it is included later in this chapter.)

Training the Mind

The awakened mind is one that knows
its Source, its Self, its Holiness.—*A Course in Miracles*[10]

Intellectual understanding or evaluation can never be an adequate substitute for direct experience on the spiritual path, just as knowledge of biology cannot substitute for sex. In fact, some masters of Eastern consciousness disciplines consider intellectual development to be an obstacle to progress on the spiritual path. Certainly intellectualization can be used defensively for the purpose of avoiding direct experience, but intellectual understanding can also be a stepping stone to self-transcendence if used appropriately. The discursive mind, like words themselves, can be either a help or a hindrance on the path. It tends to be perceived as a barrier when it is untrained or when one tries to work against it rather than with it.

In this culture, where intellectual training is valued and strong egoic and existential identification encouraged, the rational mind is not easily bypassed. Although the intuitive mind, as the part of the mind that simultaneously perceives both universal and individual awareness, can never be fully encompassed by the discursive thinking mind, given appropriate methods the discursive mind can be a help rather than a hindrance on the spiritual path. As soon as one disidentifies from it, it can become an ally instead of an adversary. Not only is it *possible* to bring the rational mind into alignment with intuitive insight, *healing and wholeness depend upon the successful integration of rationality and intuition.*

The discursive mind is a stronghold of egoic identification and a deepseated mistrust of its judgments is attributable in part to the fact that it can be trained to justify any position, as any good attorney can demonstrate. It can, for example, easily justify remaining at the egoic or existential level of consciousness, suggesting that what it does not comprehend is either a fraud or an illusion. It often becomes confused in attempting to sort out what is illusory. Learning to think clearly and to challenge assumptions about the mind can be useful preparation for self-knowledge. If one aspires to wholeness, the discursive mind cannot be rejected or discarded. In healthy psychological development it is subsumed and included in transpersonal identity. It serves specific functions and is an indispensable part of the psyche. Just as some ascetic religious practices do battle with the physical body, perceiving it to be an obstacle to spiritual progress, other spiritual disciplines tend to do battle with the thinking mind. In either case, the battle itself then becomes the main distraction that prevents awakening. Assuming responsibility for appropriate use of this faculty, like any other, is a continuing challenge.

Mastery of the mind should not be construed as suppression or judgment against it. True mastery of the mind implies using its full potential, just as physical mastery in sports implies using the body well. It implies a skillful use of faculties, rather than rigid control.

A Sufi story attributed to Gurdjieff likens the body to a carriage, the emotions to a horse, and the mind to a coachman. In our ordinary state of consciousness the coach is neglected and falls into disrepair. The horse is wild and uncontrolled, likely to bolt at the slightest provocation. The coachman is in the tavern, drinking with his friends. He has forgotten to feed the horse and oil the wheels of the carriage. The owner of the coach therefore never appears to ride in it.[11] From this perspective one must sober the mind, tame and train the emotions, and keep the body in good working order if one would attain mastery.

A basic premise of consciousness disciplines is that the mind can be trained. Training the mind is also an integral part of learning and cognitive development. Different traditions suggest different forms of training, including concentration, insight, choiceless awareness, and contemplation. In the West, meditation is often compared to contemplation or prayer, but few observers recognize its potential for mind training and self-healing. Techniques such as hypnosis, biofeedback, and systematic desensitization are Western psychological tools for mind training that have been successfully applied to specific types of healing. However, they do not necessarily contribute to Self-awareness or spiritual development when applied in a medical context. Disidentification and transcendence may be facilitated by such training, but without encouragement from the trainer—i.e., in the absence of a teacher—these potential effects are likely to remain unrecognized.

Mind training in the service of healing and wholeness depends on awareness of the purpose of the training. The mind cannot be fully healed as long as its well-being depends on submission to the domination of another mind, or the development of one mental function at the expense of another. Symptoms can be relieved and experiences can be induced, but healing that is not grounded in Self-awareness and responsibility is likely to be short-lived. One's mind can certainly be influenced by others, but sustained healing awareness depends on training the mind to recognize the power that is inherent within it.

Personal Power and Integrity

Power is defined by Webster's dictionary as the capacity to act; the ability to do. The word can be used in many different ways. The term personal power is used here to refer to the capacity of an individual to carry out intentions. In the West individual development and personal power are highly valued, but few people experience themselves as powerful. Even people who hold positions of power in government and large corporations feel powerless to affect the future.[12] However, if power is the capacity to carry out intentions, it is something that each one of us does have. The question is, how much are we willing to take responsibility for exercising intentionality in the world? Are we willing to acknowledge and use the power that is latent in the mind? Sometimes we may shy away from it, afraid that powers of the mind may get out of control and have negative repercussions. This tends to happen when power is used for personal gain or manipulation of others.

Skillful use of power depends on a willingness to take responsibility. Responsibility does not mean assigning or taking blame. It does mean recognizing that one is already carrying out intentions, shaping the environment and influencing others. One can be powerful to the extent that one is willing to be conscious rather than unconscious of one's creative potential. When one is unwilling to assume responsibility for one's own mind, one abdicates power to others. Personal power is given away whenever one claims that one is not responsible for subjective experience. Feeling powerful is inextricably linked to Self-awareness and the recognition of being a causative agent in one's own life.

Mental health depends to a great extent on taking responsibility for how one thinks about oneself and the world. Seeing oneself as an integral part of a larger whole, one can no longer pretend that one is a helpless, isolated creature existing by chance in a hostile universe. Like other creatures, human beings are shaped by the environment, but humans also shape the environment and are now capable of destroying the ecological balance that supports life. Human survival may therefore depend on our learning to see ourselves differently.

We are all affecting ourselves and each other and the environment all the time, either consciously or unconsciously. Everyone is in constant communication with others, interacting and engaging in mutually conditioned exchanges at all levels: physical, emotional, mental, and spiritual. Whoever is aware of choice can accept or reject the power of consciousness. Some people choose to remain unconscious by using drugs, others by immersion in work or distracting entertainment. Whatever the method or the rationale for abdicating responsibility for one's state of mind, choice remains available. It is always possible to change one's mind about personal power. A question one might consider is, "Am I willing to take responsibility for being powerful in my life?" Confronting this question can result in an extension of influence in the world as a natural expression of what one is. Perhaps the next challenge is the question: "Am I willing to be powerful in the world?" It often seems easier to complain about the way things are than to take responsibility for initiating change. Unconscious resistance must be confronted if one dares to act.

Personal power is not something that is dispensed by someone else. It must be claimed for oneself. One must be willing to become it. Authority is said to be twenty percent given, eighty percent taken. One person cannot make another powerful or responsible, although demonstrating appropriate behavior is itself a teaching. Power is either assumed or abdicated. As an existential choice it can be affirmed or denied. Given the opportunity for seeing options, freedom can be ignored, but it cannot be totally avoided.

The choice for ethical action and effective use of personal power depends on personal integrity. Having integrity or being integrated can mean being consistent in what one believes, what one thinks, what one says, what one feels, and what one does. Inconsistencies create conflict rather than coherence, and efforts to act effectively are thereby frustrated. When one does not act in accordance with true feelings (i.e., wholeheartedly), or when one thinks one thing and says another in order to avoid confrontation, one gives away power. One's mind may then become completely absorbed in justifying, rationalizing, and explaining one's position.

Integrity demands consistency between inner experience and outer expression. What is expressed in the world must be aligned with what is genuinely believed and felt inside if healing and integration are valued. Bringing values, beliefs, feelings, and actions into alignment with an overall purpose can be both liberating and empowering. As a laser light derives its power from its coherence, a person becomes powerful when values, intentions, and actions are coherent. A person in conflict, on the other hand, is subject to stress and fatigue. Integrity thus supports one's ability to act effortlessly and effectively in the world. Furthermore, a sense of personal integrity enables one to trust oneself and one's perception of others, and thus becomes a foundation for evaluating both systems and teachers.

Masters and Mastery

Masters of the world are those who have mastered themselves,
and mastery lies in control of the mind. If the mind becomes
your obedient servant, the whole world is at your service.
—Hazrat Inayat Khan[13]

A person who feels powerless is often drawn to submerging him- or herself in a group where responsibility for personal power can be turned over to a teacher or a guru. When major decisions are made by someone else, obedience may become a substitute for accountability. The proliferation of new religious groups in America today provides ample evidence of the attraction of surrender, not necessarily to the Self or God, but to external authority figures who are presumably better qualified to interpret truth and handle power than oneself.

Many authentic groups offer spiritual seekers a genuine opportunity to do inner work, to train the mind, and to experience transcendence. Others seem bent on indoctrination, coercion, and authoritarian control. Given the fact that the ego cannot adequately evaluate what lies beyond it and is likely to either pathologize or eulogize all non-ego states, how can a person seeking guidance on the spiritual path choose a teacher? Assuming healthy motivation for transcendence rather than an escape from responsibility and choice, a seeker may nevertheless find it useful to differentiate ego mastery from transpersonal mastery.

At any level of consciousness mastery implies superiority, and the term *master* generally refers to a male person having another being subject to his will, or to one who uses or controls at will that which is mastered. To "master" means to subdue; to become adept at a particular skill; to rule or direct. Spiritual mastery traditionally implies self-mastery, and mastery of the mind. Training in mastery of the mind often involves the practice of various forms of concentration meditation that bring the mind under control, but control may be egoic rather than spiritual.

Among the powers of mind that may become available through meditation are penetrating insight and psychic abilities. Such powers are considered by-products of spiritual work, and seekers are traditionally warned against them as traps that can lead to ego entanglements in the subtle realms. Attainment of psychic powers does not ensure ethicality or spiritual understanding. In psychological terms, familiarity with the subtleties of inner experience does not ensure healthy normalization of other levels. When an adept displays psychic powers in order to impress or intimidate followers, one might assume that motivation is in part determined by consciousness at the level of the third chakra. He or she might be at the stage of the fourth ox-herding picture. On the other hand, a spiritual master who has transcended egoic identifications might be expected to disdain the use of such powers for purposes of manipulation and control.

At the egoic level, a person is said to be a master of destiny when he or she is self-determining rather than being subject to control by others. In Western psychology, such self-determination is considered essential to mental health, but healthy functioning appears to depend on a balance between effort and surrender, control and relaxation, assertiveness and receptivity. Healing is not just a matter of increasing independence and control.

Self-determination, self-regulation, and appropriate self-concept are essential to the development of a cohesive sense of ego-identity, but attachment to this independent separate sense of self tends to impede growth beyond ego. Thus psychic powers are considered hazardous to anyone using them for ego goals. The spiritually self-realized person functioning as a bodhisattva (i.e., in the context of the tenth ox-herding picture) is therefore said to be in the world, but not of it.

The power of spiritual mastery is said to be *in* the master, but not *of* him or her. The spiritual master does not claim ownership.

This attitude can counteract the risk of ego inflation resulting from mastery of psychic abilities, but does not necessarily preclude it. Regardless of whether one claims to be a channel for Spirit, or identified with Spirit, willful claims to manipulation or control can be viewed as indicating ego mastery rather than authentic spiritual mastery. Power at the level of ego is a function of self-determination and expertise. Authentic spiritual mastery calls for integrity and self-transcendence.

In the genuine master, then, transcendence of ego goals and desires can be expected to manifest as nonattachment and acceptance of things as they are. One who has attained mastery on the spiritual path may choose to act in the world but is not attached to the outcome of particular actions. Attachment to power for its own sake at any level can be an obstacle to further development, as is attachment to recognition, success, or any form of personal achievement.

A master who actively seeks disciples may well be operating from egoic desire for recognition. In master/slave relationships that can develop at this level, the master is apt to become the slave of his own passions. In some traditions, where the master is also a trickster, invisibility rather than fame is considered a desirable attribute.[14] In yoga, when consciousness has reached the level of the sixth chakra, self-mastery gives control of inner light, and the master is said to be able to increase or decrease its brightness, becoming more or less visible at will.[15]

The person who wants to advance on the path of spiritual development is invariably instructed to practice detachment and have no expectations. Even a master who is attached to mastery is ruled by what he seeks to master. According to the Chinese sage, Lao Tsu, leadership based on love and respect is better that leadership based on fear and coercion, but leadership is best when the people say, "We have done this ourselves."[16]

It is this type of leadership that a psychotherapist may aspire to in the process of empowering individuals to take responsibility for themselves. A spiritual teacher may do likewise. As psychotherapist Sheldon Kopp says,

Of course, disciples . . . will at first be awed by the difference between his (the guru's) seeming confidence and power, on the one hand, and their own helplessness and inadequacy, on the other. The guru then tries to help his follower to see that there is no difference between them, except as the follower diminishes himself to give power to the guru. The follower maintains the imbalance to avoid the awful responsibility of being equal to everyone else in the world and completely on his own, while retaining the hope that the guru will take care of him. To maintain his own freedom, the guru must try to free the disciple from himself.[17]

In growth-oriented psychotherapy, when a therapist trains aware-ness and assists clients in personal problem solving, the aim is not to create dependency, but to enable clients to handle their own problems and empower them to continue the process of psychological growth on their own. Likewise, genuine spiritual teachers remind seekers that they must look within to find the true guru, which, translated literally from Sanskrit, means "dispeller of darkness."

The person who aspires to mastery learns, like Castaneda's war-rior, to regard everything in life as a challenge and use everything as an opportunity for inner development. The authentic spiritual master, unlike the mass leader who tries to maintain an appearance of infallibil-ity,[18] is not concerned with being right or wrong, or winning or losing. The battle has already been won. A master has nowhere to go. He or she has already arrived. He or she does not assign credit or blame, either to self or others. The authentic spiritual master knows that wis-dom and power do not belong to the individual. Wisdom and power may be manifested through the person, but one does not own any-thing. This understanding contributes to the development of trust and inner peace.

The Self that is one with the source of wisdom and power is nothing. Authentic spiritual mastery is grounded in awareness of being no-thing and every-thing, or transcendent insight. Through a process of purification the person who aspires to spiritual mastery learns to relinquish all egoic identifications. Presumably qualities as-sociated with spiritual development, such as energy, gentleness, joy, open mindedness, generosity, patience, loving kindness, truthful-ness, and calm, would be highly developed by a master. In some tradi-tions a master is not only expected to manifest these qualities, but also to be free of such negative emotions as fear, anger, and guilt.

A paradox of spiritual mastery is that it is attained through surren-der rather than control of ego. Striving therefore is counterproductive and the person who aspires to mastery must be willing to renounce even the desire for it. As the Third Zen Patriarch says, ". . . even to be attached to the idea of enlightenment is to go astray. . . . When thought is in bondage the truth is hidden."[19] Gerald May, in his thoughtful book *Will and Spirit*, points out that while psychology is objective, secular, and willful, spiritual development is essentially mysterious and calls for willing surrender. In any willful attempts to master life, whenever one is controlling or being controlled, one feels separated and lonely. A master, says Dr. May, may feel affection for a slave, but it is "an affection eternally tainted with contempt."[20]

Theoretically, an authentic spiritual master can be recognized by a person of any faith, provided he or she has the capacity for discernment at the spiritual level of consciousness. However, even when one is aware of common characteristics of mastery, in practice it may be difficult to distinguish a genuine spiritual master from a fraudulent one. Wilber points out that neither empirical nor rational knowledge can adequately evaluate transcendental reality.[21] Empirical knowledge pertains to information obtained by means of the senses and requires training in observation of the external world of space, time, and objects. Rational knowledge of philosophy, logic, and the mind itself pertains to information obtained by reason and requires training the intellect. Transcendental knowledge of a higher order of reality is obtained by pure intuition (direct apprehension of truth)[22] and requires training in contemplation. Just as the truth of a logical deduction is based on internal consistency and cannot be proved by empirical measurement of sensory objects, transcendent insight cannot be fully comprehended by either reason or empirical data.

Trying to verify the intuitive understanding of transcendental knowledge by rational or empirical means falls into the trap of attempting to define a larger, more encompassing set in terms of a smaller, component part. Such partial understanding is always hopelessly inadequate. We must accept the fact that transcendent insight into the nature of reality attained through contemplation cannot be fully comprehended without adequate training. Consensual validation does exist within the contemplative traditions. But anyone wishing to develop discernment at the level of contemplation must be willing to undertake the discipline required to do so. If one has not been adequately trained, one can hardly be expected to make appropriate evaluations in this domain.

Spiritual training is intended to culminate in an awakened state, a truly higher state of consciousness described as unchanging awareness of reality as it is, rather than a transient state of illumination. Only when flashes of insight have been stabilized into an abiding light is the mind fully awakened and spiritual mastery attained. Every tradition has its own name for the awakened state, and suggests different approaches to this goal. Writing on *The Varieties of Meditative Experience*, Daniel Goleman points out that all paths propose a diffusion of the effects of meditation into the aspirant's waking, dreaming, and sleep states.[23] What requires arduous effort at the outset becomes effortless as the meditator learns to maintain awareness in the midst of other activity. In the awakened state both origins and paths are transcended.

Discrimination and Discernment

In the absence of training, when one has perhaps attained only a glimmer of the possibility of awakening, one may nevertheless need to make discriminating evaluations with regard to a spiritual teacher. Ram Dass suggests that the best protection against being misled by false teachers on the spiritual path lies in the purity of the seeker, but a seeker with good intentions can still fall prey to false teachers. I have talked with many individuals who have left groups after being disillusioned with the leaders. Everyone had joined with pure intentions, wanting to participate in making a positive contribution to society.

Psychological health and Self-awareness can be valuable assets to the seeker who wants to avoid becoming entangled in spiritual tyranny. Initial attempts to evaluate a teacher or a group with some degree of self-awareness could begin with self-reflective questions. When a self-proclaimed master appears, for example, one might ask whether one feels peaceful in his presence. Since the presence of a spiritual master is said to have a soothing and healing effect on others,[24] one might assume that such a state could be readily discernible. If, however, one is anxious or agitated, the effect of the presence of a master could easily go unnoticed.

Other questions one might ask would be: Does the master manifest the qualities of compassion, generosity, loving kindness, honesty, calm, and open-mindedness? What attracts me to this person? Am I attracted to his or her power, showmanship, cleverness, achievements, glamor, ideas? Am I motivated by fear or love? Is my response primarily physical excitement, emotional or intellectual stimulation, or intuitive resonance? What would persuade me to trust him or her (or anyone) more than myself? Am I looking for a parent figure to relieve me of the responsibility for my life? Am I looking for a group where I feel I can belong and be taken care of in return for doing what I am told? What am I giving up? Am I moving toward something I am drawn to, or am I running away from my life as it is?

Self-awareness, however, is no guarantee of discriminating wisdom. At times when a particular leader appears to agree with one's personal biases and preconceptions, one may be willing to trust him or her without asking any questions. It is easy to question beliefs of others that seem to be irrational, funny, or bizarre. One's own beliefs, on the other hand, are usually assumed to be true.[25]

In addition to questions pertaining to Self-awareness, anyone who is considering joining a group of disciples might be advised to consider the following questions suggested by Dr. Goleman: Does the group keep secrets about its organization and the leader? How do members of the group respond to embarrassing questions? For example, does the leader have a Swiss bank account or indulge in sexual relations with group members? Do members display stereotypic behavior that emulates the leader? Does the group have a party line that does not permit members to express how they really feel? Do members see themselves as having found the only true way? Are members free to leave? Are members asked to violate personal ethics to prove their loyalty? Does the group's public image misrepresent its true nature? Are humor and irreverence permitted?[26]

Such questions are not definitive guidelines for action, but they can provide a basis of discrimination for making a decision. Just as parents cannot prevent sons or daughters from falling in love with partners they do not approve of, scholarly research is not likely to be effective in preventing fraudulent masters from gathering disciples.

It appears that neither Self-awareness nor rational discrimination is sufficient to prevent errors. Some practitioners of spiritual disciplines say that you cannot recognize a teacher as being right for you unless you have already studied and practiced the teachings in daily life.[27] Such knowledge might provide protection in some cases, but it does not prevent naive, unquestioning acceptance of corrupt leadership.

In cases of abusive spiritual authoritarianism, a return to psychological health for group members is usually based on a decision to trust oneself more than the powerful leader. Parents might ask themselves whether they are raising their children to develop independent judgment and trust themselves, or whether they are encouraging unquestioning obedience to authority. The master/slave relationship in spiritual authoritarianism is often freely chosen by the disciple who feels both unworthy and incapable of developing his or her own capacity for discernment.

On the other hand, maintaining a noncommital stance in the face of uncertainty may obscure the fact that one feels vulnerable to deception when one is inadequately trained to make informed judgments. Just as an anxious parent might try to dissuade a child from risking intimacy and thereby cripple the child's emotional development, excessive intellectual skepticism can stifle healthy spiritual development as well. If one can accept any experience in life as a challenge and an opportunity for learning, then even a difficult experience in a group can contribute to wisdom and maturity. Many people who have joined spiritual groups and later left them feel the experience was valuable, despite hardships, struggles, and disappointments. When a person leaves an organized group, his or her own sense of personal mastery may increase as a sense of integrity and authenticity is restored.

For example, one man who felt a great deal of conflict between obedience to his authoritarian teacher and his love for a woman who was not a member of the group finally resolved the issue by leaving the group, since she refused to join. In retrospect, two years later, he felt he had made the right decision. What had seemed like an act of disobedience at the time proved to be an important step for him in gaining a sense of autonomy and independence. Self-respect can be severely undermined in teacher-disciple relationships when the teacher uses coercive methods under the pretext of liberating the disciple from the confines of ego. Replacing biological parents with spiritual mentors evokes all the complications of transference familiar to psychotherapists, but few spiritual teachers are trained to handle transference issues with psychological skill and ethicality.

Unfortunately, the belief that equates suffering with purification, the assumption that if something hurts it must be good for one, while pleasure must be bad, contributes to endurance of authoritarian abuse on the part of earnest spiritual aspirants seeking self-improvement. There is little appreciation of the fact that self-condemnation can be as much of an obstacle to transcendence as self-aggrandizement on the spiritual path. The current revival of religious exploration in America is sometimes viewed as a reaction against the hedonism and narcissism of previous decades. However, overemphasis on self-sacrifice also poses a threat to psychological balance and well-being. The problem is that when spirituality is seen as an alternative to psychological development rather than as an extension of it, we continue to be faced with the same issues that led rationality to reject religion in the first place. Spiritual awareness, whether it develops inside or outside an organized system, contributes to wholeness only when it is based on psychological health and sound development of all levels of consciousness.

This does not mean that practices involving arduous discipline are not sometimes appropriate or necessary. Some may be detrimental to healthy human development, but many are ambiguous, and some do contribute to healthy psychological growth. Training the mind in contemplation may be arduous at times, and gentle at other times. Some people choose paths that are steep and narrow, others choose gentler approaches to scaling the peaks of awareness. From a psychological perspective, the mistake lies in assuming that the path one happens to be on is the only way to advance on the journey. Eventually even the idea of personal advance becomes an obstacle to transcendence.

For some people, personal devotion to a master may be stage-specific. It may benefit a person at one stage of development, whereas it would not necessarily be good for him or her at a different stage. The same may be said for specific practices. For instance, someone with a highly developed intellect might appropriately aspire to mastery in contemplation; that person might choose a rigorous meditation discipline in order to balance rational and intuitive development. Although the absence of training in contemplation is not commonly considered an imbalance, it can certainly be viewed as such from a perspective of wholeness. Contemplation also appears to be essential for spiritual understanding and realization. The same training, however, might not be beneficial for someone who had not developed integrity and responsibility at an ego level.

Writing about personal experience with spiritual teachers, Daniel O'Hanlon, S.J., a Jesuit priest who has personally explored Eastern disciplines, says:

During my years of involvement with Eastern religious practice I have had many teachers and have learned something from them all. At no time have I made that kind of total commitment to a teacher which critics of exaggerated guru-worship condemn. But I have learned something which has often been forgotten in Western spiritual practice, namely, that I can "apprentice" myself in greater or lesser degree to someone who is in some respect more advanced than I am. . . . Nowadays the trend in spiritual direction is to speak of "a friendly exchange between equals in order to discover the movement of the Spirit in our lives." It seems difficult for us to acknowledge that there may well be persons who have traveled farther than us along the path, and can guide us through those places which they have successfully passed through but are still unfamiliar to us. In this sense, anyone who is in any way more advanced than I can become my guru. In those matters in which I am more advanced, I am the guru. Nothing magical or authoritarian about that.

. . . Sharing as an equal with another person can be very helpful in enabling us to detect the movement of the Spirit within. But describing our practice and presenting our questions to someone who, out of rich experience and more advanced awareness, can give us inspiration and concrete suggestions, is even better.[28]

Implications for Psychological Investigation

Most religious institutions in the West have failed to provide training in contemplation for the lay person in any disciplined way. Understanding spiritual development as an integral aspect of wholeness calls for expanding the field of psychological investigation as well as using new methods of inquiry. The inward arc of the journey to wholeness must traverse the transpersonal domain, where each one must learn to investigate rather than to judge, condemn, or idealize spiritual disciplines. The growing concern with the well-being of humanity as a whole, and the necessity of continuing conscious evolution[29] call for discriminating wisdom in evaluating spiritual practices.

Investigators can view this domain only as participant observers. No one can understand what lies outside his or her perceptual capacity. Furthermore, observations of human development invariably reflect the level of inquiry. One tends to find what one looks for, and one can see only what perceptual limitations permit. What anyone can do is to bear in mind the limitations of one's present capacity for discernment while working on expanding the perceptual framework.

Eastern disciplines that were not designed for Western egos are not tailored to individual differences. However, apparently conflicting values can be reconciled in practice. Those who feel they have attained a degree of personal power and mastery in the world have much to learn from surrender, whether to a teacher, the will of God, service, or discipline. Those who have never claimed their freedom and autonomy may need to do that, too. It is not a matter of choosing between self-directed effort or surrender to a teacher, but of recognizing the value of both.

Egocentric identifications are outgrown naturally as consciousness evolves and awareness expands. The ego is not an enemy. Children are not less worthy for not being adults, but arrested development can be a problem. Wherever one happens to be on the path, one can recognize freedom and dignity. Likewise, spiritual growth does not justify abuse or the violation of human dignity. Guilt and self-abuse are as much obstacles to liberation as pride is. Assaults on the ego do not promote psychological balance or lead to healthy transcendence. Transcendence of ego does not require violence.

Self-awareness can no longer be considered an esoteric luxury for a few educated individuals. It has become a social necessity. We are only beginning to understand the possibilities inherent in mastering the mind, but the challenges of our time call for accelerated learning. Humanity is gaining access to vast reservoirs of undeveloped potential, but unless egoic excesses are curbed by discriminating wisdom, we run the risk of destroying ourselves. Perhaps the dilemma is a choice between ego transcendence and biological planetary death. The fact that collective suicide has become a real possibility vividly reflects the struggle between life and death, Eros and Thanatos, which is re-enacted by the soul on any path. No one is exempt from participation in this human dilemma.

Psychology as a social science is still in its infancy. In the East, spiritual understanding has rarely been applied to social problems. Sri Aurobindo and Gandhi in India were notable exceptions in this century. Gandhi recommended meditation for everyone as a contribution to world peace. Sri Aurobindo was one of the first to emphasize the interdependence of inner and outer liberation. He taught the unity of the infinite and the finite, the timeless and the temporal, and the transcendent and the immanent. Only when this unity is known can one have "peace in every action and Joy in every way."[30]

Each of us must choose where to look for guidance in unfamiliar territory. Should one surrender in obedience to another person who is deemed wiser than onself? Perhaps the cultural values of freedom and self-determination coupled with Self-awareness and a vision of transcendence, can help one avoid some of the pitfalls and develop the discriminating wisdom that is required. Each of us must undertake a subjective path of inner development as well as learn from traditional sources and external authorities. Studying the teachings and learning about something from someone else is never a substitute for direct experience. Before judging others, one may begin by acknowledging the tyranny of one's own passions, and the desire for control of both inner and outer experience. As one learns to include and balance opposites, recognizing their interdependent nature, one may also contribute more effectively to the well-being of others. Lasting peace is not purchased by surrendering one ego to another. Perhaps it is only in transcendence of egoic identification that the conditions of peace can be established.

In the final analysis, efforts at evaluation of spiritual teachers may be guided best by the words of the Buddha:

Do not believe in what you have heard; do not believe in traditions because they have been handed down for many generations; do not believe anything because it is rumored and spoken of by many; do not believe merely because the written statement of some old sage is produced; do not believe in conjectures; do not believe merely in the authority of your teachers and elders. After observation and analysis, when it agrees with reason and it is conducive to the good and benefit of one and all, then accept it and live up to it.[31]

Experiential Exercises

Guidance

Across the centuries human beings have sought guidance from many different sources. Dreams have been used as a means of tapping inner wisdom since ancient times. Divination, astrology, Tarot cards, the *I Ching*, oracles, omens, and other external tools for reflecting inner realities and determining auspicious dates and decisions are as old as human history and are still used today. Many people choose to turn over their self-determination or decision-making power to others. When they do, however, blaming others for consequences they do not like offers little consolation.

Religious mystics of all ages and all faiths have consistently told us that God dwells within, and if we want to grow, to evolve and progress on the spiritual path, we must find the inner teacher, the spirit of truth that will guide us to wholeness and Self-realization.

In contemporary society some people seek guidance from psychotherapists or teachers of various persuasions. Few people question the beliefs of the therapist or teacher or the source of their guidance.

The universal source of inner wisdom is the same source for all of us. Each of us can learn to access inner truth and the part of ourselves that can act as a teacher or a guide. No matter what part we play in life, access to truth is always available. Wisdom is found when we are willing to see things as they are, and we can see the truth about others when we are not afraid to see the truth about ourselves. As we develop the capacity to take on the roles of others, to empathize and identify with those whose life experience is different from our own, our capacity for compassion and understanding grows. Likewise, as we practice getting in touch with the source of wisdom that lies within, it becomes more easily accessible.

Some people have easy direct access to inner wisdom through well-developed intuition. Others need to do some work to clear away such obstacles as fear and self-deception. Each of us must start from where he or she is, and now is the only time we can begin. The truth is always already present, waiting only for our willingness to acknowledge its presence within us. To be wise is to accept the truth as it is, recognizing the interdependence of opposites and the transiency of all illusions. Gradually, as we learn to let go of the past and open to the present we can become more conscious of how we are co-creating our future.

In order to clarify sources of guidance that are available, take some time to reflect on the following images, accepting whatever the words evoke:

Allow a few minutes to relax and quiet your mind.

Imagine now that you are traveling backward in time to the third century B.C. Visualize yourself in your mind's eye living long ago in ancient Greece. Notice what you are wearing and the details of your surroundings. Be aware of your relationship to men and women in this society and the particular role you are playing. Who are you? Where do you look for guidance when you need to make a decision?

Moving forward in time to the Middle Ages, imagine that you are living in the country of your choice at that time. Notice your surroundings and be aware of your relationship with others. What part do you play in this society? Where do you look for guidance?

Moving forward in time again to the eighteenth or nineteenth century, imagine that you are living yet another life in another place. Notice the details of your clothes and your surroundings. Be aware of your relationships and your role in this place and time. Where do you look for guidance?

Imagine now that you are living two hundred years in the future. What is this society like? What is your part in it? How do you relate to others? Where do you look for guidance?

Now reflect on your present-day life, the part you play in it, and how you relate to others. Where do you look for guidance? Has your capacity for seeking and finding appropriate guidance evolved or changed over time? What sources of guidance do you prefer?

Teachers and Helpers

One way of becoming aware of your inner teacher is to reflect on the persons who have been significant teachers for you in the past. Who has been an important spiritual teacher in your life? Perhaps there have been several.

A spiritual teacher need not be religious. It may be someone who inspired or empowered you to grow, to transcend an old self-image or self-imposed limitation; someone who enabled you to experience yourself as expanded, liberated, free from constrictions that you did not realize you had imposed on yourself. A spiritual teacher could be someone who helped you wake up to the reality of who and what you really are, someone who allowed you to discover your own access to truth.

Make a list of the significant teachers in your life. What were the qualities in them that you most appreciated? Remember that any quality you recognize in another is also latent within you. If you choose to actualize it, you can. Pick one quality that you have appreciated in a teacher and ask yourself if you are willing to manifest that quality in your own life. If you are, ask yourself if you really intend to manifest it. Recognizing the power of intentionality is both liberating and empowering. If you truly intend to cultivate a particular quality, you will do it. Practice that follows intention leads to habit and character—to choose and intend to cultivate those qualities that you value is to assume responsibility for your own becoming, and for your part in co-creating the future. Every decision chooses the future. You are free to choose the qualities that you want to express in the world, just as you are free to choose the beliefs and attitudes that you accept into your mind. If you do not choose consciously, the choice is made unconsciously, or it is made for you by someone else. You can reclaim your capacity for choice at any time.

If you want help in the process of becoming who you are, if obstacles seem overwhelming and progress seems slow, you can always ask for assistance. Help is available, but it is easier to find if you know what sort of help you are seeking. Reflect on past experiences of having received help. Can you remember a time when you were significantly helped by someone? What was it about the person who helped you that was particularly helpful? What happened for you in the exchange with him or her? How did you feel afterward? Make a list of the qualities you found most helpful. These are the qualities you may want to look for when you ask someone for help with your process of becoming.

8 The Possible Dream: Creativity and Dreaming

Creativity and Self-Expression

Creativity has long been attributed to divine inspiration. Nowhere is the relationship between the mundane and the transcendent more explicitly revealed than in creative expression. Tapping into creativity, like dreaming, can be a way of listening to the Self. Whether creative inspiration is attributed to intuition, to a muse, a daemon, or personal struggle, it can be a source of healing and spiritual renewal for the psyche.

Every path offers opportunities for creativity, but it is valued more highly in some systems than in others. In some meditative disciplines creative ideas, like any other ideas, are seen as distractions to be ignored. Certainly excitement over what seem to be significant insights or original images during meditation can be distracting. Whether or not these "distractions" have any value either for the individual or for society is another question. Willis Harman and Howard Rheingold, writing on *Higher Creativity*, would argue for their potential value. Creative insight, they point out, has made history:

In the early part of the seventh century of the Christian calendar, a poor camel-driver in an obscure corner of the world saw an angel in a dream; by the eighth century, the armies of those who believed the revelation of Mohammed's dream had conquered an arc of territory stretching from the south of Spain to the northwest part of India. In the late nineteenth century a teenage Jewish physics student in Zurich imagined himself to be riding along a lightbeam, looking back at himself in a mirror; the resulting train of thought led to the formula $E = mc^2$, the theoretical basis for the nuclear bomb.[2]

Creativity can operate on any or all levels of consciousness—spiritual, existential, mental, emotional, and physical. Its relative value cannot be easily measured but must be taken into account. If it is stifled, inner conflict, depression, and illness are likely to ensue. Integration is necessary for healing and wholeness.

Creativity may be expressed on a concrete physical level in art, architecture, and craftsmanship in all its forms. At this level creativity shapes our environment and contributes to the quality of life in a tangible, visible way. The explicit purpose of religious art may be spiritual inspiration, but any great art can be spiritually uplifting. What is important for the person on a spiritual path, however, is to discover and honor the creative inspiration that is uniquely his or hers to express. John Curtis Gowan reports the following observation:

When Michelangelo did the Sistine Chapel he painted both the major and minor prophets. They can be told apart because, though there are cherubim at the ears of all, only the major prophets are *listening*. Here, exactly stated, is the difference between genius and talent.[3]

But one need not be a genius, or even especially talented, to learn to listen inwardly and express oneself creatively. On the emotional level creativity may be expressed in the art of loving, in relationships, in healing, nurturing, and in compassionate service. At this level creativity can contribute to the quality of life in a palpable, though invisible way. In this sense Mother Teresa of Calcutta has done very creative work among the poor. The effects of emotional creativity may be perceived as radiance, inner peace, and joy. Replacing fear with love in a healing relationship is a function of emotional creativity. Some people are skilled at using words to arouse feelings, others may express emotional creativity in music, or in other forms of art that evoke deep feeling responses. Emotional creativity is also expressed in healing emotional wounds and transforming sorrow into compassion.

On the mental level creativity is expressed in ideas, thought forms, and images. Discoveries and inventions are a product of creativity at a mental level. Mental activity is, of course, involved to some extent in all creative effort, just as feelings are involved, but the major focus of a particular creative endeavor may be physical, emotional, mental, or spiritual. The creations of mind are both visible and invisible. They shape every subjective experience, whether one is conscious of it or not.

On the spiritual level creativity may take the form of revelation as it did for Moses or Mohammed in the desert, or it may be a less dramatic sense of inner calling to a unique function in life. It may come in the form of a dream or a vision, an idea or a feeling, but it characteristically has a noetic quality, i.e., one *knows* what it is that one must do. This certainty was conveyed by Jesus' words, "I must be about my Father's business."

Stages of creativity at any level seem to follow certain patterns. One common pattern corresponds to stages of the birth process as described by Stanislav Grof in *Realms of the Human Unconscious*.[4] The first is a state of blissful union, wherein all possibilities are entertained; the second is depressive feelings of pressure and no exit; the third is passionate struggle that precipitates action; and the fourth is separation and new life. These stages appear to reflect stages of self-development in reverse: from unity (transpersonal), through despair (existential), choice (mental), passion (emotional), and separation (physical).

The creative process is one of giving birth to some new form. On the spiritual path the process of transformation is sometimes described as giving birth to the Self. A period of incubation or gestation may be followed by depression or a feeling of deadness that defies rational analysis. Although moments of inspiration may be joyous, the struggle in which the forces of eros (love) and thanatos (death) are pitted against each other is considered essential to the creative process.[5] Certainly it is highly charged emotionally, and calls for tremendous effort when viewed from an egoic or existential perspective.

The myth of Sisyphus tells the story of a man condemned to push a rock up to the top of a mountain every day, only to have the rock roll down to the bottom again, whereupon he had to begin the task of pushing it up all over again. This is analogous to the creative process when it is viewed as a struggle of the ego against forces that seem to keep it bound to an endless round of meaningless tasks. Indeed, given enough time, all human creative endeavors disappear. There is nothing permanent about creativity at the physical, emotional, or mental level. Only when the path of separation and return to unity consciousness has been traversed to completion can one look back and see how assumptions about reality are expressed in the creative process. Perhaps one may then participate wholeheartedly in the creative manifestation of spirit in all forms.

Access to creative inspiration can be gained through many different psychological methods such as hypnosis, imagery, visualization, relaxation, affirmations, etc. Methods for developing creativity and intuition have been discussed elsewhere.[6] Here we will turn our attention to dreams as a source of inspiration and guidance, since they can take us further into the hidden recesses of mind and consciousness than visualizations in the waking state, which are more susceptible to mental egoic manipulation.

Dreaming

The Way itself is like some thing
Seen in a dream, elusive, evading one. . . .
In it are essences, subtle but real,
Embedded in truth.—Lao Tsu[7]

Dreams can be a valuable source of guidance on the spiritual path, particularly if one is not formally affiliated with a teacher or religious group. Every spiritual tradition makes reference to dreaming, and it is common knowledge that God, angels, gurus, and teachers may appear in a dream to give instruction or messages to the dreamer. Dreams may also be a source of transpersonal experiences. In addition, any dream can have a healing effect on the psyche, even if it is not explicitly spiritual or psychological in content.

Some dreams are so bizarre that, were they to be experienced in a waking state, they would be called psychotic. If psychosis is defined as being trapped in a suboptimal state of consciousness that distorts reality without one's being aware of that distortion,[8] and that is dominated by fear, the term applies to most dream states. Becoming conscious in the dream state can open the possibility for a healthy, normal person to experience any or all states of consciousness. The key to memory that enables one to learn from this experience is attention. If one pays attention, dreams can be a profound source of insight.

The more attention is given to dreams, the more vital and available they become. Conscious dreaming can contribute to healing, wisdom, and creativity.[9] Dream interpretation can be approached from any level: emotional, mental, egoic, existential, or spiritual. The context in which dreams are examined tends to determine their effect. When we learn to observe them with healing awareness, dreams can become instruments of healing and wholeness.

Dreams also demonstrate that we have the power to create a world that exists only in the mind, and while it lasts we are absolutely convinced that it is real, no matter how bizarre it seems to the rational mind. Sometimes dream worlds seem to have their own reality, independent of the dreamer's participation. Dream landscapes may recur in sequential dreams, and the dreamer may encounter people and places that are never met in ordinary waking life.

Since ancient times men and women have used dreams for enhancing awareness of subtle nonphysical realities. The Bible contains many accounts of God speaking to people in dreams. For example:

God speaks in one way, and in two, though man does not perceive it. In a dream, in a vision of the night, when deep sleep falls upon men, while they slumber on their beds, then he opens the ears of men. . . . [10]

The yogic literature also gives many examples of dreams of spiritual instruction and meetings with gurus. In yoga psychology dreams are believed to communicate intuitive wisdom as well as reflect personal problems. A yogic adept may be able to maintain waking consciousness in the dream state as well as in deep sleep, as demonstrated by Swami Rama at the Menninger Clinic in Kansas.[11]

Dreams as a source of spiritual guidance are well known in religious traditions. The earliest announcement of Mohammed's mission came to him in a dream, and the Buddha's birth was announced to his mother in a dream. In ancient Egypt divine powers were believed to be conferred in dreams, and in ancient Greece dreams were thought to have an oracular as well as a healing function. In the Vedic literature of India a person is said to be "self-illuminated" in the dream state.[12]

Contemporary dream research indicates that dreams are the most common altered state of consciousness in which ESP phenomena such as telepathy and precognition occur.[13] Persistently, in all ages and in all cultures, people have reported dreams of things to come, some of which actually happen. Sometimes dreams provide accurate information about events taking place at a distance in space/time. But reading accounts of the experience of others never has as much impact as when one has the experience oneself.

One dream that I remember vividly occurred the night that my daughter did not return as planned from a backpacking expedition in the Sierras in early autumn. She was sixteen and had been hiking for a week with a group of young people and a guide. When the group failed to show up at the time they were expected, I was worried. That night I slept little, but I dreamed that she telephoned me and told me she would be out of the mountains at 1:00 P.M. the next day. I felt relief in the dream and disappointment when I awakened to find that it was "only a dream." The next day at 1:30 P.M. my daughter telephoned from a town in the mountains to tell me that she and her companions had just been rescued by helicopter from a high mountain valley where they had been trapped by a swollen river that couldn't be crossed after a night of heavy rain. She had in fact flown out of the mountain valley in the helicopter about 1:00 P.M. She said she had tried to send me telepathic messages during the night to let me know she was all right, but of course had no way of knowing when or how she would get back.

Such experiences are not uncommon among people who pay attention to their dreams. One young woman dreamed that her father had died in an accident precisely at the time when he was killed in an automobile crash. Another woman dreamed that her father came to say goodbye, and the next day she received a telephone call informing her that her father had died the preceding day. Another dreamed of meeting her "soul mate" a few days before meeting the man she later married. Sometimes dreams warn us of impending danger, as in the case of a woman who dreamed of driving off the edge of a cliff the day before an accident in which a car on the road in front of her did skid off the edge of the road and roll down the embankment.

More often, however, dreams portray subjective rather than objective reality. The fact that dreams reflect events in the external world should not obscure the fact that they also constantly monitor the inner life of the psyche and give us insight into the state of our physical, emotional, mental, existential, and spiritual health. Ever since Freud's pioneering dream research and his publication of *The Interpretation of Dreams*[14] at the turn of the century, dreams have been considered the royal road to the unconscious. Freud interpreted dreams as disguised wish fulfillments. Jung suggested that dreams reveal more than they conceal, and saw them serving a compensatory function that helped restore balance to the psyche.[15] By highlighting psychological processes that are beyond conscious control, dreams point to areas of psychic life that need attention and make us aware of self-deception.

Dreams can also be a source of inspiration. Many creative inspirations find their way to consciousness through dreams. Robert Louis

Stevenson dreamed the plots for many of his stories, and Mozart heard music in his dreams which he subsequently wrote. Artists in all fields have been inspired by dreams, but dreams are fruitful for creativity only when the dreamer is prepared to make the effort to capture their elusive contents and pay attention to them.

In some cultures, such as among some of the American Indians, young men are expected to determine their lifelong vocation on the basis of their dreams. People who take their dreams seriously often consult them in making life-changing decisions and career choices. For instance, one man who was offered a job that would have meant taking on what he felt was an overwhelming responsibility dreamed that he was being sentenced to the twelve labors of Hercules and decided not to accept the offer. A woman considering marriage had a dream of living in a gingerbread house with her new husband. Everything seemed artificial and make-believe. The relationship broke up when she began to question some of her assumptions and look behind appearances.

Another woman who had been getting a better sense of herself in therapy dreamed of being in a king's bedroom and stepping into his shoes, which fit perfectly. She was indeed learning to be her own authority and rule her own life.

Dreams of illness or danger when a person is apparently in good health are often interpreted as warning dreams. I find it useful to assume the dream is letting us know what is actually happening now in the psyche, outside of conscious awareness. If one ignores the dream, it may well manifest more concretely as physical sickness or accident, but if one is alert to its subtle messages, the concrete manifestations of these difficulties may be prevented.

From a Jungian perspective, Max Zeller writes,

When the dream says that someone is sick, we take it as just such a diagnostic statement about a disease occurring *in the psyche* and acknowledged there. The sickness that the unconscious brings into focus is hidden from the patient's consciousness. It is like a hidden sickness, a secret suffering not known before. The unconscious opens up a new dimension which becomes manifest through the dream and widens and balances the onesided conscious outlook. . . .

Dream images of illness, then, communicate a disturbance in the flow of life. Although the dreamer himself may have felt that all is not well and that he is in a bad way, frus-

trated, cut off and depressed; although he may be tormented
and complain and bemoan his fate, he will hardly ever think of
himself as being sick.[16]

Dreams seem to conceal as well as reveal the meaning we long for
in our lives. They distort, reverse, condense, and disguise ordinary
reality, and show us another dimension in which thoughts are in-
stantly manifested. They reveal truth about subjective inner experience, and what is consciously denied tends to surface in nightmares. If
we are angry, upset, anxious, guilty, or sad, these emotions may be
expressed in dreams, even more violently for having been suppressed
in waking consciousness. If I have not acknowledged my anger, for
instance, I am likely to project it onto dream images that will then appear to be angry or threatening.

Dream Interpretation

One effective method for deciphering the messages the psyche offers
to convey to consciousness through dreams is role playing the various
figures in the dream. When one is willing to take the part of every figure in the dream, to own the projections and recognize each one as an
aspect of the whole Self, the process of differentiation and reintegration begins. By learning to do this one can experience what it feels like
to be other than that with which one is consciously identified. This
enables one to view the self and the world from different points of
view, recognizing the relativity and plasticity of them all.

This approach to dreamwork, based on Gestalt therapy, is particularly effective in the process of ego integration that calls for healing the
split between persona and shadow and owning projections. It is also
helpful in identifying various polarities in the psyche and bringing
them into balance. Learning to identify with the context of a dream,
e.g., describing oneself as a house in which the action of the dream
unfolds facilitates the process of disidentification from the melodrama
or the contents of consciousness. When one views oneself as a figure in
the dream from the point of view of the Self as context, one assumes an
altogether different perspective from the ordinary egocentric one.

Sometimes dreams reveal archetypal images that evoke powerful
responses when one is open to encountering them. By interacting with
them with healing awareness, one affirms their healing influence without imposing preconceived egocentric ideas on them. Archetypal images are sometimes experienced as energizers that call forth a variety

of latent potentials. Their power and creative abundance is unfathomable. The problem with symbolic interpretation is that symbols may have different meanings for different people or in different contexts. It seems advisable therefore to investigate such images with an open, inquiring mind, allowing the images to speak for themselves, given the context of the dreamer's personal history and the particular dream in which they appear. Many books on dream interpretation are now available, and perhaps any approach is better than none. However, I would caution the inexperienced observer of dreams to refrain from cookbook interpretations that provide definitive meanings for specific symbolic images. Dreams can best serve their creative and healing functions when viewed in the context of the life of the dreamer, and it is up to the dreamer to accept or reject specific interpretations.

There is no one right way of working with dreams. But methods that do not presume to interpret dreams out of context, that are open-ended and take individual life circumstances into account, seem to be most valuable. Dreaming is a faculty everyone possesses, but awareness of it is often repressed or undeveloped. Learning to use dreams as a source of guidance requires attention, but is possible for anyone.

Dreams can convey messages from any level of consciousness. They are difficult to categorize, however, since they often represent multiple levels and can be deciphered and re-experienced from a variety of perspectives. Some analysts who work with dreams believe that it is a mistake to interpret a dream, and prefer to focus on the feelings evoked by the dream, or allow dream images to speak for themselves in a process of active imagination. Dreams bring to life the imaginal world of the psyche, a powerful resource of inexhaustible abundance. Sometimes dreams have such a powerful emotional impact that interpretations seem superfluous. Nevertheless, I have found that familiarity with the various levels of meaning that can be discerned in a particular dream can deepen understanding and avoid reductionistic approaches that attempt to interpret all dreams from a single perspective.

Wilber suggests reviewing interpretations from all levels of consciousness to find the ones that fit best from the perspective of the dreamer.[17] He suggests beginning from a psychoanalytic viewing frame that presumes classic Freudian psychosexual messages, and moving up to other perspectives such as the humanistic, existential, and transpersonal, in order to view the dream through these frameworks as well. In addition, a dream may be examined for both manifest and latent content. The dream may be conveying literal information or a symbolic message.

When working with dreams in the context of psychotherapy, I usually follow a flexible process that includes the following steps:

1. Getting acquainted with the images as they are.

2. Inquiring into the feeling tone of the dream.

3. Exploring subjective associations and interpretations.

4. When it seems appropriate, role playing or active imagination to complete the process.

Transcendental or transpersonal messages that are inherent in the dream are, in my experience, apprehended intuitively and do not usually require explanation. However, if the dreamer is confused, upset, or anxious in response to a dream that carries transpersonal overtones, the dream can be discussed from whatever perspective the dreamer is prepared to explore. Wilber comments that the more consciously developed a person is, the more he or she will respond to higher levels of interpretation. In any event, whenever one fails to acknowledge multiple ways of perceiving a dream, one may be depriving the dreamer of an opportunity to uncover layers of meaning that are contained within it. For practical purposes, however, one may intuitively respond to a particular dream from one perspective that seems to be an obvious fit and not bother to spend much time on others. The main thing to remember is that interpretations are always partial, colored by feelings, projections, and viewing frames. As long as one is aware of the inherent limitations of interpretation, one can gain both insight and understanding of psychological processes by analyzing content as well as feelings in dreams.

On the other hand, in some cases any interpretation may be superfluous. For example, the following dream of mine had a powerful impact and conveyed an important message, but interpretations seemed unnecessary:

I am riding a bicycle along a muddy, rutted road. It is difficult and I am trying to avoid all sorts of obstacles. Then I remember that I can shift my attention and need not concentrate solely on the road and its obstacles. I focus instead on my pedaling, which is difficult. I need to make an effort to keep going. If I just keep pedaling, I will be all right. Then I notice that someone is riding beside me, and if we pedal in synch—if I adjust

my pedaling to keep time with his—it is easier. I begin to feel
the rhythm of our pedaling and it feels more and more enjoyable. Suddenly we are lifted off the ground and are riding
through the air, quite effortlessly. I feel a strong humming
vibration that seems to connect us as we continue riding joy-
ously above the ground.

Healing Dreams

All healing is essentially the release from fear.—*A Course in Miracles*[18]

Any dream can be viewed as a healing dream. Some dreams can have
a healing effect on the psyche with no interpretation; others become
instruments of healing only if they are perceived in this context. All
dreams can contribute to a sense of wholeness when integrated into
the overall pattern of perception that gives coherence to experience.
When we fall asleep each night, consciousness is freed from the domination of the rational mind, and those aspects of ourselves that are
unavailable in the ordinary waking state come into view.

Healing dreams have been noted in many cultures throughout
history. In ancient Greece people in need of healing would visit the
Temple of Asclepius and ask for a healing dream. The god of healing
was expected to appear in a dream to perform healing. Rituals of purification were performed in preparation for the visitation. In shamanic
cultures, the shaman performs healing in his or her own dream, rather
than in the patient's dream.[19] Both approaches have claimed effectiveness. But healing dreams need not be literally dreams of healing. Any
dream that helps correct imbalances and brings awareness to what has
been repressed or ignored can facilitate healing.

Shamanic traditions view dreaming as a means of healing the soul
of a person who is sick. The sick person is thought to be in trouble
when he or she has lost power or is dis-spirited. The shaman then undertakes a journey to the other worlds, the lower world or the upper
world, in order to retrieve the soul that has been lost or stolen and return it to the sick person. When the person's soul or power is restored,
he or she is healed or made whole again. The process is also healing for
the shaman. In *The Way of the Shaman*, Michael Harner says, "In
shamanism there is ultimately no distinction between helping others
and helping yourself. By helping others shamanically, one becomes
more powerful, self-fulfilled, and joyous."[20]

Modern rituals of dream incubation have also been developed in
connection with healing. Research studies on dream incubation, in

which participants request guidance for specific issues from their dreams, indicate that significant dreams can have a major impact on life decisions. Whether one participates in group rituals of dream incubation or simply records dreams on a regular basis, they can be an inner source of profound healing wisdom.

Dreams also contribute to healing and wholeness insofar as they are a source of empowerment and liberation of intuition. As one learns more about oneself through dreams, one becomes naturally more intuitive.[21] Intuition as a way of knowing that transcends empirical and rational modes of knowing can be an important source of guidance on the spiritual path, but must be tested for validity in order to prevent self-deception. Intuition is subtle and one must remember not to try too hard to grasp it. Given attention, it unfolds spontaneously.

The following dream illustrates for me how intuition operates in relation to our usual methods of trying to figure things out:

I was walking along a familiar path in the country, going steeply uphill. The path became more difficult, almost impassable. I struggled to continue to climb. Suddenly I realized that I did not have to struggle. I could just relax. When I did I began to fly.

Letting go of resistance, as experienced in this dream, can be a significant step in the process of healing and self-transcendence.

Another, more explicit healing dream provided instructions for forming "a healing circle." In the dream, the following communications were received:

Healing occurs when two minds recognize their oneness and become glad. (I recognized this as a quotation from *A Course in Miracles*.) Forming a healing circle is a way of joining for the purpose of mutual Self-healing. These are the steps to be followed:

1. Ask for guidance. Remember that you are not doing anything. Turn the process over to the Holy Spirit, God, or Self.

2. Join hands with palms touching; right palm facing down, left palm facing up.

3. Experience the current of light energy flowing through heart and hands. Self-healing is mutual. The more you

allow, the more you receive, the more you give. (The feeling was very powerful.)

The next morning, when I shared the dream with a friend who was in the hospital recovering from an automobile accident, she seemed grateful. I was reminded again that healing can take place on all levels.

All dreams are creations of the psyche, whether they be sleeping, waking, or lucid dreams. The dreams we seek to actualize in life, the dreams that are fulfilled as well as those that are broken, are given meaning by the dreamer who believes in them. Dream images reflect our interpretations of experience, which can be psychological and/or spiritual. At the same time, if we take them too literally we fall into the trap of mistaking them for ultimate reality. They reflect both fear and desire, and until we know ourselves as dreamers, they seem to have control over us. As mirrors of the psyche they rearrange and impose order on experience, calling attention to what we already know intuitively.

In dreams the psyche asserts its autonomy, upsetting egocentric interpretations of reality and ideas of how things should be. Dreams can literally be revelations of a different order of reality in which the separate self-sense is either maintained or transcended, but is not subject to natural laws of physical reality. Thus one may have dreams of flying or going through solid objects, as well as dreams of death and rebirth.

Fears of physical harm, old age, disease, and death can be confronted and transcended in the dream state, since the dream body has no physical substantiality and dreams of dying are survived. One may experience intense fear in anticipation of physical harm, but the actual experience of pain in dreams of death and dismemberment is insubstantial. However, since the emotional and mental identifications of self remain intact, dreams can create intense emotional anguish and mental agony. If the dream world is viewed as a realm of pure thought and wish fulfillment, the prevailing state of emotional and mental health can be clearly observed.

An intuitive approach to dreams works well when one maintains an attitude of healing awareness with respect to the dream itself and the accompanying associations. I find that even after many years of experience with dream interpretation, deciphering my own dream messages is greatly enhanced by the presence of someone who is willing to provide supportive noninterfering attention. Learning to facilitate dream recall and doing intuitive dreamwork can offer anyone a way of self-healing and guidance on the spiritual path.

Dream Yoga and Subtle Realities

Your sleeping and your waking dreams have different forms, and that is all.—A Course in Miracles[22]

In addition to being a source of healing and inspiration, dreams teach us about nonphysical dimensions of reality where thoughtforms manifested as images appear to be objectively real. This reality interpenetrates our everyday waking reality and tends to be undifferentiated in the absence of Self-awareness. In lucid dreams (i.e., those dreams in which one knows that one is dreaming), awareness may be clearly differentiated from the dream ego that is engaged in the activity of the dream.

Sometimes a *déjà vu* experience in waking life may feel like a lucid dream. A person, place, or event may seem familiar, even when one "knows" that it is being experienced in the ordinary waking state for the first time. Some people have identified *déjà vu* experiences as scenes from dreams that were dreamed prior to the waking event that unfolds in the same way. Others have suggested that thoughts or images that preceded the event in time actually contributed to creating it, and that the *déjà vu* is a remembered image. This suggests waking precognition, in contrast to dreaming precognition. Others suggest that *déjà vu* experiences provide evidence of reincarnation. Whatever the explanation, there are moments when the boundaries between dreaming and waking consciousness seem more permeable. Memories also take on a dreamlike quality, especially as they become blurred with the passage of time. Memories of real events are often confused with dreams or imagined memories and sometimes become indistinguishable. In fact, the boundaries between waking and dreaming consciousness may never be clearly differentiated. Perception of any level of reality is invariably filtered through personal projections, hence the importance of recognizing them.

Self-awareness in the dream state is an integral part of self-knowledge and has its place on the spiritual path. Some spiritual teachers ask their students to tell them their dreams. However, treatment of dreams varies in different traditions. For example, in Zen Buddhism dreams are dismissed as illusion, not to be taken seriously, whereas in some types of yoga, dreaming is said to be the permanent state of mind of a God-tuned master.[23] In some dream yogas sleeping dreams are considered more real than waking perceptions of what we call objective reality. Whether one visits heaven or hell or other regions in the dreamstate, the task is to maintain awareness and develop the capacity for witnessing experience, becoming increasingly lucid in this state. Lucid dreams provide an experience of a subtle level of consciousness that can be used for learning more about how the mind creates subjective reality.

Dream yoga as mental training offers a gateway to self-knowledge that transcends bodily egoic identifications. Tibetan dream yoga suggests the practice of viewing dreams as reality and waking life as a dream. As we become more aware of dreaming we tend to become more conscious in any state of mind. Life itself may be viewed as a lucid dream for a better understanding of the power of beliefs that govern everyday experience. When the ordinary waking state is viewed as a lucid dream, the creations of the mind of the dreamer are more easily recognized. By practicing self-observation in dreams as well as in waking life one may begin to see how one creates experience that seems beyond conscious control and how change occurs with shifting attention and perception.

In my own experience the following dreams provided a taste of the relative reality of different states of consciousness:

I dreamed that I was exploring different realities. A thread of awareness that was sustained through various discontinuous dream scenes allowed me to realize that each one was a world unto itself. I left a nightclub scene that did not hold my interest, and went down a long tunnel into another world. As I made my way into this new reality, I saw that I had entered through a maze, and it would now be impossible to turn back and return the way I had come. So I kept on going, feeling all the time a sense of make-believe, as though I were in Disneyland, experiencing the landscape and the strange creatures that inhabited it as if they were not altogether real, although they seemed perfectly natural. Various monsters that reminded me of dinosaurs, wild animals, and unknown territory all appeared frightening, but failed to terrify me. I knew that if I was dreaming, I could proceed unharmed if I kept my attention on finding my own way. I did not know where to go, but it seemed to make no difference, since I knew it was impossible to find my way out. The further I went, the more real and solid everything became. I followed a little dog for a while, then I found myself walking along a beach, wading in the surf. Eventually I met a group of people and walked with them among the rolling hills. They were also trying to find their way out of this make-believe reality. Each one had a theory about what could get us out of here. One said we should put more effort into walking. In fact, we should all be jogging. Another said we should be doing breathing exercises. Each person had a different idea about what would enable us to escape from this world that was pretty enough, but with which we all seemed dissatisfied. I realized as I watched each one trying to practice the preferred technique more effectively, that the more effort we put into trying to get out, the more deeply immersed and imbedded we became, forgetting that this reality was not the only one. In the moment I felt the "Aha!" of my insight, I woke up.

I dreamed I was at home among the stars in an ocean of bliss, being everything, wanting nothing. Into my vision came a pearl of great beauty, reflecting a brilliant light. It caught my attention and I was drawn into swirling soft mists that enveloped me. I knew I could rest here, for some time, in some place. Then I plunged into darkness and emerged from an ocean to ride horseback on beaches and drive my own car on a road to a city. I entered a marketplace of goods and ideas and carried a ladder on which to climb higher for a better view. I wanted to see more, forgetting that ladders are burdens to be discarded . . . then I remembered the source of my love . . . going nowhere.

Learning to operate in subtle realms of consciousness requires letting go of the exclusive identification with the body or ego as self. This shift is facilitated when death is consciously experienced in dreams, particularly if the dream is lucid. Attitudes toward death can change radically as a result of dreams of dying. One woman who experienced a number of dreams of dying, including dismemberment, found that her fears of dying seemed to disappear as a result of these dreams, and she was able to be with her dying mother with a sense of peace and serenity that would have been inconceivable to her before these dream experiences.

Dreams of awakening, like dreams of dismemberment, death, and resurrection, can be viewed as initiations into realms of subtle consciousness and knowledge. The image of dismemberment is often associated with the beginning of the spiritual journey. When a significant transformation from one level of consciousness to another occurs and one experiences dying to the former identification, the event may be marked by a major dream.

Initiation Dreams

In addition to dreams of awakening and dreams of dying, dreams of initiation ceremonies and esoteric spiritual practices are part of the experience of many spiritual seekers. Meeting the guru on the inner plane of experience is common. For example,

. . . on Wednesday night, as I slept, I became aware of Bhagawan Nityananda's Presence. Then he appeared to me, and he spoke to me throughout the night of my experiences. He told me I should prepare to leave immediately, Thursday, the day before I had planned.[24]

Here we have an example not only of felt presence, but of specific advice, which, in this case, the dreamer chose to follow.

Dreams of initiation or mystical revelation, in which consciousness is temporarily transported into a state that permits a new perception of reality, can have a powerful and long-lasting effect on the dreamer's awareness. The following initiation dream was recorded by a woman, several months prior to a spontaneous awakening of kundalini energy:

I was in India participating in an initiation ceremony of some kind. I felt strange in this exotic environment and a bit frightened about what might take place. I was led from an anteroom, through a series of colorful and extravagantly appointed byzantine-style rooms, down into the earth. I didn't know any of the other initiates who were with me. We went through one room hung with heavy velvet draperies and decorated with intricate filigree carving and colored mosaic windows, and another that was filled with the smoke of incense. I felt I might want to leave, as incense makes me feel claustrophobic, but it seemed imperative that I stay. I knew I must go through this initiation, no matter how uncomfortable I felt. I was seated at a large oval wooden table with about eight other initiates, and we were told that during the ceremony we would

be visited by spirits representing good and evil, love and
death, and each one of us would experience these visitations
differently. We were instructed to rate them on score cards,
according to the level of intensity we felt in their presence. I
decided I was not going to score anything. The ceremony
began and I became aware of a mixture of very subtle energies
and I knew I was undergoing an invisible but powerful change
internally. I felt this was the initiation, but on some level I also
doubted that it was happening—I seemed so peaceful and it
was not particularly dramatic. We were given something to
smoke and some fish to eat. While I was in the process of
analyzing and doubting what I was experiencing an older man
in white robes came into the room and looked at me directly in
the eyes, and then stepped up on a dais behind me and sat
down. Later, still unsure of what had happened, I turned
around and he told me he had been with me all along. He was
aware of my skepticism and encouraged me not to doubt my
experience. I knew he had access to my unconscious and I
knew that he would be with me always. I felt I had completed
the initiation and was prepared to return to the outside world.

Another initiation dream is reported by Da Free John:

One night, in the spring of 1970, I passed from this body during sleep and arrived in subtle form on the inner plane of the
world. There I stayed with an old man who had white hair and
a closely cut white beard. He wore a bandanna around his
forehead, which was the custom of the late saint Sai Baba of
Shirdi. I had met the Siddha, Sai Baba, on the subtle plane.
I was received as if I had been awaited. I was greeted by
the family, friends, and devotees of the old man. He embraced
me with love and told the company I was his son. Then I was
received by all in a celebration that had the informal, family air
and importance of a Jewish Bar Mitzvah.[25]

I remember that when a prominent Tibetan teacher first came to
California many people who met him would subsequently dream
about him. Of these, a significant number felt it was a sign that they
should become his disciples. Spiritual teachers who are adept at working at this level often encourage this form of communication. Sometimes communication exchanges that take place in dreams between

teachers and students are taken quite literally. The following dream is an example of this type of teaching/learning:

I dreamed that my meditation master asked me what I would give him in return for his instruction. I asked him what it was he had actually given me. He said that he had given me courage. "In that case," I replied, "Your reward will be great bliss."

The numinous quality of dreams in which one experiences subtle energies, or tunes into a sense of resonance with creation, or feels filled with light, can be indications of receptivity and readiness in the mind of the dreamer for a new subtle level of consciousness, as well as being important learning experiences in themselves.

Spontaneous awakenings of kundalini energy experienced as electrical currents in the spine are sometimes experienced in a half-sleep state, when conscious controls are relaxed. When there is no major obstruction these occurrences need not be psychologically disruptive. However, in cases where the person is unprepared and does not understand what is happening, such experiences can be extremely frightening and stressful. The person who, by virtue of listening to dreams with some consistency, is not taken by surprise by a powerful experience that may erupt when conscious controls are deeply relaxed is better prepared to integrate the experience.

When such experiences are appropriately integrated they can have powerful healing effects. One client reported frequent jolts of energy in the spine that resembled electrical currents when dreaming of a spiritual teacher. Being able to discuss the experience and allow it rather than trying to suppress it was helpful. She began paying more attention to diet and physical fitness, and also became more disciplined in her meditation practice. As her work in therapy continued and some emotional blocks were dissolved, she experienced less violent disruptions of sleep by the flow of energy and found herself better able to function effectively with more energy.

A dream that is clearly numinous, conveying a feeling of supernatural healing within it, can be a turning point in the life of the dreamer. For example, shortly after beginning therapy one man dreamed that he was caught in a pit, with only head and shoulders above the ground. The earth was unstable, as if in an earthquake. He was afraid of being swallowed up and buried alive. He called for help and a Christ figure appeared, extending his hand. When the dreamer reached out and touched the extended hand he felt himself become charged with radiant light energy. He woke up with renewed intention to change his life's work. The powerful impact of this dream was such that it did not require interpretation for its healing effect to become apparent.

Examining similarities between waking reality and the dream state can help in understanding subtle levels of consciousness and how they operate. One learns to recognize the role one plays in creating experiences that seem to happen spontaneously in each moment. Paying attention to how reality operates in the dream state can also facilitate seeing how subtle changes in attitude and perception influence experience. When one is very active on the physical, emotional, and mental levels of consciousness, awareness of this subtle realm may be suppressed, but becomes available when attention is directed to it. In Tibetan practice lucid dreaming is said to be enhanced by meditation on the throat center prior to falling asleep. In this way awareness of the fifth chakra can be consciously integrated.

Sleeping and waking dreams emanate from the same sources of personal and collective consciousness. Self-knowledge enhances understanding of dreams and vice versa. Becoming more conscious of our dreams and in our dreams can have a profound effect on awareness of every aspect of well-being.

The Way of Dreams

Those who are awake have one world in common. Those who are asleep live each in a separate world.—Heraclitus[26]

Spiritual awakening is in part a recognition of the pervasiveness of dreaming in every aspect of our lives. The shared reality that shapes our common destiny is a world of dreams. Dreams of healing, dreams of progress, dreams of future events can and do come true. In the search for wisdom and healing, dreams offer important information, particularly in regard to the nature of mind as the source of good and evil, pleasure and pain, and all the dichotomies and conflicts of the human condition.

Although dreams and fantasies are often terrifying to the ego, the life of the psyche is not limited to the egoic identity that lives in terror of its own demise. Dreams of fear can be changed to dreams of healing in the light of consciousness. Shamans are masters of this process. Michael Harner writes,

Shamanism goes far beyond a primarily self-concerned transcendence of ordinary reality. It is transcendence for a broader purpose, the helping of humankind. The enlightenment of shamanism is the ability to light up what others perceive as darkness, and thereby to *see* and to journey on behalf of . . . humanity. . . .[27]

Dreams are persistent. They come and go in different forms, engendering fear and desire, hope and despair. Dreams can infuse life with meaning. They transcend the ordinary limitations of time and space and reveal subtle realms of consciousness where the power of the mind in creating experience is uncontested. Dreams bring formlessness into form and then dissolve again into nothingness. In dreams we taste heaven and hell, higher and lower levels of consciousness that contain the seeds of healing and wholeness. Understanding dreams transforms them into instruments of healing. Perhaps as we learn to expand awareness in the dream state we may also learn to transform collective waking dreams of fear to healing dreams for humankind.

Experiential Exercises

Recording Your Dreams

In order to remember dreams accurately, it is best to record them as soon as you wake up. It is a good idea to keep a paper and pencil or a tape recorder next to the bed in order to be able to make a record of dreams immediately upon waking up. A good practice is to record the dream exactly as you remember it, without any explanations or commentaries. After the dream is completely recorded, add any associations or insights or memories that are triggered by the dream. Later you may want to review the account again to see if anything else occurs to you which was not apparent at first. If you choose to work on the dream with a partner or a therapist, you may want to record their comments and insights as well. No matter who offers to interpret your dream, remember that you are the final authority on what it means in the context of your life. It is up to you to decide whether or not a particular interpretation fits.

The following questions may be useful for understanding your dream more clearly:

1. What is an appropriate title for this particular dream? Is there an obvious message to this dream? Is there a particular message that might have some relevance to your life at present?

2. What is the predominant feeling tone of this dream?

3. What are the principal qualities of the different characters in the dream? Are you aware of these qualities in yourself?

4. Can you view the dream from the point of view of one of the other characters in the dream?

5. Is this dream a recurring dream? Is the theme familiar, or does it seem entirely new?

6. Does this dream seem to be a "big dream" or does it seem to be an ordinary dream?

7. If you were to make an affirmation for yourself from this dream, what would it be?

8. Is there any particular action you would like to undertake as a result of what you have learned from this dream?

9. Would you like to continue this dream in your imagination?

10. Would you like to give this dream a different ending?

11. If you could redream this dream, how would you change it?

When a dream seems particularly significant, it is a good idea to review it soon after you have recorded it, and then again at a later time, perhaps the next day. Many times when you return to a dream after some time has passed you are able to see it more clearly and find meaning in it that was not apparent at first. Some people prefer to wait a few days before working on a dream, simply allowing the images to remain in awareness in order to get better acquainted with them. If you choose to follow a particular method of dream interpretation, remember that no one method is final or absolute. It is better to keep an open mind about possible interpretations than to assume that the first interpretation is complete.

Dream recall tends to improve when there is an intention to work with dreams. Dreams respond to consistent attention, and become more available when they are valued. Everyone dreams every night. Remembering your dreams may be easier if you take some time to be quiet when you first wake up in the morning and reflect on what you were dreaming before getting up. Some people find that setting an alarm allows them to remember dreams more easily since they are more likely to awaken in the middle of the dream when the alarm goes off. However, you can experiment and try out different methods to see which one works the best for you. It is particularly helpful to have a dream friend or a partner with whom you can share your dreams. Many of my clients in psychotherapy report remembering dreams much more easily after we start discussing them in therapy. If you have a friend or a family member who enjoys sharing dreams, this can be very supportive in paying attention to them.

If you are listening to someone else's dream, it is best not to offer interpretations but to invite the person who is sharing the dream to articulate and communicate their own associations and interpretations in order that the meaning of the dream can emerge from the psyche of the dreamer. Sharing your dreams can contribute to healing and wholeness by maintaining balance in the psyche.

Dream Reflections

In addition to paying attention to the dreams you have when you sleep each night, you can also become more conscious of dreams you are living out in the ordinary waking state. If life can be a lucid dream rather than an unconscious dream, creative changes may be initiated more skillfully.

If we want to live in peace in a world where health and wholeness is possible for everyone, we need to be open to understanding both waking and sleeping dreams. Have you lived all your life in your own secret dream world? Have you been willing to view the world through the eyes of another person's dream?

In psychotherapy we sometimes use words to transform dreams from nightmares into pleasant adventures. Anyone can learn to change subjective reality by developing healing awareness and choosing to live more consciously. Every dream has both a positive and a negative aspect.

If, for example, you were to dream that you entered the world for the purpose of healing, you might be expected to transform this world from the dreary one that some have made into one that they would rather have. Some people might want you to perform miracles for them without bothering to learn how to heal themselves. Others might want to learn a few tricks of the trade for personal gain. You might want to learn to teach others how to heal themselves. Remember that becoming identified with the archetype of the wounded healer is to remain unhealed.

If you dream of a quality that you want to cultivate, it can become yours if you remember every day that you want it. Make up an affirmation for yourself. For example, "I am a loving person," or "I am at peace." You can affirm any quality by naming it, experiencing what it feels like, becoming it in imagination, and giving it away. Ideas and qualities increase in power by being shared.

It is possible to awaken from dreams of separation to awareness of the transpersonal Self we share. The timeless unity that is forgotten in private egocentric dreams of heroism can be remembered. The awareness we need for healing and wholeness is available. Even dreams of death and dismemberment can help us remember the Self. As we learn to see the Self in others and begin to listen to dreams in the context of healing, we may contribute to creating a shared vision of a peaceful world.

9 Healing Relationships

Spiritual practice always involves going beyond simply finding out who one is to a level of finding out also what one needs to do in the world.
—*Gerald May*[1]

Psychological health on the spiritual path depends to a great extent on healing relationships. How one responds to others reflects one's state of consciousness, and wholeness depends not only on personal health, but on satisfying relational exchange at each stage. Jonas Salk points out that evolution itself is a process of changing relationships.[2]

The purification required by spiritual disciplines is partly a process of transcending egoic desires in relationship and letting go of pride, guilt, and unworthiness. Relationships with teachers, guides, or peers can be particularly helpful in reflecting projections and preventing self-deception. Truth is recognized, not learned, and those who would travel the spiritual path to completion must be willing to recognize themselves in others without pretenses or defenses.

Every relationship is partly determined by who and what we think we are. Self-concept influences *who* we relate to, and *how* we relate to them. As we change, our relationships change, but whatever form they take, they can serve as mirrors of unacknowledged parts of ourselves. Intimate relationships can be particularly helpful in preventing what Arthur Diekman calls "premature sanctity" on the spiritual path. As one transcends the desire for spiritual specialness and grows into awareness of the transpersonal Self, one may choose consciously to work on healing relationships.

Improving the quality of relationships, like improving self-concept, depends in part on the quality of attention that is given to them. Healing awareness can be expanded by learning to listen to others as well as to oneself. It is relatively easy to feel quiet, peaceful, and self-transcendent when one is alone in a quiet place. It is a far greater challenge to extend that peace to others when one is in close contact with them.

Traditional wisdom cautions that spiritual development cannot be completed alone. The spiritual journey that begins as a solitary pursuit can come to completion when it is expressed in conscious relationships. For some, marriage becomes a consciously shared journey.[3] Others may find companionship in community. Whether one travels the spiritual path alone or in partnership, one needs relationships to help one recognize blind spots, acknowledge interdependence, and transcend illusions of isolation. Everyone can benefit from relationships with spiritual friends. Relationships based on mutual love and respect are essential to healing and wholeness. In Buddhism the sangha, the community of fellow seekers, is considered a jewel—one of the gifts or treasures of the spiritual path.

As one becomes increasingly sensitive to states of consciousness, one may be drawn to seeking relationships with others who, by virtue of their own awareness, can reflect and amplify attitudes that are conducive to healing. Eventually one may see the Self reflected in everyone, not only in those who are conscious of it. Along the way it can help to be among people who share an appreciation of it.

Meeting someone who is truly awake can be an experience of feeling transparent. If someone seems to be able to see right through you and know you as intimately as you know yourself, it may be exhilarating or frightening, depending on whether or not you are trying to hide something. Ram Dass used to tell stories about his guru, who seemed to know everything about him and yet was totally accepting.

Everyone longs for such unconditional love, but removing the veil of separation and leaving the psyche totally exposed can be frightening. Sometimes one worries that another will find fault and be critical. But fear of being seen is based on a presumption of guilt. The criticism one fears is often a projection. To the extent that one has not accepted oneself, one cannot expect to be accepted by others, nor can one accept others as they are. The overall quality of one's relationships depends on how willing one is to be open, accepting, and loving rather than fearful, covert, and defensive.

If the risk of dropping pretenses is taken, feeling seen and accepted can help one feel loved and whole. An experience of unconditional love can also help one accept oneself and others better. Sometimes unconditional love is mistakenly equated with passivity or martyrdom in relationship. One way of recognizing a relationship in which unconditional love is present is that it is always safe to tell the truth in any communication within it. Unconditional love is a source of healing in any relationship, but only when one is willing to hide nothing can one open to giving and receiving this love. In the meantime, practicing healing awareness in relationships can be a way of expanding a capacity for love and trust.

The healing power of unconditional love is no secret, but as long as one is afraid to trust, one can neither receive it nor offer it. Unfortunately, fear of loneliness, rejection, and loss cuts one off from both inner and outer sources of love and thus exacerbates feelings of deprivation. As long as one feels guilty, needy, or deprived, one inhibits the very expression of love that is desired.

Attachment to an egoic self-concept can be a major obstacle to the experience of intimacy and love in relationship. Yet the thought of giving up separateness makes the ego shudder. The transition from an egoic to transpersonal sense of identity is often marked by a dark night, not of the soul, but of the ego. The egoic self likes to think of itself as separate, independent, and in control of things. Those experiences that it cannot control it resists. Just as the normal developmental transition from dependence to independence is experienced as frightening and difficult at times, the transition from independence to interdependence can also seem threatening. Nonetheless it is essential to healing and wholeness.

When identification with a mental egoic self-concept is relinquished in favor of transpersonal Self-awareness, the desire for control in relationship may be abandoned in favor of mutuality and joining in a co-creative process. This change implies a shift away from the polarity of dominance/submission to a position of transcendent witnessing. It does not mean that one becomes a passive observer of life, but rather that one is less concerned with personal gain, recognizing that one's own best interests need not be opposed to the best interests of others. From this viewpoint, what one does for others one does for oneself, quite literally, since consciousness is fundamentally one. Attempts to manipulate and control relationships may then be replaced by a willingness to delight in surprise and to surrender to a process of mutual discovery.

Transcending egoic identifications further affects relationships insofar as it enhances a capacity for empathy and compassion, inner vision, and understanding. Accepting and understanding others depends on a willingness to accept and understand oneself. Social knowledge, the knowledge required for establishing harmonious relationships among people, said E. B. Schumacher, can only be obtained by understanding the inner experiences of other human beings. Schumacher felt that obtaining access to this knowledge was one of our most important tasks as social beings. This access can be gained only through self-knowledge. He said,

It is a grave error to accuse a man who pursues self-knowledge of 'turning his back on society.' The opposite would be more nearly true: that a man who fails to pursue self-knowledge is and remains a danger to society, for he will tend to misunderstand everything that other people say or do, and remain blissfully unaware of the significance of many of the things he does himself.[4]

To the extent that consciousness remains undeveloped, mistaken assumptions about the consequences of certain actions may indeed be dangerous to ourselves and others.

The Social Self

Healing at any level may be considered a function of the social self insofar as it involves relational exchange between people. The social self refers specifically to the self as expressed through relationships. It can be differentiated from the personal (egocentric) self and the universal (transpersonal) Self. These distinctions do not correspond to levels of consciousness or stages of self-development, since they are present at all levels. In other words, one may experience physical, emotional, mental, existential, and spiritual levels of consciousness in both personal growth and social development. Likewise, one may view the personal, social, and universal aspects of Self from the position of identifying with a mental egoic, existential, or transpersonal self-concept.

The social self can be a bridge between the personal and universal aspects of self. It may be an expression of either or both. Relationships are not the same when they are viewed from a purely personal perspective as when they are viewed from the perspective of shared universal consciousness. From a transpersonal perspective the universal Self is expressed *through* the personal self in relationship and social interaction. The universal underlies both personal and social expressions of self.

Characteristics of the social self can be discerned in archetypal patterns that shape behavior. When these patterns are recognized they can be changed. For example, the tendency to re-enact a family pattern by choosing a spiritual teacher or marriage partner that resembles a parent is one way in which unconscious patterns can be perpetuated. When the social self is differentiated from the personal and universal self, it may be experienced as a creative free agent that can contribute to healing, rather than being confined to patterns of conditioned reactivity.

The social self is perceived differently from a transpersonal perspective than from a strictly egocentric one. A direct experience of the universal Self that reveals unity consciousness can radically alter experiences of the social self. Instead of using relationships for personal growth or getting something for oneself, one may see them as an opportunity for healing and mutually expanding Self-awareness. Just as one cannot know others without knowing oneself, one cannot know oneself fully unless the social self and relationships are understood. Qualities of the social self are evident in the way one treats oneself as well as other people. If you think you are more tolerant of others, or that you expect more or less from yourself than from others, you may be mistaken. One cannot truly accept others unless one also accepts oneself, and self-acceptance at any level is essential for satisfying relationships. Whereas psychotherapy tends to focus on self-acceptance and self-forgiveness, Christian spirituality tends to emphasize the importance of forgiving others. Both aspects seem necessary if the social self is to become an effective healing agent.

In the absence of self-acceptance, relationships with an intimate other, with family, community, the world, nature, and the universe may be confined to fulfillment of social role expectations. When the social self is largely governed by social rules and conditioning, unsatisfying, conditioned patterns of behavior in relationships tend to be repeated until a conscious choice is made. One can persist in the same pattern or risk change. As one becomes more aware of existential freedom, social roles may be freed from early conditioning and used appropriately to promote healing and wholeness. If every encounter with another is viewed as an opportunity to heal and extend love, one may learn to heal and be healed in relationship. This can happen more easily when the universal Self is experienced as a shared source of healing, not as an attribute that is personally possessed. Universal love may then be reflected through the social self in any relationship.

A relationship can be defined as a healing relationship if it nurtures growth toward wholeness and removes barriers to Self-awareness and love. When the inward arc of consciousness is given priority,

a loving relationship with a teacher may become increasingly important. If one finds a teacher who can guide one toward wholeness, a
genuine healing relationship may develop.

In secular Western cultures the therapeutic relationship, when
developed in depth, can be a source of genuine healing. Insofar as
depth psychology is concerned with healing the psyche, it provides a
useful model of a healing relationship in which the social self is the
instrument of healing, while the universal transpersonal Self is the
source that informs the interaction. Observation of relationship, like
self-observation, seems most reliable when it is dispassionate, free
from judgments and evaluations. We will therefore examine the
therapeutic relationship not to evaluate it, but to deepen our understanding of how healing takes place.

Therapeutic Relationships

Therapeutic relationships are often viewed as healing relationships,
but most psychotherapists readily acknowledge that they are "unhealed healers." They may or may not be coping adequately with their
personal relationships and may or may not make clear the distinctions
between medical and growth-oriented models of therapy. Few are
trained in contemplative disciplines and many have hardly begun the
journey of the inward arc. Some may have had some experiences of
self-transcendence, but it is rare to find one who has attained self-mastery or transcendent insight. This does not mean that a therapist of
limited experience cannot be helpful in resolving personal problems
and facilitating growth at stages of development up to and including
his or her own. But the depth of the work is necessarily limited by the
stage of the therapist.

A recent survey conducted by the California State Psychological
Association's task force on spirituality pointed to the total lack of education in spiritual issues in most graduate training programs, despite
the fact that clinicians often have to deal with these issues in their
work. Therapists who are unfamiliar with the inward arc of human
development and some of the difficulties that may be encountered are
ill-prepared to provide guidance in this domain. Those who have not
read the literature in transpersonal psychology may not even realize
that they could develop greater skills in this area. Fortunately, the
number of therapists who are undertaking spiritual disciplines on their
own is rapidly growing. Many psychotherapists who consider the essence of psychotherapy to be caring for the soul and healing the psyche
are not satisfied with traditional training. As they continue to grow

toward wholeness themselves, they may become increasingly effective as healers without claiming spiritual specialness.

Acknowledging that one may be an unhealed healer can be a useful safeguard against identification with the healer archetype,[5] but this does not imply that being unhealed is a desirable condition. Romanticizing the unhealed healer as one who participates in the suffering of humanity does not necessarily promote healing. Furthermore, the assumption that healers must remain in a condition of partial incompleteness can become a self-fulfilling prophecy. Acknowledging incompleteness is wise, but not if it is used as an excuse to justify perpetuating it.

Healing at a particular level of consciousness tends to be effective to the extent that the healer has already transcended that particular level. A competent therapist may be able to work effectively *with* others who are at any level on the developmental spectrum, since the *process* of moving through psychological blocks to further development is the same at each level. However, the further the therapist has evolved through the stages of Self-awareness at various levels of consciousness, the more effective he or she is likely to be as a healer. In Tibetan medicine emptiness and compassion are said to be the principal weapons of the healer.[6]

Being an effective healer does not mean that one will necessarily identify with the role of being a healer. Wholeness presupposes transcendence of any social role, no matter how lofty. From a transpersonal perspective the healed healer is not one who has resolved all conflicts on an ego level, for this is impossible. The mental egoic self always perceives itself as incomplete, dissatisfied, and conflicted. By definition it is not whole. Rather, a healed healer, like a spiritual master, is one who has *transcended* ego, one who is no longer concerned with issues of approval, power, or personal gain in relationship. By virtue of identifying with the transpersonal Self rather than the mental egoic or existential self, a healer is capable of *acting on* the mind, emotions, and body for the purpose of facilitating self-healing and wholeness.

A healed healer, by his or her presence, can provide the context of a healing relationship for any interaction. This does not imply that the healer has no ego, but that he or she is free of egocentric objectives in the relationship. The therapeutic relationship, then, can be a healing relationship to the extent that the personal concerns of the therapist are out of the way. The social self can then become an effective instrument of healing, provided it is grounded in transcendent insight and Self-awareness.

The therapist as healer may know that the psyche is naturally inclined toward self-healing and wholeness. When this natural impulse for development is impaired, painful symptoms may develop. Help may be sought only if the pain becomes unbearable. Therapy often begins with symptom relief, and it may end there. The effectiveness of a therapist as healer, however, can be greatly enhanced by training awareness.

Working in a context of transpersonal rather than egoic identification can have a liberating effect on both therapist and client, who are then free to choose the level of their work and the depth of their relationship. A healed healer does not *do* anything from an egoic perspective. But in bringing healing awareness to any relationship he or she provides the optimum conditions for the natural self-healing process of the psyche to unfold.

Personal Relationships

Formal therapeutic relationships are by no means the only ones in which healing occurs. Healing can be facilitated through any relationship in which open communication is established in a context of healing awareness. The same principles that pertain to healing the individual psyche can be applied to relationships. A relationship can then be viewed as both the object and the instrument of healing.

Conscious love is of central importance to healing relationships, but it may not seem easy to practice. Different relationships call forth different types of love. For example, a good therapeutic relationship may evoke filial love, which is quite different from passionate, erotic love. Yet the source of all types of love is the universal, transpersonal Self. Knowing that the source is within every one can make giving and receiving love less threatening than thinking that love must be earned or manipulated out of somebody else. While everyone longs for unconditional love, it is the direct experience of one's own capacity for love, as in the opening of the heart chakra, that conveys knowledge of its universal presence.

A healing relationship can be any one that favors the development of awareness, self-esteem, trust, growth, freedom, well-being, and transcendence. A healing relationship makes it safe to let go of masks and defenses, and allows one to be fully present in a free feeling-exchange with another person. Genuine satisfaction in relationship is enhanced by letting go of egoic defensiveness and practicing healing awareness. When one learns to give loving, noninterfering attention and communicate truthfully, favorable conditions for healing are established. Removing barriers of fear, expectation, and pretense facilitates release at the emotional level and correction of perceptual distortion at the mental level.

This process may begin by identifying barriers that inhibit communication in order to let them go. Some of these barriers may be familiar and easy to identify. Some that have served a purpose at one stage of development may become impediments to healing and wholeness at a later stage. Other barriers may be unconscious. Ego defenses, for example, may be consciously justified or quite unconscious. Familiar habitual defenses can be barriers to healing and effective communications in any relationship.

Defenses

Ego defenses are coping devices used primarily to protect a self-image. They are learned early and used unconsciously, in the belief that they are necessary for survival. During the early years of ego development they protect the emerging egoic self-concept against whatever is perceived as threatening or unacceptable. Unfortunately, defenses also constrict awareness and distort perception, and tend to perpetuate the conditions that are defended against. For example, repressing anger in fear of disapproval can result in a buildup of resentment that increases the likelihood of angry, alienating behavior. This is not to say that anger should always be expressed, but appropriate expression and appropriate suppression are often confused with pathological excesses.

When defenses remain unconscious, inner and outer reality may become indistinguishable (projection). In relationships this is typically expressed as justification for being angry because the other person is angry. Projection as a defense attributes to others the qualities one does not want to see in oneself. Other common defenses exclude reality (denial), reverse reality (reaction formation), avoid reality (repression), redefine reality (rationalization), or withdraw from reality (regression).[7] Unconscious defenses may be appropriately used for the protection of ego identity at earlier stages of development, but they can be major obstacles to Self-awareness and healing relationships on the inward arc.

Working through defenses is, once again, a process of differentiation, observation, disidentification, and transcendence. The major defenses may be identified as follows:

1. Projection
Projection of internal feelings on the external world usually means

seeing what one does not like about oneself in somebody else. For example, one of my clients was always angry with her coworkers whom she regarded as "competitive cutthroats." As she became more accepting of her own ambitions she gradually became less critical and more successful. Scapegoating is an example of projection that involves a whole group of people projecting their own shadow onto the group or individual that is a scapegoat. The term itself is derived from the ancient practice of sacrificing goats for the purification of the tribe among the Hebrews. The sins of the tribe would be "projected" into the goat, which would then be slain or driven out into the desert, and presumably everyone would feel better temporarily. Unfortunately, the relief that projection provides is temporary and ineffective. Projection can also be positive, such as when one attributes wisdom and intelligence to someone who seems to embody good qualities that one fails to recognize in oneself. Projection always influences perception.

2. Denial

Denial is the refusal to acknowledge what one does not want to see. For example, pretending not to care about a lover or spouse being unfaithful is one form of denial that is prevalent in open relationships. Denial is also evident in refusal to acknowledge a particular problem, such as alcoholism. Both alcoholics and co-alcoholics are notoriously good at denial. Perhaps the most prevalent form of denial in our culture is the denial of death.[8]

3. Reaction Formation

Reaction formation is the process whereby one becomes the opposite of what one fears. For example, a male in a culture that values machismo may be fearful of his own homosexual inclinations and become adamantly antihomosexual. If his own homosexual feelings are ruthlessly repressed, he finds himself hating homosexuals.

4. Repression

Repression involves selective forgetting of unpleasant memories or painful feelings. Guilt is often repressed. Consequently incidents in early childhood associated with guilt are forgotten. Unfortunately painful feelings that are repressed and consciously forgotten do not go away. Given the appropriate stimulus they sometimes resurface in a seemingly incomprehensible and distorted form. Repression also binds energy and has a deadening effect. When repressed emotion is released through catharsis in therapy, more psychic energy becomes available. Re-experiencing and releasing feelings in a safe healing relationship can be a great relief. On the other hand, when repression remains unconscious, it contributes to maintaining projection, denial and reaction formation.

5. Rationalization
Rationalization is the process whereby one explains and justifies whatever thoughts, feelings or actions one has judged to be unacceptable. For example, angry outbursts may be rationalized as therapeutic when they are actually self-indulgent.

6. Regression
Regression is reverting to an earlier level of development in an attempt to avoid anxiety. Feeling overwhelmed by some problem can result in behaving in a helpless, childlike manner, hoping that someone will come to the rescue. If the ploy is successful, it may become a habit. If it fails, it is likely to breed resentment. At later stages of development on the inward arc, regression may involve reverting to egocentric behavior.

All defenses are used in the service of ego for the purpose of maintaining an acceptable self-concept and ostensibly for maintaining relationships with others. Defenses are considered essential for building ego structure and are therefore necessary at earlier stages of development. However, once established, they tend to become obstacles to further growth. Furthermore, they tend to perpetuate the threats they are used to defend against. Denial, for example, does not get rid of painful feelings. On the contrary, denial prevents discharge and release. What is avoided and buried becomes entrenched. Likewise, if one projects shadow qualities onto others, refusing to recognize such qualities in oneself, one tends to become fearful of intimacy in relationship and feel helpless and unable to change.

The more defensive one is, the more perception is distorted and the more one is subject to self-deception. Self-deception can be a major obstacle to healing, and almost everyone needs help from an outside observer, be it a therapist, teacher, or friend, in clearing it up. When one does not see oneself clearly, one cannot see others clearly, and one remains caught in a world of illusion where genuine presence and authentic contact with others is impossible.

When one is defensive, one has perceived others as threatening. If this is the case, one would not want anyone to get too close. Thus defenses designed to protect self-image effectively keep others away and preclude trust. Healing occurs when one is willing to risk being and expressing all that one is in relationship.

Letting Go of Defenses

Even when one can see that the image one is protecting is not the Self, but an illusory, unnecessary self-concept, letting go of defenses may not be easy. One must trust enough to risk defenselessness in a relationship if one wants to participate in healing relationships.

Unfortunately, trying to get rid of defenses only reinforces them. Resistance causes persistence. The more one tries to avoid a certain experience, such as feeling rejected, the more one tends to encounter it. Conversely, the willingness to experience it in spite of fear provides an opportunity for new learning. When undesirable experiences are defensively avoided (e.g., "I'll reject you before you reject me," or "I won't get close to anyone so I won't be rejected"), one deprives oneself of opportunities for change and healing. It is easy to spot an individual with a "chip on the shoulder," who alienates others by continually justifying and explaining his or her behavior in an effort to appear acceptable. It is more difficult to become aware of the subtle habits of thought and behavior that reinforce patterns in one's life that one wants to change. When this is recognized, one may find that communication in a healing relationship is more effective than doing battle with defenses and trying to change oneself.

Asking oneself the question, "What am I defending against?" can be useful as part of the process of differentiating fears. Naming what one most fears in a relationship, whether it is rejection, abandonment, or violence, can help overcome the fear. When one tries to hide fear, it tends to get worse and inhibit both self-expression and communication. Identifying specific fears and communicating them to someone who does not share them can provide relief and reassurance.

Examining fears with healing awareness may reveal that all fears are future-oriented. What one fears is always in the future. Being present in this moment one may be fine, yet plagued with anxiety of what might happen or might not happen sometime later.

John was a man who had grown up on the streets of a big city and had frequently been beaten up on his way to school as a youngster. He recalled that when actually being hurt he was not afraid, but he lived with constant fear, anticipating the next time. He had learned to cope adaptively, though unconsciously, by reaction formation. He consis-

tently sought out situations that frightened him in order to confront
them. He discovered that when he confronted his own worst specific
fears they disappeared. By the time I talked with him there was not
much in the external world that he was afraid of, but he was still
plagued by feelings of anxiety, and was afraid of his own anger.

John was ready to own his projections. He realized that when he
felt hostile, others appeared to be hostile; whenever he was scared, he
would get angry and this gave him the illusion of feeling powerful.
When he was angry he did not have to feel the underlying fear. But the
nonspecific anxiety did not go away until he was able to acknowledge,
confront, and communicate his fear. As it dissolved, his anger also
abated. He recognized that he was afraid of his own hostility projected
onto others. Feelings of guilt generated fear of retribution, and he always found ways of punishing himself either consciously or unconsciously. As he continued to work on uncovering fears he slowly
realized that everything he feared, moment by moment, was in his
own mind. What he most feared were his own thoughts. Gradually, as
he practiced developing awareness and risking open communication,
he became increasingly at ease with himself and others. His willingness to trust the process in a healing relationship enabled him to let go
of the past and reclaim his capacity for intimacy.

When fears are examined, they can usually be traced to a thought,
an image, or a fantasy about what might or might not happen in the
future. Occasionally one might be in physical danger, but many people
who enjoy dangerous sports feel exhilarated rather than afraid in moments of danger. What concerns us for healing purposes is not the
appropriate flight or fight response, but the inappropriate ones that
occur in response to perceived psychological threats in relationships.
Egoic fears of what people think, of being wrong, or of making mistakes interfere with communication, satisfaction, and healing in relationships. Awareness reveals that this type of fear stems mainly from
disowned prejudices that are projected onto others. If one wants to be
free from interpersonal fear one must be willing to reclaim projections
that are hostile and frightening. We literally scare ourselves, not only
in nightmares but in ordinary consciousness as well.

Approaching Defenselessness

On the spiritual path difficulty is encountered by the aspirant who
unconsciously projects fearful impulses such as anger onto deities.
The vengeful God or wrathful deities threaten death and destruction

to the ego as punishment for sins, real or imagined. In medieval Christianity the devil personified unacceptable impulses. "The devil made me do it" became a common excuse for avoiding personal responsibility.

Guilt has often been used as a weapon of control and manipulation by parents and organizations. Many people regard guilt as necessary for maintaining social order. Yet guilt breeds fear and resentment, stress and tension, anxiety and conflict. Guilt can be a major obstacle to healing relationships. Feelings of guilt always interfere with trust and invite punishment in some form. Once again, it is in open communication rather than concealment that release from guilt can be found.

Letting go of defenses and releasing fear and guilt are essential for healing relationships. When one has examined what one is defending and what one is defending against, one may be willing to risk being vulnerable. By risking defenselessness in a healing relationship one learns to trust the process and the inner guidance that leads to wholeness. Psychological health and self-esteem are not contingent on what other people think, say, or do, but on Self-awareness and understanding. As one learns to trust oneself, one becomes trustworthy, and in healing oneself one becomes capable of healing relationships.

Letting go of defenses means forgiving oneself for past mistakes and present inadequacies. It also means forgiving others for not being what one thinks they should be. If to understand all is to forgive all, then lack of forgiveness implies inadequate understanding. If, in the light of consciousness, there is nothing to forgive, forgiving oneself and others can be considered an expedient teaching that has a healing effect on the psyche as long as one believes that there is something to be forgiven. Practicing forgiveness can be powerfully effective in healing relationships.

Forgiving others has always been advocated in Christianity, but all too often the need for it is associated with judgment and guilt. In psychotherapy, forgiving oneself is more likely to be emphasized, as in learning to accept and express negative emotions such as anger. Healing the psyche, like healing relationships, however, depends on forgiving both oneself and others. In the Christian mystical teachings of *A Course in Miracles*, forgiveness is said to be "the key to happiness," and "a key to meaning in a world that seems to make no sense."[9] Certainly practicing forgiveness in relationships seems to benefit everyone and harm no one.

Risking defenselessness for healing does not mean that one cannot feel hurt or experience disappointment, but such feelings are no longer perceived as a threat to self-image. The compassionate love of a healing relationship, based on genuine concern for the other, need not be frightening. In a romantic relationship the challenge to be truthful and defenseless may seem more difficult, but is not essentially different. If the person with whom one's ego is identified leaves or betrays the relationship, one may feel devastated. Yet this wound too can be healed in the presence of the unconditional love of a healing relationship.

Activating the healing power of the inner source of love in the psyche is essentially what is required for developing trust and healing relationships. Self-awareness, grounded in experience of the universal Self, is not only an asset in relationship, it is also the basis of healing. In growing toward wholeness and developing a deeper understanding of the psyche, one becomes trustworthy by learning to trust. If I think my survival and well-being depends on your behavior, I will find it difficult to let go of defensiveness even in the best of circumstances. Only when we can both see our relationship as an opportunity to express love from the inner wellsprings of the universal Self, can we have a truly healing relationship that will nurture our wholeness and enable us to extend healing awareness to others.

When trust has been experienced in the context of a therapeutic relationship where agreements are clearly defined, trust may be extended more easily in other relationships. As long as risk is avoided, belief in the necessity of defenses is constantly reinforced by experience. For example, if I react defensively to someone who questions what I am doing, that person may also feel attacked and react defensively. If I have assumed that people who question me are hostile, I will perceive my assumptions as being correct. On the other hand, if I respond in a friendly way, the interaction could result in a useful healing exchange for both of us.

Instead of strengthening one, ego defenses tend to perpetuate feelings of inadequacy and vulnerability. As long as one feels it is necessary to hide pain, fear, guilt, or anger, a healing relationship will not be very effective. Only when one can risk letting go can one discover that defenses are appropriately outgrown as consciousness evolves.

Every defense that distorts perception presents an obstacle to awareness of wholeness. When one avoids what seems threatening in relationships, one cannot see that the threat itself is a subjective interpretation of reality that can be changed. One cannot discover that a situation is harmless as long as one avoids it. Thus defenses that were useful in establishing ego identity become major barriers to growing beyond ego.

Mutually satisfying, healing relationships depend on trusting experiences of the universal Self. This means seeing through egoic distinctions and appreciating the common ground of being. Humanity shares a common biological, psychological, and spiritual potential. Everyone experiences birth and death and finds ways of relating to other people. Everyone experiences aspects of the personal, social, and universal Self at some level, with more or less awareness. Everyone experiences love and fear and choice in some form, and we all share the possibility of learning to heal both ourselves and our relationships.

As we become whole, relationships become an opportunity for synergy and extending love as an expression of who we are, rather than compensating for deficiencies or meeting personal needs. From time to time anyone may feel the need of a healing relationship, and a great deal of emotional pain can be alleviated if one is willing to ask for such a relationship. Acknowledging the need for healing and the deep desire for healing relationships that nurture wholeness is essential to optimum health and conscious evolution.

Healing Relationships and Liberation

A person who is able to listen with awareness and provide unconditional love and acceptance is a natural healer. When one makes contact with such a person one may begin to feel at peace with oneself. Once these conditions are established, the relationship can also become a vehicle for liberation and spiritual awakening. Liberation implies freedom from internal constrictions and distortions of awareness, as well as consciousness of choice and personal power. Only when we know and accept ourselves fully can we love wholeheartedly. The form of the relationship is not what matters. Whenever the inner attitude is free from clinging and expectation, grounded in the awareness of the universal Self, unconditional love is possible. A therapist who demonstrates this in a professional context, or a friend who does it in a personal context, can make an invaluable contribution to healing and wholeness.

Love, trust, and safety are qualities that we can bring to our relationships when we have found them in ourselves by letting go of fear, guilt, and defensiveness. When we do, all our relationships can be healing relationships. When healing awareness has been discovered in ourselves, it can be extended in relationships. We grow toward wholeness as we learn to heal ourselves and each other, trusting our own essential nature and the universal Self.

Unconditional love cannot be produced on demand, and trust cannot be forced, but both can be encouraged and supported by healing awareness. Every day provides opportunities for practice in healing relationships. Free feeling-exchange allows a direct experience of open communication. We all need the emotional nurturing and reflection that enable us to release defenses that prevent us from experiencing wholeness. Relationships are the mirrors in which we can learn to see ourselves and experience the transpersonal Self.

Experiential Exercises

Reviewing Relationships

If we are willing to examine defenses we usually uncover a number of inner conflicts that need to be healed if we want to heal our relationships. Conflicting wishes and desires that reflect a split between persona and shadow, male and female, sex and spirituality, or any other pair of opposites can make ambivalent feelings painfully apparent. Many of these conflicts can be healed in the context of a healing relationship, and indeed must be healed if relationships are to become a source of peace and joy rather than pain and conflict.

Using attention skillfully in relationship is primarily a process of training awareness. Beliefs, habits, assumptions, expectations, judgments, and preconceptions all interfere with clear perception and effective communication. Thus the process of healing relationships is partly one of uncovering obstacles that interfere with awareness.

Reflecting on the following questions may be useful for identifying patterns in relationships and may begin the process of healing.

1. Reflect for a moment on the important relationships in your own life. Are they truly satisfying to you? Are you getting what you want in your relationships? What do you bring to your relationships? What are the predominant qualities that you experience in your relationships at this time? Do you feel competitive, manipulated, victimized, or rejected? Do you experience joy, vitality, synergy, love, and shared purpose? What qualities do you bring to your relationships?

2. What patterns of relationship are you aware of? Do you consistently

feel misunderstood or mistreated? Do you think you give more than you get? Do you experience the universal Self as the source and context of relationships? Do you take responsibility for initiating change?

3. What beliefs and assumptions do you hold about relationships? Recognizing patterns can help uncover assumptions such as "Loving someone means always doing what the other person wants." "I can't tell him or her how I really feel because it would hurt him or her." "Caring for someone means not telling him or her what he or she does not want to hear." Any beliefs that cannot be questioned constrict awareness. After taking an inventory of beliefs, notice which ones you are unwilling to question.

4. Who/what do you think you are? Whether you identify predominantly with a physical, emotional, mental, existential, or transpersonal self-concept, this identification affects every relationship. If you have made a commitment to authenticity, your relationships will undoubtedly be more satisfying than if you are still attempting to derive your sense of self-worth only from appearances and the approval of others. If you are well grounded in both the personal self and the universal Self, this will certainly affect the quality of your relationships.

5. What is the purpose of relationship? Responses to this question will reflect the answers to the previous questions. Values in relationship tend to mirror personal attitudes. For example, if you feel manipulated, you are probably manipulative or would like to be. If you are aware of others' longing for love, you have no doubt experienced it yourself. At times everyone experiences alienation, loneliness, and separation. Sometimes compassion is born in the depths of despair, when personal pain can be seen as only a microcosm of human suffering.

  Relationships can be a source of pleasure and pain, teaching and learning, love and co-creation. When relationships are devalued or used in the service of fulfilling ego goals, they tend to be shallow and frustrating. When a relationship becomes an end in itself and one tries to live only for another, one is invariably disappointed. Relationships seem to be the most satisfying when two people share a sense of purpose that transcends personal desires. When the relationship is a source of enrichment rather than a means of survival, it can be free from coercion or manipulation. Be honest in examining your motives and your purpose in relationships. Only when you bring all of your secret desires into awareness can relationships become a source of healing.

6. What relationships in your life have been most important to you? Everyone learns about relationships from parents or parenting adults. Early conditioning exerts a strong, though not insurmountable, influence on all relationships. Blaming parents for difficulties is not useful. Only when one claims autonomy in relationships can one free oneself from the past and initiate change in a desired direction. Patterns that were established early can be changed in subsequent relationships, whenever one is willing to risk new levels of open exchange.

7. Imagine that you are old now and ready to die. Reflect on the quality of relationships in your life. Do you have any regrets? Is there anything you would like to have changed with respect to your relationships?

   In retrospect, people facing death often say that relationships are what really mattered most in their lives. Accomplishments and achievements that appeared momentous at one time seem to lose their lustre with the approach of death. On the other hand, the ability to give and receive love and to contribute to the well-being of others seems more valuable. Times of giving or receiving unconditional love may be cherished long after successes and failures are forgotten. Regrets often focus on not having communicated love to someone when the opportunity was there. Is there anyone to whom you want to express love or appreciation now?

8. If you could change your relationships unilaterally, what qualities would you want to cultivate in your relationships?

   Awareness of what you want in relationships is the first step toward getting it. When you don't know what you want you are not likely to get it. On the other hand, when you see clearly what's missing or what you would like to have, it more easily becomes available. For example, if you know you want more love in your life, you begin to look for it. Looking for it includes finding the source inside yourself that allows you to love beauty, harmony, and your own creative spirit. An experience of transpersonal identity may provide this. Seeing such a thing in others may precede seeing it in yourself. The shift in perception that allows one to see love in others is an essential stepping stone on the path of liberation.

9. Assuming that others remain just as they are, what would have to change in order for your relationships to be healed? What are you offering? What are your hidden demands or agendas?

10. Are you willing to forgive past mistakes rather than cling to grie-

vances? What have you had the most difficulty forgiving yourself for? Are you willing to intend healing for yourself and others in all your relationships?

Removing Obstacles in Relationship

The following exercise is designed for healing a specific relationship. It is best done with a partner. In the absence of a partner, reponses can be written down.

1. Identify and describe a relationship that is troublesome for you.

2. List your grievances and resentments in this relationship.

3. Clarify your wants, demands, expectations of this relationship.

4. Communicate your fears with respect to this relationship.

5. Communicate guilt feelings in this relationship.

6. Visualize the relationship as it would be if it were healed. What would it be like? How would it be different?

7. What do you believe you would have to give up to move in this direction?

Receptive Role Playing

An effective exercise for healing a troubled relationship is a form of role playing that can be called receptive, since it involves only listening on the part of the person who is sitting in for someone who is not present. The listener should not give any feedback while you are talking. He or she may choose to listen with eyes closed in order to avoid responding with facial gestures or expressions. The listener should monitor internal responses to your monologue, but reserve any comments or feedback for later. Talk to your listening partner as if he or she were the person with whom you are having difficulty in relationship. Tell him or her everything that is on your mind. Express whatever you have been withholding for any reason, and say absolutely everything. Tell him or her what you have been afraid to say, and communicate whatever you are feeling right now. When you have finished, your partner should not respond as if he or she were the person addressed, but should communicate whatever he or she was aware of as you were speaking.

This exercise can be very effective in precipitating unexpected changes. For example, one woman who used this exercise for clearing up a communication problem with her brother, to whom she had not spoken for more than a year, was astonished to hear from him only four days after she had released her anger and frustration and decided to let go of the longstanding resentment.

Shifting Attitudes

Sometimes changes in relationships following shifts in attitudes are not contingent on formal exercises. In my own life the following experience occurred spontaneously:

Shortly after I was divorced I seriously considered looking up a college boyfriend whom I had thought about occasionally as someone I might have married. We had dated and cared a lot for each other in college, but had gone our separate ways and married other people. After some deliberation, I decided not to try to resurrect the past and I let go of my fantasies of seeing him again. After all, I had not heard anything from him for nearly twenty years. About a month after I released the past internally, he telephoned, out of the blue. He was in town for a few days and called because he had recently had two dreams about me.

Other less dramatic instances can happen in the most ordinary circumstances. For example, a client reported the following incident:

When I went to pick up my car at the garage the other day I noticed that one of the taillights was out. I asked the mechanic who was working on the car to change it, but he said no because it was lunch time. I was annoyed but resolved to forgive him as I didn't want to feel angry. I had no sooner dismissed the whole incident from my mind than he came over and said he would change it after all—it would only take a minute.

Coincidence? Maybe. But I have heard so many reports like these and experienced similar incidents myself so many times, I cannot dismiss them altogether. Without resorting to simplistic explanations we can at least assert that when we change our mental attitude, changes in relationships ensue. Healing relationships does not have to be contingent on others. It can begin whenever we are willing to try it.

Expanding Healing Relationships

Take a few minutes to reflect on the nature of your relationship with one person who is very important to you. How do you feel about yourself in relation to this person? What is the quality of exchange in this relationship? How much responsibility are you willing to take for the quality of this relationship?

Turn your attention now to your relationship with your family or group. How do you feel about the whole group? How would you describe your relationship to it? What is the quality of that relationship?

Think about the nature of your relationship to the community in which you live. How do you relate to your community? What do you feel or think about this community and your relationship to it?

Think about your relationship to the country in which you live. How do you feel about being a citizen of your country? What is your relationship to your country?

What is your relationship to the earth? How do you relate to the planet as a whole?

Beyond the earth, how do you experience your relationship to the universe? Take time to find the thread of relationship that connects you to each of these complex systems of which you are a part. What do you contribute to each of these relationships?

Be aware of the emotional tone you set for yourself in your relationships. If you judge yourself harshly, you will find harsh judgments in all your relationships. Although emotions tend to be inconsistent (i.e., at times you may be gentle and caring, at other times irritable and angry), they exert a powerful influence on relationships. Emotions seem to come and go and change of their own accord, but they are also affected by values, attitudes, and beliefs. If there is a predominant affect or feeling that colors all your interactions, examine the assumptions that may be perpetuating it.

Consider the following questions in connection with creating what you want in relationships: What would you have to give up in order to feel free in relationships? Responses to this question have included the following:

"I would have to give up fear."

"I would have to drop my pretenses."

"I would have to give up my defenses."

"I would have to give up my helplessness."

"I would have to give up blaming."

"I would have to give up feeling small."

Naming the obstacles that appear to be in the way is the first step to removing them.

In a time of accelerating social change, conscious men and women tend to become what they intend to be. Change, freedom, choice, and responsibility are existential realities. Transcending existential identity in transpersonal awareness carries with it the potential of healing relationships.

10 Transpersonal Vision

Where there is no vision, the people perish.   —*Proverbs 29:18*[1]

Vision arises from emptiness or a state of nondual awareness. The spaciousness of mind that is not preoccupied with thought may be likened to a clear sky in which images appear and disappear as clouds drifting by in everchanging patterns to which the mind ascribes symbolic value. Bliss and liberation are the states of mind that result in awakening, from seeing through appearances of duality and apprehending the truth that is always already present in each moment, here and now.

Vision sees the unity as well as the duality of experience, whereas perception splits the world into subject and object, perceiver and perceived. Perception focuses on particular objects of consciousness, whether they be physical objects, sensations, feelings, or thoughts. Vision sees the context in which they exist as well as the relationships between them. It allows simultaneous awareness of unity, diversity, and interconnecting relationships. Wilber has called the primary function pertaining to the transpersonal level of consciousness vision/logic, thus emphasizing the fact that while vision transcends reason, these functions are complementary, not oppositional.

Huston Smith writes:

To those who, their hearts having been opened, can see with
its eye (the Sufi's *"eye of the heart,"* Plato's "eye of the soul"),
spiritual objects will be discernible and a theistic metaphysics
will emerge. The final "night vision" which can detect the

awefilled holiness of everything is reserved for those
whom . . . I have called mystics . . .

The divisions between the levels of reality are like one-
way mirrors. Looking up, we see only reflections of the level
we are on; looking down, the mirrors become plate glass and
cease to exist. On the highest plane even the glass is removed,
and immanence reigns . . . looking up from the planes that
are lower, God is radically transcendent . . . looking down,
from the heights that human vision can to varying degrees
attain, God is absolutely immanent.[2]

Vision depends on Self-knowledge and awareness that transcends
egoic and existential identifications. As long as we are prisoners of
limited self-concepts, insight can point the way to liberation. Beyond
the mental realm, where knowledge is apprehended by intuition
rather than reason, concepts become irrelevant. But concepts are not
to be dismissed lightly. Like anything else, they can either help or hin-
der the process of awakening depending on how they are used. They
can be either stepping stones or obstacles to vision. Transpersonal
vision empowers one to transcend conceptual limitations. Great
spiritual teachers are individuals of great vision.

Vision depends on light, and in many cultures fire is a symbol of
purification, as in "baptism by fire," where everything false is con-
sumed by fire and only what is true remains. Mastery of mind over
matter is dramatically demonstrated by our ability to walk unharmed
over a bed of hot coals that would normally burn unprotected flesh.
Having participated in one such ceremony myself, I know it is possible.
This type of experience can have a powerful influence in revising beliefs about what is possible when we put our minds to it. Fire represents light that is made by humans. It has the power to overcome darkness and consume impurities. It is part of many religious ceremonies,
in the form of candles.

Since light is necessary for vision, whatever one fears to see, whatever one hides in darkness, becomes an impediment to vision. When
inner vision is ignored, one is caught in illusions that constrict awareness. Inner vision is a gift that is always available, requiring only attention for recognition. The light is everpresent, awaiting only our willingness to experience it.

Enlightenment, as the goal of the spiritual path, is partly a result
of awakening vision. In the introduction to his book *What is Enlightenment?* John White writes:

Enlightenment is understanding the perfect poise of being-amid-becoming.

The truth of all existence and all experience, then, is none other than the seamless here-and-now, the already present, the prior nature of that which seeks and strives and asks: Being. *The spiritual journey is the process of discovering and living that truth.* It amounts to the eye seeing itself—or rather, the I seeing its Self. In philosophical terms, enlightenment is comprehending the unity of all dualities, the harmonious *compo*-site of all *op*posites, the oneness of endless multiplicity and diversity. In psychological terms, it is transcendence of all sense of limitation and otherness. In humanistic terms, it is understanding that the journey is the teaching, that the path and the destination are ultimately one.[3]

There is no one true path. Any path can serve as a means of awakening vision when truth is the goal. All paths are metaphors of change or movement through time and space, whereas vision encompasses the totality of experience and is not bound by concepts of relative change in form or space/time. A spiritual path is not a destination. Truth is the destination, although as a goal it can never be reached. The destination, therefore, like destiny itself, does not lie in the future, but in each moment, whenever one is prepared to meet it. Being always present here and now, truth is not reached by change or movement in time or space. Only by removing obstacles to awareness and accepting the totality of limitless being can one begin to see through the veils of illusion that seem to hide truth.

Vision, as knowledge of truth, does not require going anywhere or doing anything. Any pursuit becomes an obstacle to awareness of what can be experienced in the present. Thus, whenever we remember the past or try to imagine the future we are imposing our own ideas, interpretations, and concepts (i.e., the products of the thinking mind) on the immediate experience of formless truth. Any such movement in time, into either the past or the future, distracts attention from the present.

This eternal present in which we can experience the fullness of being is not just a discontinuous moment separated from what preceded it and what follows it, i.e., the passing present. It is, rather, an inclusive totality that includes the awareness of both past and future as existing now. Past and future do not exist anywhere except in the mind, therefore all of the past and all of the future are included in the fullness of this moment. Vision of the past, like vision of the future, depends on selective perception that is subject to change with any shift in perspective.

Intuition as a mode of knowing that takes as its object the domain of spirit can function as an inner guide to the recognition of everpresent (always, already) truth. Intuitively one may apprehend immediately and with absolute certainty what is true. The experience of insight, the sudden flash of revelation, the "Eureka!" or "Aha!" of inspiration, the recognition of something forgotten, are examples of this intuitive perception. Intuition allows one to see into the nature of things and apprehend truth directly. When intuition is used to envision possibilities, the process may activate both insight and imagination, giving form to formlessness in the mind, thereby creating something out of nothing. Just as formal operational thinking enables us to think about thinking at the mental level, vision enables us to see how intuition works at the transpersonal level.

Training awareness in contemplative disciplines activates intuition and clears vision. In the Sufi tradition, intuition is said to be an organ of perception that must be trained in order to be developed.[4] The training itself, as in all spiritual disciplines, starts with a process of undoing, or unlearning, those concepts that limit vision by imposing interpretations on reality. As intuition develops, one begins to see how perception structures both the inner and the outer world, while insight attributes meaning to the process.

For example, if I am preoccupied with a philosophical concept such as existential *angst*, anything arising in my awareness will be filtered through this preoccupation, and meaning will be attributed accordingly. Likewise, if I am preoccupied with something in the external world, such as a creative project, I will tend to notice only what is relevant to my project, and focus on getting the information I need while overlooking or ignoring other aspects of reality. In the absence of training, whatever captures my attention rules my consciousness. Even obsessive preoccupation with observation of the mind and its processes can become a trap.

Vision is further limited by beliefs and mental habits such as "I can't," "I should," "If only," "What if," "Someday. . . ." Such phrases indicate that what *is* does not match the pictures of what I want or what I think reality *should* be. More attention and importance may be given to what is *not* than to what *is*. Vision is cleared when interpretations and preconceptions are relinquished and one is willing to see things as they are.

Perception, be it intuitive, rational, emotional, or sensory, reflects both fear and desire. Perception imposes conceptual limitations on vision, just as interpretation imposes meaning on experience. In an effort to transcend this limitation, a practice such as za-zen, for example, is said to be "meaning-free," and a student may cultivate emptiness.

Perception may be considered a function of looking (narrow focus), whereas vision is a function of seeing (open focus). Truth, which is all-encompassing, cannot be perceived; it can only be experienced as open focus. Absolute subjectivity or awareness that cannot be objectified is likened to the eye that sees everything, but can never hope to see itself. Likewise, the experience of truth in which subject/object dualism is transcended cannot be fully communicated in language. Nevertheless, the language of vision can be used as a metaphor to illustrate shared experience in this domain.

The Language of Vision

There is no sight, be it of dreams or from a truer Source, that is not but the shadow of the seen through inward vision.
—*A Course in Miracles*[5]

The metaphoric language of vision has been used throughout the ages, in all cultures, in attempts to communicate contemplative truth. Whereas words and concepts serve adequately to describe the relative reality of perception, vision is subject to distortion when it is communicated conceptually. Enlightenment and illumination, for example, are terms that describe states of consciousness that cannot be conceptualized; they can only be experienced. Vision, like truth and love, can be shared only to the extent that it resonates with direct awareness. It cannot be measured or quantified, but it can be acknowledged as shared experience.

Vision itself is formless. Visions, on the other hand, as manifestations of vision, are perceptions that by their specificity and focus exclude a part of the totality. In consciously choosing what one attends to, one takes responsibility for experience. By training in self-observation, vision can be freed from the distortions of unconscious wishes. However, it remains colored by expectations and constricted by any consciously determined focusing of attention.

The capacity to envision freedom from perceptual distortion is a function of formless vision. Likewise, the ability to comprehend the paradoxical nature of truth that transcends and includes all opposites is also a function of vision. Vision is one, and in its wholeness encompasses totality, whereas visions, as products of the mind, are many. Visions are contents of consciousness. Vision includes context and process as well. Vision provides insight into the nature of reality and plumbs the depths of inner wellsprings of inspiration, yet never sees itself.

Symbolic representations of reality, perceived in either the dreaming or the waking state, simultaneously reveal and conceal truth. Sometimes the form is confused with the essence; the image may be mistaken for the reality it represents. Nonetheless, a glimpse of the potentiality of vision afforded by a specific symbolic vision can be a strong incentive to waking up. It depends whether one chooses to turn attention to consciousness itself or only to the objects of consciousness that can impede clear vision. The danger is always that the symbol, the path, or the teacher may be idolized and hence become a limiting entrapment. The very vehicle of revelation becomes, when perceived as an end in itself, another illusion to be transcended.

A Buddhist teacher of Vipassana meditation tells the following story:

Hinayana Buddhism is known as the lesser vehicle of individual liberation.

Mahayana Buddhism is known as the greater vehicle of liberation for all beings.

Lesser vehicle, greater vehicle, in the end all vehicles are towed away at the owner's expense.[6]

The vehicles that serve well at one stage of the journey must be abandoned at another, and dreams that disclose hidden meanings at one level of consciousness may be perceived as illusion from another perspective. Just as pursuit of consciously determined goals distracts attention from truth that is always already present, whenever we look for vision or prepare for enlightenment, we separate ourselves from it and place it in the future, making it subject to space and time, forgetting that as a transcendent function it is ever present and eternal.

Outside of time there is no path and no achievement. In time vision gives a sense of direction to the journey of awakening consciousness. The goal of this journey is unity consciousness, or the truth of existence that can be apprehended intuitively by clear vision, free from constricting distortions of perception. The path that leads to awakening vision leads through dreams and illusions to knowledge, liberation, and enlightenment. The awakened mind is one that sees its wholeness.

Attributes of Vision

The scope of external physical vision is extended by the use of instruments that amplify the physical eye, such as the microscope, telescope, or periscope, and aid the collection of empirical data. When spiritual realities are viewed through a mental lens, it is analogous to using a periscope to extend the perception of intellect into contemplation. The eye of reason searches for meaning and responds to symbolic representations of those dimensions of consciousness that transcend mental identifications. The eye of contemplation, however, can awaken inner vision that encompasses the transcendent reality that remains forever a mystery to the rational mind.

Wisdom is an attribute of one who, by virtue of inner vision, understands the nature of illusion and duality. The archetypal image of a wise old person or a god that may emerge as a symbolic representation of wisdom can only be a partial representation, at best. The inherent wisdom of the psyche as a whole may become accessible as an inner teacher that is always available, waiting only to be perceived. Yet the inner teacher, the archetypal representation of wisdom in any form, remains a perceptual construct imposed on the totality. Universal symbols, as collective images, give form to the formless and fix in time that which is eternal. Even the loftiest, most numinous perceptions and symbols of vision are time-bound. Vision itself is timeless. Keeping these distinctions in mind can help prevent us from idolizing images, falling in love with them, or mistaking them for absolute truth.

From a transpersonal perspective, archetypes are the exemplary forms on which creation is patterned. Strictly speaking, the term *archetype* refers to the first form in involution, the first manifestation of form emerging from the formless, undifferentiated void. It can refer to those Platonic ideals that in philosophy are said to exist *a priori*, independently of any particular manifestation, e.g., truth, beauty, perfection, harmony, etc. As patterns of creation, archetypal forms are not identical with primordial images, although primordial images are based on the archetypes. An archaic image may be the first manifestation in evolution of a particular archetype, but the image itself is not the pattern, nor is it the underlying principle that it represents. Freud and Jung agreed that we inherit phylogenetic images, but the universal images that appear crossculturally are not necessarily transpersonal. What is transpersonal is not the particular manifestation of an image, but the vision that sees the pattern or principle on which an image is based, existing *a priori* or independently of any particular manifestation in space/time.

Certainly it can be argued from an existential point of view that only the specific particular form exists and any abstraction is merely speculation or illusion. There is no rational argument that suffices to establish transcendental realities. Only a direct experience of transcendence of form, a direct awareness of vision, can validate the claim. Reality can never be explained, but it can be experienced universally, as the contemplatives and mystics of every tradition have ascertained.

The Self as source of archetypes is known by means of vision that sees formlessness as well as form. As an unmanifest abstraction, an archetype cannot be known concretely, but it can be apprehended intuitively, by training in contemplation. It is known not as an object, but as a potentiality existing in the psyche, awaiting the creative expression that brings it into existence as an image. In the manifest realm it exists only as expressed through human beings. Confusion of the particular manifestation (e.g., the primordial image) with the archetype as abstraction or pattern on which all forms are based can lead to mistaken attempts to locate archetypes in some other time or place. It might be more accurate to say that they exist outside of time, always and only in present awareness. As thoughtforms, they become available when one chooses to turn attention to them.

Vision enhances awareness of archetypes as templates for present experience. Archetypal forms and patterns can be differentiated when one is not identified with any one of them. Once this distinction is made, identification is less likely, since it can be understood as a limitation. When one becomes aware of all potentialities through vision, one is not separate from them, but joined with them as aspects of Self. Experiencing Self as limitless being at one with all and everything means relinquishing attachment to the subtle separateness of the transpersonal Self and accepting the totality that we did not create.

Vision is a resource of inexhaustible abundance and unlimited possibility that can inform the mind with boundless creativity. Vision gives access to an infinite source of inspiration that transcends narrow viewing frames of perception. Vision sees time as well as eternity, emptiness and consciousness as well as objects. Vision has no qualities or allegiances. It is priceless, and has no cost. It becomes available when we accept everything as it is. We have only to remove the illusion of obstacles to awareness imposed by dreams and self-concepts. It is renewed, never depleted, by being accessed and shared.

Vision, as illumination, dawns naturally on the mind that is at peace within itself. The empty mind and open heart is the matrix of vision. Here all possibilities in the realm of form may be conceived.

Vision needs no justification and inspires gratitude in accordance with its value. It is sufficient unto itself. It offers access to Spirit, however it is conceived. With the awakening of vision, perception of reality may be radically altered.

Vision beholds; it does not separate or categorize. As awareness of distinctions, it beholds both the unity of the Self and the particular viewpoints of self-identification. Just as analytical faculties provide consensual validation in the mental realms of reason, vision can provide consensual validation in the realms of contemplation and intuition.[7]

In language, vision can be distinguished from rational knowledge in the following terms:

Vision	*Rational Knowledge*
illumination	understanding
trans/form	in/form
formless	in/formation
be/hold (hold being)	compare/contrast
discover	prove
awakening	probing
reveal	report
review	research
intuitive	rational
revise	restore
encompassing	differentiating
creative	ordering
circular	hierarchical
empowering	controlling
perceptual	conceptual
insight	ideation
inherent wisdom	acquired wisdom
recognized	learned
seeing	looking
spontaneous	intentional
inspires	codifies
views	categorizes
looking out	putting into
images (shared vision)	facts (shared knowledge)

Vision, like truth, is not attained by striving. Whereas knowledge can be acquired by sustained effort, vision requires letting go and opening to what is already present. As a function of awareness of the transpersonal Self, vision can enhance every dimension of experience.

The Healing Vision

In the history of the collective as in the history of the individual, everything depends on the development of consciousness. This gradually brings liberation from imprisonment in "agnoia," "unconsciousness," and is therefore a bringer of light as well as healing.—C. G. Jung[8]

The healing vision is a vision of wholeness. Wholeness is not perceived as an end state because it is never static. It is, rather, a dynamic integration of intrinsic, organismic wholeness and optimum participation in the larger whole that includes all and everything. The whole person is one whose vision of wholeness includes Self as source in the seamless web of reality.

Religions can be viewed as interpretations of vision from various perspectives. Philosophical and theological approaches to the study of comparative religions that compare and contrast beliefs and practices offer what Fritjof Schuon calls the exoteric view.[9] Exoteric refers to the outward aspects of religious observance. An esoteric view, on the other hand, is concerned with essence rather than form of spirituality, and as such remains hidden to outside observation, but is accessible to vision and may be discerned by anyone who undertakes the necessary training. Esoteric religion generally refers to the advanced or inward aspects of spiritual practice and constitutes the mystical core of all the world's great religions.

In a discussion of the sociology of religion, Wilber has made a distinction between legitimacy and authenticity. Legitimacy is the extent to which religions meet psychological needs such as the desire for meaning, immortality symbols, and ethical precepts. Authenticity is the extent to which religions facilitate genuine transcendence.[10] A psychological investigation of religion may be concerned with both legitimacy and authenticity, but it is the latter that pertains to the effects of spiritual practice on consciousness. Huston Smith, an eminent religious scholar, points out that all revealed religions converge in what appears to the discerning intellect as Unity. This unity can be known only by means of direct intuitive knowing that identifies the knower with what is known.

The Absolute Unity that is God defies visualization or even consistent description, but is nonetheless required. . . . Intimations and realizations of this supreme identity appear in varying degrees of explicitness in all revealed religions and constitute the point at which they are one. But this establishes religious unity on the esoteric plane: it is hidden and secret not because those who know will not tell, but because the truth to which they are privy is buried so deep in the human composite that they cannot communicate it. . . .[11]

Schuon explicitly states that this knowledge is not possessed by the individual insofar as he is an individual, but only insofar as in his innermost essence he is not distinct from the Divine Principle. Whether we call this divine principle Buddha-nature, Christ, Atman, or Self, it bespeaks a universal understanding of that in us which transcends individual identity. First this may be seen as a possibility, then one may begin to understand it; but seeing it or understanding it should not be confused with illumination or realization. Realization occurs only in direct experience, and this may be fleeting at first. Only when one learns to live in this awareness is one likely to experience its healing effects.

For this, spiritual practice is required. Profound insights into reality and our true nature can be irrelevant if dissociated from everyday life. Awakening to vision is therefore only a step in the ongoing process of becoming. Vision must be actualized in everyday life in thoughts, relationships, and practice. Possibilities are limited by impoverished vision. Spiritual practice can be a way of training awareness and awakening vision. Any path that leads to revelation of unity consciousness may be useful.

Through practice in contemplation or meditation, understanding may gradually become realization. Spiritual practice may be understood with the discursive mind, but awakening to vision is a function of transpersonal consciousness. Both Eastern and Western spiritual disciplines employ similar methods to facilitate realization. In Christianity the word *contemplation* is used by Thomas Merton and others to designate a simple direct awareness, beyond words or concepts, of divine presence. In Buddhism meditation can be both a method for training awareness and an expression of intrinsic Buddha-nature.

For the first time in history humanity is confronting the necessity of seeing the world as a whole. Spirituality, too, must be addressed in global terms. Healing awareness that transcends cultural distinctions may be essential to human survival. The healing vision that sees beyond appearance and duality to the unity of transcendence does not require belief in a personal God; it does require a willingness to be aware, moment by moment, of what is true in both inner and outer experience. When we are healed we become conscious of our wholeness, complete in each moment, an essential part of it all.

Gradually, the desirability of sharing experiences, not just doctrines and ideas, among various traditions, is becoming more widely accepted. If we are to become universal persons of global vision, self-knowledge must deepen into awareness of universal spirituality. As Maslow said many years ago, self-actualizing people are always involved in something beyond themselves.[12] The wisdom needed for healing the world cannot be taught by words alone. It must be discovered within and applied in relationship. As we grow toward wholeness we may become more aware of our shared psychological and spiritual resources. Any situation may be perceived as an opportunity to heal the split mind that generates conflict while caught in the illusion of separateness. A mind possessed by illusions is healed when it awakens to vision and Self as Spirit, eternally free.

As a journey of a thousand miles begins with a single step, healing the whole begins with healing ourselves, our relationships, and our world. Our inherent capacity for self-healing is empowered when we awaken the vision of unity consciousness. We are challenged to see ourselves whole, free from egocentric attachment to form or outcome. If we would participate in co-creating a future different from the past, a future that could heal the earth, we may begin by envisioning possibilities. In *Up from Eden*, Ken Wilber has suggested some possibilities:

For those who have matured to a responsible, stable ego, the next stage of growth is the beginning of the transpersonal, the level of psychic intuition, of transcendent openness and clarity, the awakening of a sense of awareness that is somehow more than the simple mind and body. To the extent that it does start to occur, there will be profound changes in society, culture, government, medicine, economics. . . .

[This] will mean a society of men and women who, by virtue of an initial glimpse into transcendence, will start to understand vividly their common humanity and brother/sisterhood; will transcend roles based on bodily differences of skin color and sex; will grow in mental-psychic clarity; will make policy decisions on the basis of intuition as well as rationality; will see the same Consciousness in each and every soul, indeed, in all creation, and will start to act correspondingly; will find mental psychic consciousness to be transfigurative of body physiology, and adjust medical theory accordingly; will find higher motivations in men and women that will drastically alter economic incentives and economic theory; will understand psychological growth as evolutionary transcendence, and develop methods and institutions not just to cure emotional disease but foster the growth of consciousness; will see education as a discipline in transcendence, body to mind to soul, and regear educational theory and institutions accordingly, with special development; will find technology an appropriate aid to transcendence, not a replacement for it; will use mass media, instant telecommunication, and human/computer linkages as vehicles of bonding-consciousness and unity; will see outer space as not just an inert entity out there but also as a projection of inner or psychic spaces and explore it accordingly; will use appropriate technology to free the exchanges of the material level from chronic oppression; will find sexuality to be not just a play of reproductive desire but the initial base of kundalini sublimation into psychic spheres—and will readjust marriage practices accordingly; will see cultural/national differences as perfectly acceptable and desirable, but will see those differences on a background of universal and common consciousness; . . . will realize fully the transcendent unity of all Dharmakaya religions, and thus respect all true religious preferences while condemning any sectarian claim to possess "the only way"; will realize that politicians, if they are to govern all aspects of life, will have to demonstrate an understanding and mastery of all aspects of life—body to mind to soul to spirit. . . .

In short, a true Wisdom Culture will *start* to emerge. . . .[13]

A vision of a world that is healed and whole, that provides a supportive environment for humanity and all other forms of life, is a possible dream. We must dare to dream those qualities and values that are needed for well-being. Everyone is given opportunities for service and creative participation. The challenge of our time is for each of us to do our part in creating a world we want for everyone. If we fail to choose our future, we may not have one. The state of the world, reflecting the state of our collective mind, indicates that we are badly in need of healing. We have become as gods, with the power to destroy the world. Will we awaken in time to the vision that allows us to see that we also have within us the wisdom to preserve it? Consciousness has, by necessity, become both the object and the instrument of change.

We must learn to apply what we know about healing ourselves to healing the world, and empower ourselves and each other in co-creating peaceful evolutionary alternatives to self-destruction. This is not a task that can be undertaken by anyone alone. We can no longer afford to wait for a hero to rescue us. The heroic journey is no longer a viable myth for our time. We have learned the hard way that evil cannot be conquered in battle. Doing battle perpetuates the problem. It is, rather, our mutual capacity for transcendence that must be recognized if we want to transform present danger into opportunity for renewal. If we persist in our folly of wishful thinking and blaming others for our predicaments, we may forfeit the chance to grow into wisdom.

It is not impossible to envision a world where we can learn to live in harmony, in the light of the perennial wisdom of the great traditions. As we awaken from the dream of being isolated entities in a fragmented universe where individual thoughts, feelings, and actions make no difference, we can see that our destiny is shared.

By perceiving the unity of opposites we may begin to envision a world in which all beings may recognize their oneness in Spirit and their capacity for love and compassion, while respecting and appreciating differences. The emergence of a global spirituality, concerned with the welfare of the whole rather than particular forms of religious practice,[14] is one of the most promising signs that a shared dream of healing and wholeness is no more improbable than any of the others we collectively entertain.

Each one of us has a unique function in healing the whole. We can discover it by listening to the Self and seeing things as they are. We have a capacity for turning problems into challenges and empowering each other in sharing a vision of wholeness. We can no longer afford to pretend to be children playing while the home we inhabit is being destroyed. We must acknowledge our reponsibility for the world as it is and for consciously choosing to change. By sharing a vision that transcends present limitations, and inspires creative imagination, we become the visionmakers and healers of our time. We have only to shift the focus of our attention from the part to the whole, from the content to the context, in order to transcend limited perceptions and expand vision.

Facing the collective challenge calls for a willingness to witness the pain of the human condition. To open the heart is to become a source of love that can heal the wounds of deprivation—physical, emotional, mental, existential, and spiritual. Peace is an attribute we must value in ourselves if we want to have it in the world.

Awakening to vision does not impose a new image on reality or provide answers to the questions of the way-seeking mind. It is a process of self-transcendence that allows each of us to see for ourselves what is true. We can never be fully satisfied with lies or illusions. We can delude ourselves temporarily into believing what we want to believe, but true vision is never deceived. When we are afraid or confused we may ask others for guidance, but ultimately we must learn to see for ourselves. There is no one way to awaken vision. Any way can be subject to distortion. But healing vision sees the unity of wholeness.

As we practice removing obstacles to vision on the inward arc, we begin to see that vision is not on the path, but actually created the path in the first place. Thus the person who sets out on the spiritual path never arrives at the destination. Who we thought we were when we set out, turns out to be only a figment of imagination, an illusory fragment of being that we mistakenly identified as self. To Self as Spirit, the absolute subjectivity that is forever unconditioned and unbound, nothing can be attributed, for it is beyond perception, devoid of qualities, yet infusing everything with life.

Experiential Exercise

Identifying Illusions

We become more aware of our capacity for vision when we recognize illusions.

What is your favorite illusion?

Your responses to this question can give you a glimpse of personal dreams and illusions that can be mistaken for vision. For example, here are some possibilities:

My favorite illusion is the illusion that I have no illusions.
. . . the illusion that I am a fascinating person.
. . . the illusion that I am earning brownie points in heaven by spiritual practice.
. . . the illusion that I am becoming a sage.

A sage is said to be one who restores humor to the world, who is able to play with opposites, who contributes to the well-being of everyone, and who no longer strives for self-improvement. Wei Wu Wei says,

Intention can make you a saint,
But it can prevent you from becoming a sage.
Appearance only: there is no entity to be either.[15]

This final truth is a beginning, not an end. It is from this place of emptiness, having relinquished all illusory self-concepts, that possibilities for healing and wholeness may be envisioned.

May you awaken to vision that inspires you,
may your heart be guided by love
and your mind by divine wisdom,
that all beings may find a better way.

Notes

Introduction

1. A. Einstein, cited in J. Goldstein, *The Experience of Insight*, Boulder, CO: Shambhala, 1983.
2. A. Huxley, *The Perennial Philosophy*, New York: Harper & Row, 1944.
3. K. Wilber, *Up from Eden: A Transpersonal View of Human Evolution*, Garden City, NY: Doubleday, 1981.
4. D. Bohm, *Wholeness and the Implicate Order*, Boston: Routledge & Kegan Paul, 1980.
5. K. Wilber (ed.), *The Atman Project: A Transpersonal View of Human Development*, Wheaton, IL: Theosophical Publishing House, 1980.
6. Wilber, *Up from Eden*.
7. K. Wilber, "A Developmental View of Consciousness," *Journal of Transpersonal Psychology*, 1979, 11(1), pp. 1–22.
8. R. Walsh, *Staying Alive: The Psychology of Human Survival*, Boulder, CO: Shambhala, 1984.
9. CSPA Task Force Report, California State Psychological Association *Newsletter*, 1983.

Chapter 1

1. Anonymous, *A Course in Miracles*, New York: Foundation for Inner Peace, 1975, vol. 1, p. 595.
2. I. Yalom, *Existential Psychotherapy*, New York: Basic Books, 1980; J. Bugental, *The Search for Authenticity*, 2nd ed., New York: Irvington Publishers, 1981; J. Bugental, *Psychotherapy and Process*, Reading, MA: Addison Wesley, 1978.
3. R. Walsh and F. Vaughan (eds.), *Beyond Ego: Transpersonal Dimensions in Psychology*, Los Angeles: J. P. Tarcher, 1980.

4. K. Wilber (ed.), *Quantum Questions*, Boulder, CO: Shambhala/New Science Library, 1984, pp. 15–16.
5. M. S. Peck, *The Road Less Traveled*, New York: Simon & Schuster, 1978.
6. Dharma teaching, Insight Meditation Center, Barre, MA, 1983.
7. F. Capra, *The Turning Point*, New York: Simon & Schuster, 1982.
8. D. Shapiro and R. Walsh (eds.), *Meditation: Classic and Contemporary Perspectives*, New York: Aldine Press, 1984.
9. W. Harman, "Peace is Possible," Sausalito, CA: Institute of Noetic Sciences, 1984.
10. R. May, *Existential Psychology*, New York: Random House, 1969, p. 35.
11. K. Wilber,
12. W. McGarey, "An Adventure in Health," *New Realities*, vols. 5 and 6, 1964.

Chapter 2

1. H. Smith, *Beyond the Post Modern Mind*, New York: Crossroads, 1982.
2. G. Allport, "The Fruits of Ecclecticism: Bitter or Sweet," *Acta Psychologia*, 23, 1964, pp. 27–44.
3. J. Bugental, *Psychotherapy and Process*, Reading, MA: Addison Wesley, 1978.
4. K. Wilber, *Eye to Eye*, New York: Doubleday, 1983.
5. K. Wilber, *The Atman Project: A Transpersonal View of Human Development*, Wheaton, IL: Theosophical Publishing House, 1980.
6. M. Mahler et al., *The Psychological Birth of the Human Infant*, New York: Basic Books, 1975.
7. Wilber, *Eye to Eye*, p. 89.
8. Ibid.
9. K. Wilber, *Up from Eden: A Transpersonal View of Human Evolution*, New York: Doubleday, 1982, p. 8.
10. Wilber, *Eye to Eye*.
11. E. Erikson, *Childhood and Society*, New York: Norton, 1963.
12. Wilber, *The Atman Project*.
13. R. May, E. Angel, and H. Ellenberger (eds.), *Existence*, New York: Basic Books, 1958, p. 52.
14. L. Kohlberg, *The Philosophy of Moral Development*, New York: Harper & Row, 1981.
15. E. Becker, *The Denial of Death*, New York: Free Press, 1974.
16. W. James, *The Varieties of Religious Experience*, New York: Collier, 1961.
17. J. Welwood, "Vulnerability and Power in the Therapeutic Process: Existential and Buddhist Perspectives," *Journal of Humanistic Psychology*, 14(2), 1982, pp. 125–140.
18. Anonymous, *A Course in Miracles*, New York: Foundation for Inner Peace, 1975, vol. 2, p. 431.
19. Wilber, *The Atman Project*.
20. F. Capra, *The Turning Point*, New York: Simon & Schuster, 1982.
21. Wilber, *The Atman Project*.
22. C. Tart, *Transpersonal Psychologies*, New York: Harper & Row, 1975.
23. R. Walsh and F. Vaughan (eds.), *Beyond Ego: Transpersonal Dimensions in Psychology*, Los Angeles: J. P. Tarcher, 1980.

24. Wilber, *Eye to Eye*.
25. Walsh and Vaughan, *Beyond Ego*.
26. I. Prigogine, *From Being to Becoming*, San Francisco: W. H. Freeman, 1979, cited in *Brain/Mind Bulletin*, 4(13), May 21, 1979, pp. 1–4.
27. K. Wilber, *No Boundary*, Boulder and London: Shambhala/New Science Library, 1981.
28. L. von Bertalanffy, *General Systems Theory*, New York: George Braziller, 1968.
29. *A Course in Miracles*, vol. 2, p. 155.

Chapter 3

1. K. Wilber, concept of a person according to Heidegger, personal communication, 1982.
2. M. L. von Franz, "The Process of Individuation," in C. G. Jung, *Man and His Symbols*, New York: Doubleday, 1964, p. 162.
3. R. Walsh and F. Vaughan, "Toward an Integrative Psychology of Wellbeing," in R. Walsh and D. Shapiro (eds.), *Beyond Health and Normality*, New York: Van Nostrand, 1983.
4. Y. Kaufman, "Analytical Psychotherapy," in R. Corsini (ed.), *Current Psychotherapies*, 3rd ed., Itasca, IL: F. E. Peacock Publishers, 1984, p. 109.
5. A. Guggenbuhl-Craig, *Power in the Helping Professions*, Zurich, Switzerland: Spring Publications, 1971, p. 139.
6. C. G. Jung, *Psychological Commentary on Kundalini Yoga*, Zurich: Spring Publications, 1975, p. 31.
7. Ibid.
8. A. Maslow, *The Farther Reaches of Human Nature*, New York: Viking, 1971.
9. L. Hixon, *Coming Home*, New York: Anchor Press, 1978.
10. M. Stein (ed.), *Jungian Analysis*, LaSalle, IL: Open Court, 1982.
11. C. G. Jung, *Letters*, ed. G. Adler, Princeton, NJ: Princeton University Press, 1973.
12. M. Friedman, "Aiming at the Self: The Paradox of Encounter and the Human Potential Movement," *Journal of Humanistic Psychology*, 16(2), 1976, pp. 5–34.
13. B. Bettelheim, "Freud and the Soul," *The New Yorker*, March 1, 1982, p. 63.
14. Ibid. p. 86.
15. J. Hillman, *Revisioning Psychology*, New York: Harper & Row, 1977, p. 74.
16. K. Wilber (ed.), *Quantum Questions*, Boulder, CO: Shambhala/New Science Library, 1984.
17. K. Wilber, *The Atman Project: A Transpersonal View of Human Development*, Wheaton, IL: Theosophical Publishing House, 1980, p. 175.
18. J. Needleman, *Lost Christianity*, New York: Doubleday, 1980, p. 189.
19. Sri Nisargadatta Maharaj, *I Am That*, trans. Maurice Frydman, Bombay: Chetana, 1973, Part 1, p. 183.
20. Wilber, *The Atman Project*.
21. Mahatma Gandhi, words attributed to Gandhi in film on his life, 1983.
22. R. Walsh, *Staying Alive: The Psychology of Human Survival*, Boulder, CO: Shambhala/New Science Library, 1984.
23. R. May, *Love and Will*, New York: Norton, 1969.

24. C. G. Jung, "Aion: Researches into the Phenomenology of the Self," *Collected Works*, Vol. 9, in J. Campbell (ed.), *The Portable Jung*, New York: Viking, 1971, p. 148.
25. J. Campbell, lecture on *The Tibetan Book of the Dead*, Esalen Institute, 1982.
26. K. Wilber, *No Boundary*, Boulder, CO: Shambhala/New Science Library, 1981.
27. K. Wilber, *Eye to Eye*, New York: Doubleday, 1983.
28. Kaufman, "Analytical Psychotherapy."
29. K. Wilber, unpublished manuscript in preparation.
30. A. Diekman, *The Observing Self*, Boston: Beacon Press, 1982, p. 63.
31. Jung, "Aion: Phenomenology of Self."
32. B. Roberts, *The Experience of No-Self: A Contemplative Journey*, Boulder, CO: Shambhala, 1984.
33. Huang Po, *The Zen Teaching of Huang Po on the Transmission of Mind*, trans. John Blofeld, New York: Grove Press, 1958.
34. J. Goldstein, *The Experience of Insight*, Boulder, CO: Shambhala, 1983.
35. D. Shapiro and R. Walsh (eds.), *Meditation: Classic and Contemporary Perspectives*, Chicago: Aldine, 1984.
36. J. Krishnamurti, *Freedom from the Known*, New York: Harper & Row, 1969.
37. Anonymous, *A Course in Miracles*, New York: Foundation for Inner Peace, 1975, Vol. 2, pp. 170–171.

Chapter 4

1. C. G. Jung, cited in I. Oyle, *The Healing Mind*, Millbrae, CA: Celestial Arts, 1975.
2. F. Perls, *Gestalt Therapy Verbatim*, Lafayette, CA: Real People Press, 1969, p. 16.
3. E. Green and A. Green, *Beyond Biofeedback*, New York: Delacorte, 1977.
4. C. Simonton and S. Simonton, *Getting Well Again*, Los Angeles: Tarcher, 1982.
5. Green and Green, *Beyond Biofeedback*.
6. P. Russell and A. Shearer, *The Upanishads*, New York: Harper & Row, 1978.
7. C. G. Jung, *The Secret of the Golden Flower*, New York: Harcourt, Brace & World, 1969, p. 93.
8. K. Wilber (ed.), *Quantum Questions*, Boulder, CO: Shambhala/New Science Library, 1984.
9. Anonymous, *A Course in Miracles*, New York: Foundation for Inner Peace, 1975, Vol. 1, p. 418.

Chapter 5

1. Anonymous, *A Course in Miracles*, New York: Foundation for Inner Peace, 1975, vol. 2, p. 182.
2. J. Jacobi (ed.), *C.G. Jung: Psychological Reflections, A New Anthology of His Writings*, Princeton, NJ: Princeton University Press, 1970.
3. *A Course in Miracles*, vol. 2, p. 182.
4. A. Maslow, *The Farther Reaches of Human Nature*, New York: Viking, 1971, p. 36.

5. G. May, *Will and Spirit,* New York: Harper & Row, 1982, p. 16.
6. Sri Nisargadatta, *I Am That,* trans. Maurice Frydman, Bombay, India: Chetana Pvt. Ltd., 1973, vol. 1, p. 238.
7. Yogananda, *Sayings of Yogananda,* Los Angeles: Self-Realization Fellowship, 1968, p. 60.
8. Sri Nisargadatta, *I Am That,* p. 237.
9. D. Doig, *Mother Teresa: Her People and Her Work,* San Francisco: Harper & Row, 1976, p. 155.
10. Dante Alighieri, *The Divine Comedy of Dante Alighieri,* trans. Carlyle-Wicksteed, New York: Random House, 1950.
11. N. Cousins, *Anatomy of an Illness,* New York: Norton, 1979.
12. M. S. Peck, *The Road Less Traveled,* New York: Simon & Schuster, 1978, p. 119.
13. J. Sampson (ed.), *William Blake,* London: Oxford University Press, 1928.

Chapter 6

1. J. White (ed.), *What is Enlightenment?* Los Angeles: J. P. Tarcher, 1985.
2. E. Underhill, *Mysticism,* New York: E. P. Dutton, 1961.
3. Dante Alighieri, *The Divine Comedy of Dante Alighieri,* trans. Carlyle-Wicksteed, New York: Random House, 1950.
4. J. Campbell, *The Masks of God: Creative Mythology,* New York: Viking, 1968, vol. 4.
5. J. Campbell, *The Hero with a Thousand Faces,* New York: Pantheon, 1949, p. 30.
6. Ibid. p. 391.
7. B. Roberts, *The Experience of No-Self,* Boulder, CO: Shambhala, 1982, p. 174.
8. Ram Dass, *Grist for the Mill,* Santa Cruz, CA: Unity Press, 1977.
9. A. Govinda, *Foundations of Tibetan Mysticism,* New York: Samuel Weiser, 1969.
10. Swami Radha, *Kundalini: Yoga for the West,* Spokane, WA: Timeless Books, 1978.
11. K. Wilber, "Are the Chakras Real?" in J. White (ed.), *Kundalini, Evolution and Enlightenment,* New York: Doubleday/Anchor, 1979.
12. E. Neumann, *The Origins and History of Consciousness,* Princeton, NJ: Princeton University Press, 1973.
13. K. Wilber, *Up from Eden: A Transpersonal View of Human Evolution,* New York: Doubleday, 1981.
14. Campbell, *Masks of God,* p. 154.
15. C. G. Jung, "Psychological Commentary on Kundalini Yoga," Lectures 1 and 2, Autumn, 1932, Zurich, Switzerland: Spring Publications, 1976, pp. 2–33; ibid. Lectures 3 and 4, Autumn, 1932, pp. 1–31.
16. S. Bhatnagar, "The Chakra Paradigm: The Inner Tuning System of Therapy," paper delivered at the Seventh International Conference of the International Transpersonal Association, Bombay, India, Feb. 14, 1982.
17. Ibid.
18. Jung, "Kundalini Yoga."
19. Bhatnagar, "Chakra Paradigm."
20. Jung, "Kundalini Yoga."

21. K. Wilber, *The Atman Project: A Transpersonal View of Human Development*, Wheaton, IL: Theosophical Publishing House, 1980.
22. Ibid.
23. Bhatnagar, "Chakra Paradigm."
24. Jung, "Kundalini Yoga."
25. Govinda, *Tibetan Mysticism*.
26. Swami Radha, *Kundalini*.
27. K. Wilber, Heidegger's concept of a person, personal communication, 1982.
28. R. Metzner, "Ten Classical Metaphors of Self-Transformation," *Journal of Transpersonal Psychology*, 1979, 12(1).
29. Jung, "Kundalini Yoga."
30. Swami Radha, "Kundalini."
31. Jung, "Kundalini Yoga."
32. Swami Radha, "Kundalini."
33. T. Byrom, *The Dhammapada: The Sayings of the Buddha*, New York: Vintage, 1976.
34. Swami Radha, "Kundalini."
35. K. Wilber, *No Boundary*, Boulder, CO: Shambhala, 1981.
36. Dogen, *The Way of Everyday Life*, trans. H. T. Maezumi and J. D. Loori, Los Angeles: Center Publications, 1978.
37. Govinda, *Tibetan Mysticism*, p. 80.
38. L. Hixon, *Coming Home: The Experience of Enlightenment in Sacred Traditions*, New York: Doubleday/Anchor, 1978.
39. W. Rahula, *What the Buddha Taught*, New York: Grove Press, 1974.
40. C. M. Owens, "Zen Buddhism," in C. Tart (ed.), *Transpersonal Psychologies*, New York: Harper & Row, 1975.
41. D. T. Suzuki, *Mysticism: Christian and Buddhist*, New York: Harper and Row, 1957, p. 41.
42. The ox-herding illustrations are original drawings by Eugene Gregan, Lookout Farm, Napanoch, NY.
43. Hixon, *Coming Home*; P. Kapleau, *The Three Pillars of Zen*, Garden City, NY: Anchor Books, 1980.
44. C. Trungpa, *Cutting Through Spiritual Materialism*, Berkeley, CA: Shambhala, 1973.
45. Hixon, *Coming Home*.
46. Wilber, *Atman Project*.
47. Hixon, *Coming Home*.
48. Wilber, *Atman Project*.
49. Sengstan, Third Zen Patriarch, *Hsin Hsin Ming: Verses on the Faith Mind*, trans. from Chinese by Richard Clark, Sharon Springs, NY: Zen Center, 1976.
50. Hixon, *Coming Home*.
51. Wilber, *Atman Project*.
52. Ibid.
53. Hixon, *Coming Home*.
54. S. Suzuki, *Zen Mind, Beginner's Mind*, New York: Weatherhill, 1977.
55. Satprem, *Sri Aurobindo or the Adventure of Consciousness*, Pondicherry, India: Sri Aurobindo Ashram Trust, 1970.
56. Hixon, *Coming Home*.

57. Wilber, *Atman Project.*
58. Hixon, *Coming Home.*
59. Wilber, *Atman Project.*
60. Hixon, *Coming Home.*
61. Wilber, *Atman Project.*
62. Hixon, *Coming Home.*
63. Wilber, *Atman Project.*
64. K. Wilber, "Odyssey: A Personal Inquiry into Humanistic and Transpersonal Psychology," *Journal of Humanistic Psychology,* 22(1), pp. 59–70.
65. T. S. Eliot, "Little Gidding," in *The Complete Poems and Plays,* New York: Harcourt Brace, 1952.
66. Kapleau, *Three Pillars of Zen,* p. 24.
67. Suzuki, *Zen Mind, Beginner's Mind.*

Chapter 7

1. G. W. F. Hegel, *Lectures on the Philosophy of Religion,* London: Kegan Paul, Trench, Trubner, 1895, Vol. 1, p. 75, cited in J. Rowan, "Mystical Experiences," *Journal of Humanistic Psychology,* 23(2), 1983, pp. 9–27.
2. R. May, *The Courage to Create,* New York: Norton, 1975.
3. G. Marcel, *Philosophy of Existence,* New York: Philosophical Library, 1949.
4. F. Vaughan, *Awakening Intuition,* New York: Anchor Books, 1979.
5. C. Castaneda, *The Teachings of Don Juan,* Berkeley: University of California Press, 1968.
6. J. Krishnamurti, *Freedom from the Known,* New York: Harper & Row, 1969.
7. Castaneda, *Teachings of Don Juan.*
8. H. I. Khan, *Spiritual Dimensions of Psychology,* Lebanon Springs, NY: Sufi Order Publications, 1981.
9. F. Vaughan, "A Question of Balance: Health and Pathology in New Religious Movements," *Journal of Humanistic Psychology,* 23(3), 1983.
10. Anonymous, *A Course in Miracles,* New York: Foundation for Inner Peace, 1975, vol. 2, p. 312.
11. C. Tart, personal communication, 1984.
12. P. Hawken, J. Ogilvy, and P. Schwartz, *Seven Tomorrows: Toward A Voluntary Tomorrow,* New York: Bantam, 1982.
13. Khan, *Spiritual Dimensions of Psychology.*
14. Castaneda, *Teachings of Don Juan;* R. deRopp, *Warrior's Way,* New York: Dell Publishing Co., 1979.
15. Swami Radha, *Kundalini: Yoga for the West,* Spokane, WA: Timeless Books, 1978.
16. Lao Tsu, *The Way of Life,* trans. W. Bynner, New York: Perigee Books, 1980.
17. S. Kopp, *Guru: Metaphors from a Psychotherapist,* Palo Alto, CA: Science & Behavior Books, 1971, p. 8.
18. H. Arendt, *The Origins of Totalitarianism,* New York: Harcourt, Brace & World, 1966.
19. Sengstan, Third Zen Patriarch, *Hsin Hsin Ming: Verses on the Faith Mind,* trans. Richard B. Clark, Sharon Springs, NY: Zen Center, 1976.
20. G. May, *Will and Spirit,* New York: Harper and Row, 1982.
21. K. Wilber, *Eye to Eye,* New York: Doubleday/Anchor, 1983.

22. F. Vaughan, *Awakening Intuition*, Garden City, NY: Anchor Books, 1979.
23. D. Goleman, *The Varieties of the Meditative Experience*, New York: E. P. Dutton, 1977.
24. Khan, *Spiritual Dimensions of Psychology*.
25. T. Hersh, "The Phenomenology of Belief Systems," *Journal of Humanistic Psychology*, 20(2), 1980.
26. D. Goleman, "Early Warning Signs for the Detection of Spiritual Blight," *Association for Transpersonal Psychology Newsletter*, Palo Alto, Summer, 1981.
27. Swami Radha, *Kundalini*.
28. D. O'Hanlon, S.J., "Integration of Spiritual Practices: A Western Christian Looks East," *Journal of Transpersonal Psychology*, 13(2), pp. 105–106.
29. R. Walsh, *Staying Alive: The Psychology of Human Survival*, Boulder, CO: Shambhala, 1984.
30. Satprem, *Sri Aurobindo or the Adventure of Consciousness*, Pondicherry, India: Sri Aurobindo Ashram Trust, 1970, p. 243.
31. Kalamas Sutra, cited in Boorstein (ed.), *Transpersonal Psychotherapy*, Palo Alto, CA: Science and Behavior Books, 1981.

Chapter 8

1. Anonymous, *A Course in Miracles*, New York: Foundation for Inner Peace, 1975, vol. 1, p. 139.
2. W. Harman and H. Rheingold, *Higher Creativity: Liberating the Unconscious for Breakthrough Insights*, Los Angeles: J. P. Tarcher, 1984, p. xxii.
3. J. C. Gowan, "Incubation, Imagery and Creativity," *Journal of Mental Imagery*, vol. 2, 1978, cited in Harman and Rheingold, *Higher Creativity*, p. 8.
4. S. Grof, *Realms of the Human Unconscious*, New York: Viking, 1975.
5. R. May, *The Courage to Create*, New York: Norton, 1975.
6. P. Goldberg, *The Intuitive Edge*, Los Angeles: J. P. Tarcher, 1983; F. Vaughan, *Awakening Intuition*, New York: Anchor Press, 1979.
7. Lao Tsu, *The Way of Life*, New York: Mentor Books, 1955.
8. R. Walsh and F. Vaughan, *Beyond Ego: Transpersonal Dimensions in Psychology*, Los Angeles: J. P. Tarcher, 1980.
9. G. Delaney, *Living Your Dreams*, New York: Harper & Row, 1979; A. Faraday, *The Dream Game*, New York: Harper & Row, 1974; P. Garfield, *Creative Dreaming*, New York: Ballantine Books, 1976; S. LaBerge, *Lucid Dreaming*, Los Angeles: J.P. Tarcher, 1985.
10. *The Holy Bible*, Revised Standard Version, New York: Thomas Nelson & Sons, 1952, Job 33:14–16.
11. Swami Rama et al., *Yoga and Psychotherapy: The Evolution of Consciousness*, Honesdale, PA: Himalayan Institute, 1976, p. 135.
12. R. Woods and H. Greenhouse, eds., *The New World of Dreams*, New York: Macmillan, 1974.
13. A. Hastings, "Dreams of Future Events: Precognitions and Perspectives," *Journal of the American Society of Psychosomatic Dentistry and Medicine*, 1977, pp. 51–60; M. Ullman et al., *Dream Telepathy*, New York: Macmillan, 1973.
14. S. Freud, *The Interpretation of Dreams*, 3rd ed., trans. J. Strachey, New York: Avon Books, 1967.
15. C. G. Jung, *Man and His Symbols*, Garden City, NY: Doubleday, 1964.

16. M. Zeller, *The Dream: The Vision of the Night*, Los Angeles: C. G. Jung Institute, 1975, pp. 134–135.
17. K. Wilber et al., *The Pathology of Consciousness: Conventional and Contemplative Developmental Approaches*. Boulder, CO: Shambhala/New Science Library, 1985.
18. Anonymous, *A Course in Miracles*, New York: Foundation for Inner Peace, 1975, vol. 1, p. 19.
19. M. Harner, *The Way of the Shaman: A Guide to Power and Healing*, New York: Bantam, 1982.
20. Ibid., p. 139.
21. Vaughan, *Awakening Intuition*.
22. *A Course in Miracles*, vol. 1, p. 351.
23. P. Yogananda, *Autobiography of a Yogi*, Los Angeles: Self-Realization Fellowship, 1969.
24. F. Jones, *The Knee of Listening*, Los Angeles: The Dawn Horse Press, 1972, p. 104.
25. Ibid., p. 145.
26. Heraclitus, cited by Ralph Metzner in address to International Transpersonal Association, New York, 1982.
27. Harner, *The Way of the Shaman*, p. 139.

Chapter 9

1. G. May, *Will and Spirit: A Contemplative Psychology*, New York: Harper & Row, 1982, pp. 160–161.
2. J. Salk, *Anatomy of Reality: Merging of Intuition and Reason*, New York: Columbia University Press, 1983.
3. Ram Dass, *Grist for the Mill*, Santa Cruz, CA: Unity Press, 1977.
4. E. B. Schumacher, *A Guide for the Perplexed*, New York: Harper & Row, 1977, p. 119.
5. A. Guggenbuhl-Craig, *Power in the Helping Professions*, Zurich, Switzerland: Spring Publications, 1971, p. 139.
6. T. Clifford, *Tibetan Medicine and Psychiatry*, York Beach, ME: Samuel Weiser, 1984.
7. J. Fadiman and R. Frager, *Personality and Personal Growth*, New York: Harper & Row, 1976.
8. E. Becker, *The Denial of Death*, New York: Macmillan, 1973.
9. Anonymous, *A Course in Miracles*, New York: Foundation for Inner Peace, 1975, vol. 2, p. 210.

Chapter 10

1. *Holy Bible*, Authorized King James Version, Oxford: Oxford University Press.
2. H. Smith, *Beyond the Post Modern Mind*, New York: Crossroads, 1982.
3. J. White (ed.), *What is Enlightenment?* Los Angeles: J. P. Tarcher, 1985.
4. A. Diekman, *The Observing Self*, Boston: Beacon Press, 1982.
5. Anonymous, *A Course in Miracles*, New York: Foundation for Inner Peace, 1975, vol. 2, p. 347.
6. J. Goldstein, *The Experience of Insight*, Boulder, CO: Shambhala, 1983.

7. K. Wilber, *Eye to Eye*, New York: Doubleday, 1983.
8. C. G. Jung, *The Collected Works of C. G. Jung*, vol. 9, part I, *Four Archetypes*, trans. R. F. C. Hull, Princeton, NJ: Princeton University Press, Bollingen Series XX, 2nd ed., 1969, p. 272.
9. F. Schuon, *The Transcendent Unity of Religions*, Wheaton, IL: Theosophical Publishing House, 1984.
10. K. Wilber, *A Sociable God*, New York: Macmillan, 1983.
11. H. Smith, Introduction to Schuon, *Transcendent Unity of Religions*, pp. xiii, xv.
12. A. Maslow, *The Farther Reaches of Human Nature*, New York: Viking, 1971.
13. K. Wilber, *Up from Eden: A Transpersonal View of Human Evolution*, New York: Doubleday, 1981.
14. R. Muller, *New Genesis: Toward a Global Spirituality*, New York: Doubleday, 1982.
15. Wei Wu Wei, *Open Secret*, Hong Kong: Hong Kong University Press, 1982, p. 49.

Bibliography

Anonymous. *A Course in Miracles*. New York: Foundation for Inner Peace, 1975.

Arendt, H. *The Origins of Totalitarianism*. New York: Harcourt, Brace and World, 1966.

Becker, E. *The Denial of Death*. New York: Free Press, 1974.

Bettleheim, B. "Freud and the Soul." *The New Yorker*, March 1, 1982: 63.

Bhatnagar, S. "The Chakra Paradigm: The Inner Tuning System of Therapy." Paper delivered at the Seventh International Conference of the International Transpersonal Association, Bombay, India, February 14, 1982.

Bohm, D. *Wholeness and the Implicate Order*. London, Boston, and Henley: Routledge & Kegan Paul, 1980.

Boorstein, S., ed. *Transpersonal Psychotherapy*. Palo Alto: Science and Behavior Books, 1981.

Brain/Mind Bulletin 4 (13): 1–4

Bugental, J. *Psychotherapy and Process*. Reading, Mass.: Addison Wesley, 1978.

———— *The Search for Authenticity*. New York: Irvington Publishers, 1981.

Byrom, T. *The Dhammapada: The Sayings of the Buddha*. New York: Vintage, 1976.

Campbell, J. *The Hero with a Thousand Faces*. New York: Pantheon, 1949.

———— *The Masks of God: Creative Mythology*. New York: Viking, 1968.

————, ed. *The Portable Jung*. New York: Viking, 1971.

Capra, F. *The Turning Point*. New York: Simon and Schuster, 1982.

Castaneda, C. *The Teachings of Don Juan*. Berkeley: University of California Press, 1968.

Clifford, T. *Tibetan Medicine and Psychiatry*. York Beach, Me.: Samuel Weiser, 1984.

Corsini, R., ed. *Current Psychotherapies*. Itasca, Ill.: F. E. Peacock Publishers, 1984.

Cousins, N. *Anatomy of an Illness*. New York: Norton, 1979.

CSPA Task Force Report. California State Psychological Association *Newsletter*, 1983.

Dante. *The Divine Comedy of Dante Alighieri*. Translated by Carlyle-Wicksted. New York: Random House, 1950.

Delaney, G. *Living Your Dreams*. New York: Harper & Row, 1979.

deRopp, R. *Warrior's Way*. New York: Dell Publishing Company, 1979.

Diekman, A. *The Observing Self.*Boston: Beacon Press, 1982.

Dogen. *The Way of Everyday Life*. Translated by H. T. Maezumi and J. D. Loori. Los Angeles: Center Publications, 1978.

Doig, D. *Mother Teresa: Her People and Her Work*. San Francisco: Harper & Row, 1976.

Eliot, T. S. *The Complete Poems and Plays*. New York: Harcourt, Brace & World, 1952.

Erikson, E. *Childhood and Society*. New York: Norton, 1963.

Fadiman, J., and Frager, R. *Personality and Personal Growth*. New York: Harper & Row, 1976.

Faraday, A. *The Dream Game*. New York: Harper & Row, 1974.

Freud, S. *The Interpretation of Dreams*. Translated by J. Strachey. New York: Avon Books, 1967.

Friedman, M. "Aiming at the Self: The Paradox of Encounter and the Human Potential Movement." *Journal of Humanistic Psychology* 16, 2 (1976): 5–34.

Garfield, P. *Creative Dreaming*. New York: Ballantine Books, 1976.

Goldberg, P. *The Intuitive Edge*. Los Angeles: J. P. Tarcher, 1983.

Goleman, D. *The Varieties of the Meditative Experience*. New York: E. P. Dutton, 1977.

———. "Early Warning Signs for the Detection of Spiritual Blight." *Association for Transpersonal Psychology Newsletter* (Summer 1981).

Govinda, A. *Foundations of Tibetan Mysticism*. New York: Samuel Weiser, 1969.

Green, E., and Green, A. *Beyond Biofeedback*. New York: Delacorte, 1977.

Grof, S. *Realms of the Human Unconscious*. New York: Viking, 1975.

Guggenbuhl-Craig, A. *Power in the Helping Professions*. Zurich: Spring Publications, 1971.

Harman, W. "Peace is Possible." Sausalito, Calif.: Institute of Noetic Sciences, 1984.

———, and Rheingold, H. *Higher Creativity: Liberating the Unconscious for Breakthrough Insights*. Los Angeles: J. P. Tarcher, 1984.

Harner, M. *The Way of the Shaman: A Guide to Power and Healing*. New York: Bantam, 1982.

Hastings, A. "Dreams of Future Events: Precognitions and Perspectives." *Journal of the American Society of Psychosomatic Dentistry and Medicine* (1977):51–60.

Hawken, P.; Ogilvy, J.;and Schwartz, P. *Seven Tomorrows: Toward a Voluntary Tomorrow.* New York: Bantam, 1982.

Hersh, T. "The Phenomenology of Belief Systems." *Journal of Humanistic Psychology* 20, 2 (1980).

Hillman, J. *Revisioning Psychology.* New York: Harper & Row, 1977.

Hixon, L. *Coming Home: The Experience of Enlightenment in Sacred Traditions.* New York: Doubleday/Anchor, 1978.

Huang Po. *The Zen Teaching of Huang Po on the Transmission of Mind.* Translated by John Blofeld. New York: Grove Press, 1958.

Huxley, A. *The Perennial Philosophy.* New York: Harper & Row, 1944.

Jacobi, J., ed. *C. G. Jung: Psychological Reflections, A New Anthology of his Writings.* Princeton: Princeton University Press, 1970.

James, W. *The Varieties of Religious Experience.* New York: Collier, 1961.

Jones, F. *The Knee of Listening.* Los Angeles: Dawn Horse Press, 1972.

Jung, C. G. *Man and His Symbols.* Garden City, N. Y.: Doubleday, 1964.

——— . *Four Archetypes.* Translated by R. F. C. Hull. In *The Collected Works of C. G. Jung,* Vol. 9, part 1. Princeton: Princeton University Press, 1969.

——— . *The Secret of the Golden Flower.* New York: Harcourt, Brace & World, 1969.

——— . *Letters.* Princeton: Princeton University Press, 1973.

——— . *Psychological Commentary on Kundalini Yoga,* Zurich: Spring Publications, 1975, p. 31.

Kapleau, P. *The Three Pillars of Zen.* Garden City, N. Y.: Anchor Books, 1980.

Khan, H. I. *Spiritual Dimensions of Psychology.* Lebanon Springs, N. Y.: Sufi Order Publications, 1981.

Kohlberg, L. *The Philosophy of Moral Development.* New York: Harper & Row, 1981.

Kopp, S. *Guru: Metaphors from a Psychotherapist.* Palo Alto: Science and Behavior Books, 1971.

Krishnamurti, J. *Freedom from the Known.* New York: Harper & Row, 1969.

LaBerge, S. *Lucid Dreaming.* Los Angeles: J. P. Tarcher, 1985.

Lao Tsu. *The Way of Life.* New York: Mentor Books, 1955.

——— . *The Way of Life.* Translated by W. Bynner. New York: Perigree Books, 1980.

Mahler, M., et al. *The Psychological Birth of the Human Infant.* New York: Basic Books, 1975.

Marcel, G. *Philosophy of Existence.* New York: Philosophical Library, 1949.

Maslow, A. *The Farther Reaches of Human Nature.* New York: Viking, 1971.

May, G. *Will and Spirit: A Contemplative Psychology.* New York: Harper & Row, 1982.

May, R. *Existential Psychology.* New York: Random House, 1969.

——— . *Love and Will.* New York: Norton, 1969.

——— . *The Courage to Create.* New York: Norton, 1975.

——— ; Angel, E.; and Ellenberger, H., eds. *Existence.* New York: Basic Books, 1958.

McGarey, W. "An Adventure in Health." *New Realities*, Vols. 5 and 6 (1964).

Metzner, R. "Ten Classical Metaphors of Self-Transformation." *Journal of Transpersonal Psychology* 12, 1 (1979).

Muller, R. *New Genesis: Toward a Global Spirituality*. New York: Doubleday, 1982.

Needleman, J. *Lost Christianity*. New York: Doubleday, 1980.

Neumann, E. *The Origins and History of Consciousness*. Princeton: Princeton University Press, 1973.

O'Hanlon, D., S. J. "Integration of Spiritual Practices: A Western Christian Looks East." *Journal of Transpersonal Psychology* 13, 2: 105–106.

Oyle, I. *The Healing Mind*. Millbrae, Calif.: Celestial Arts, 1975.

Peck, M. S. *The Road Less Traveled*. New York: Simon & Schuster, 1978.

Perls, F. *Gestalt Therapy Verbatim*. Lafayette, Calif.: Real People Press, 1969.

Radha (Swami). *Kundalini: Yoga for the West*. Spokane, Wash.: Timeless Books, 1978.

Rahula, W. *What the Buddha Taught*. New York: Grove Press, 1974.

Ram Dass. *Grist for the Mill*. Santa Cruz, Calif.: Unity Press, 1977.

Rama (Swami), et al. *Yoga and Psychotherapy: The Evolution of Consciousness*. Glenview, Ill.: Himalayan Institute, 1976.

Roberts, B. *The Experience of No-Self: A Contemplative Journey*. Boulder: Shambhala, 1984.

Rossi, E. *Dreams and the Growth of Personality*. New York: Pergamon Press, 1972.

Rowan, J. "Mystical Experiences." *Journal of Humanistic Psychology* 23, 2 (1983):9–27.

Russell, P., and Shearer, A. *The Upanishads*. New York: Harper & Row, 1978.

Salk, J. *Anatomy of Reality: Merging of Intuition and Reason*. New York: Columbia University Press, 1983.

Sampson, J., ed. *William Blake*. London: Oxford University Press, 1928.

Satprem. *Sri Aurobindo or the Adventure of Consciousness*. Pondicherry, India: Sri Aurobindo Ashram Trust, 1970.

Schumacher, E. B. *A Guide for the Perplexed*. New York: Harper & Row, 1977.

Schuon, F. *The Transcendent Unity of Religions*. Wheaton, Ill.: Theosophical Publishing House, 1984.

Sengstan. *Hsin Hsin Ming: Verses on the Faith Mind*. Translated by Richard Clarke. Sharon Springs, N. Y.: Zen Center, 1976.

Shapiro, D. and Walsh, R., eds. *Meditation: Classic and Contemporary Perspectives*. New York: Aldine, 1984.

Simonton, C., and Simonton, S. *Getting Well Again*. Los Angeles: J. P. Tarcher, 1982.

Smith, H. *Beyond the Post-Modern Mind*. New York: Crossroads, 1982.

Sri Nisargadatta Mahjaraj. *I Am That*. Translated by Maurice Frydman. Bombay: Chetana, 1973.

Stein, M., ed. *Jungian Analysis*. LaSalle, Ill.: Open Court, 1982.

Suzuki, D. T. *Mysticism: Christian and Buddhist*. New York: Harper & Row, 1957.

Suzuki, S. *Zen Mind, Beginner's Mind*. New York: Weatherhill, 1977.

Tart, C., ed. *Transpersonal Psychologies*. New York: Harper & Row, 1975.

Trungpa, C. *Cutting Through Spiritual Materialism*. Berkeley: Shambhala, 1973.

Ullman, M., et al. *Dream Telepathy*. New York: Macmillan, 1973.

Underhil, E. *Mysticism*. New York: E. P. Dutton, 1961.

Vaughan, F. *Awakening Intuition*. Garden City, N. Y.: Anchor Books, 1979.

————. "A Question of Balance: Health and Pathology in New Religious Movements." *Journal of Humanistic Psychology* 23, 3 (1983).

von Bertalanffy, L. *General Systems Theory*. New York: George Braziller, 1968.

Walsh, R. *Staying Alive: The Psychology of Human Survival*. Boulder: Shambhala, 1984.

————, and Shapiro, D., eds. *Beyond Health and Normality*. New York: Van Nostrand, 1983.

————, and Vaughan, F., eds. *Beyond Ego: Transpersonal Dimensions in Psychology*. Los Angeles: J. P. Tarcher, 1980.

Wei Wu Wei. *Open Secret*. Hong Kong: Hong Kong University Press, 1982.

Welwood, J. "Vulnerability and Power in the Therapeutic Process: Existential and Buddhist Perspectives." *Journal of Humanistic Psychology* 14, 2 (1982):125–140.

White, J., ed. *Kundalini, Evolution and Enlightenment*. New York: Doubleday/Anchor, 1979.

————, ed. *What is Enlightenment?* Los Angeles: J. P. Tarcher, 1985.

Wilber, K. "A Developmental View of Consciousness." *Journal of Transpersonal Psychology* 11, 1 (1979):1–22.

————, ed. *The Atman Project: A Transpersonal View of Human Development*. Wheaton, Ill.: Theosophical Publishing House, 1980.

————. *No Boundary*. Boulder: Shambhala, 1981.

————. *Up From Eden: A Transpersonal View of Human Evolution*. Garden City, N. Y.: Doubleday, 1981.

————. "Odyssey: A Personal Inquiry into Humanistic and Transpersonal Psychology." *Journal of Humanistic Psychology* 22, 1 (1982):59–70.

————. *Eye to Eye*. New York: Doubleday/Anchor, 1983.

————. *A Sociable God*. New York: Macmillan, 1983.

————, ed. *Quantum Questions*. Boulder: New Science Library/Shambhala, 1984.

————, et al. *The Pathology of Consciousness*. Boston: New Science Library/Shambhala, 1985.

Woods, R., and Greenhouse, H., eds. *The New World of Dreams*. New York: Macmillan, 1974.

Yalom, I. *Existential Psychotherapy*. New York: Basic Books, 1980.

Yogananda, P. *Sayings of Yogananda*. Los Angeles: Self-Realization Fellowship, 1968.

————. *Autobiography of a Yogi*. Los Angeles: Self-Realization Fellowship, 1969.

Zeller, M. *The Dream: The Vision of the Night*. Los Angeles: C. G. Jung Institute, 1975.

Index

Also in New Science Library:

The Tao of Physics: An Exploration of the Parallels between Modern Physics and Eastern Mysticism, second edition, revised and updated, by Fritjof Capra

Transformations of Consciousness: Conventional and Contemplative Perspectives on Development, by Ken Wilber, Jack Engler, and Daniel P. Brown

The Tree of Knowledge: The Biological Roots of Human Understanding, by Humberto Maturana and Francisco Varela

Up from Eden: A Transpersonal View of Human Evolution, by Ken Wilber

Waking Up: Overcoming the Obstacles to Human Potential, by Charles T. Tart

The Wonder of Being Human: Our Brain and Our Mind, by Sir John Eccles and Daniel N. Robinson